WHO WROTE THE TAO?

The Literary Sourcebook for the *Tao of Jeet Kune Do*

James Bishop, Ph.D.

PROMETHEAN PRESS™
Dallas   Vancouver

Published by Promethean Press™
A division of Promethean Multimedia, LLC
Dallas, TX
www.promethean-press.com

Cover design by Carl Fox and James Bishop
Digital cover art by James Bishop

First Paperback Edition - March 2023

Grateful acknowledgement is made to the following people for their assistance in preparing this book:

Carl Fox
Chris Kent
Richard Torres

© 2022 James Bishop

The material in this book is provided for educational and informational purposes. Copyright Disclaimer under section 107 of the Copyright Act of 1976, allowance is made for "fair use" for purposes such as criticism, comment, news reporting, teaching, scholarship, education, and research. The rights for the material quoted in this book reside with the authors.

Printed in the United States of America
ISBN 978-1-77331-005-3

TABLE OF CONTENTS

Foreword 3
Introduction 4
A Zen Poem 6
Zen 7
Buddhism's Eight-Fold Path 9
Art of the Soul 9
Organized Despair 14
Jiddu Krishnamurti 23

PRELIMINARIES

Training 27
Warming Up 28
On-Guard Position 29
Charles Louis de Beaumont 31
Frank Gilmer 34
Progressive Weapons Charts 35
Eight Basic Defensive Positions 37
D. T. Suzuki 38
Some Target Areas 40

QUALITIES

Coordination 43
Precision 45
Power 45
Endurance 46
Balance 47
Philadelphia Jack O'Brien 50
Good Form 51
Economy of Motion 53
Vision Awareness 54
Speed 57
Timing 59
Movement Time 61
Broken Rhythm 62
Cadence 63
Tempo 64
Stop-Hit 65
Counter-Time 67
Attitude 68

TOOLS

John Kardoss 71
Four Basic Methods of attack 72
Jim Driscoll 74
Kicking 78
Edwin Haislet: The Man Behind the Book 80
Eric Hoffer: The Longshoreman Philosopher 86

Thomas Inch 89
Jack Dempsey 92
Barney Ross 94
Lead to Body 96
Lead Jab 98
Leading Finger Jab 100
Straight Lead Rear Thrust to Body 101
Rear Cross 101
In a Right Stance 103
The Hook 106
Lead Hook 106
Shovel Hook 110
Uppercut 113
Grappling 116
Studies on Judo and Ju-Jitsu 122

PREPARATIONS
Feints 125
Julius Palffy-Alpar: Renaissance Man 129
Parries 132
Julio Martinez Castelló 135
Manipulations 136

MOBILITY
Distance 139
Footwork 142
Rocky Marciano 153
Slipping 154

ATTACK
The Psychological Process of Attack 161
Primary and Secondary Attacks 162
Preparation of Attack 164
Simple Attacks 166
Roger Crosnier: Maître d'Armes 171
Compound Attack 170
Counterattack 173
Peter McInnes 176
Riposte 181
Renewed Attack 184
Tactics 186
Ways of Attack 195
Circle With No Circumference 200
It's Just A Name 206
Joseph J. Snyder, Jr.: The First *Tao of Jeet Kune Do* Scholar 209
Afterword 213
List of Publications Found in the *Tao of Jeet Kune Do* 214
Statistics on the *Tao of Jeet Kune Do* 218
Word Usage in the *Tao of Jeet Kune Do* 221

FOREWORD

I am very honored to write a foreword to this wonderful book. James Bishop's previous book on Bruce Lee, *Bruce Lee: Dynamic Becoming*, was a remarkable, well-researched contribution to the literature on the founder of Jeet Kune Do. That book brought to light a number of quotes wrongly attributed to Lee and ended with a very comprehensive list of many of the books Lee owned in his library. Now, with his new book, *Who Wrote the Tao? The Literary Sourcebook for the Tao of Jeet Kune Do,* Dr. Bishop has created another treasure.

As many fans and students of Bruce Lee may already know, Bruce Lee injured his back while performing weight training exercises in 1970, which prevented him from participating in martial arts as well as any physical activity for several months. While convalescing, Lee took this time at home to gather his books and write down the underlinings and marginal notes that he previously made in the books in his library. A portion of those notes were published posthumously by the Lee estate in the 1975 book, *The Tao of Jeet Kune Do.*

James Bishop has undertaken exhaustive research and investigation to track down these books and show the reader where much of the material included in *The Tao of Jeet Kune Do* originated. In this new book, you will see the sources of Bruce Lee notes on martial arts and philosophy as well as the conclusions he drew from them that formed the basis of Jeet Kune Do. As we get to know Bruce Lee and his genius, we learn from this book who his "teachers" were and what they taught him; we learn how they helped create and mold the man who became a phenomenal martial artist, philosopher, actor, and human being. I hope the reader can enjoy this wonderful book and appreciate the work that James Bishop took to put it together. Enjoy.

Richard Torres
Jeet Kune Do Instructor

INTRODUCTION

If you have picked up this book expecting to read the writings of Bruce Lee, then I am sorry to disappoint you; the truth is that not a single word spoken or written by Bruce Lee appears in this book. But if you have come with an honest desire to understand the contents of the *Tao of Jeet Kune Do*, then you are in luck, because this book is the most authoritative, scholastic resource ever produced on the subject.

In 1975, the Estate of Bruce Lee and Ohara Publications published the *Tao of Jeet Kune Do,* a 208-page book purported to contain the writings and ideas that formed the basis of Bruce Lee's martial art of Jeet Kune Do. Taken from Bruce Lee's handwritten notes, it soon became clear that at least some of the contents of the book were verbatim passages from other authors. Over the years, as more items in the *Tao of Jeet Kune Do* were discovered to be borrowed from other authors, a nagging question began to emerge: "Who really wrote the *Tao of Jeet Kune Do*?"

As its title implies, *Who Wrote the Tao? The Literary Sourcebook for the Tao of Jeet Kune Do* intends to answer that question. The book will illuminate the true origins of the uncredited material contained in the *Tao of Jeet Kune Do* and give recognition to the actual authors for their contributions to the body of knowledge that informed Bruce Lee's development.

This book came into existence as part of an extensive research project to identify the true sources of texts attributed to Bruce Lee. Since beginning this project five months ago, I have identified over 2,000 unique instances of Bruce Lee being credited for the work of other people, including significant portions of the *Tao of Jeet Kune Do*. And as my research progresses, I continue to find more instances of wrongful attribution. *Who Wrote the Tao? The Literary Sourcebook for the Tao of Jeet Kune Do* is the first of what will be at least three books resulting from my research.

Now a few notes about the text. While the majority of the items were taken verbatim from other sources, not all of the items contained in this book represent verbatim passages. In the case of many of the non-verbatim items contained in this book, I was able to determine the source of the item because Bruce Lee's notes, as published, appear to have largely been printed in the order in which he wrote them. I could see Bruce Lee's progression through the text of a particular book from verbatim quote, to not-verbatim quote, to yet another verbatim quote. In many ways I feel as if I was looking over the Jeet Kune Do founder's shoulder as Bruce Lee was reading these books and taking his notes.

I've designed this book to make it as easy as possible to compare the passages between *Who Wrote the Tao?* and the *Tao of Jeet Kune Do*. To that end, I have attempted to follow the pagination of the *Tao of Jeet Kune Do* as closely as possible, so that the reader may more easily find the relevant passage for comparison. You will also notice some quotes encapsulated in gray boxes; I discovered, during my research, Bruce Lee's tendency to combine pieces of verbatim quotes from multiple sources into one single quote; wherever this occurred, I used the boxes to make it easier to recognize them. I have also retained the spelling of the original sources, so the contents will reflect both American and British spelling. In all, this book represents the original sources for about 85% of the *Tao of Jeet Kune Do*. If a source for a particular passage does not appear in this book, that means I have not yet identified an original source. This does not necessarily mean that the passage originated with Bruce Lee, but it does make the case more likely.

I want to thank Richard Torres for his assistance in providing some of the materials for my research and for being a resource for all things Bruce Lee; Alan Davies and Dwight Woods for bringing to my attention several additional sources, and I would also like to extend a special thanks to Professors Todd Kettler and Laila Sanguras of Baylor University for their friendship and encouragement of this project.

Finally, I want to acknowledge the work of some individuals who previously attempted to shine a light on the sources of the ideas contained in the *Tao of Jeet Kune Do* and other Bruce Lee texts: Joe Snyder, Robert Colet, and Kip Brockett. I also want to acknowledge Tommy Gong and Teri Tom, Jeet Kune Do instructors who produced recent works of scholarship on Bruce Lee and Jeet Kune Do that, where they were aware of misattributed text, credited the proper authors.

Now grab that dog-eared copy of the *Tao of Jeet Kune Do* from your personal library, set this literary sourcebook directly beside it, and rediscover the *Tao of Jeet Kune Do* in an entirely new way. And when you are done, I encourage you to take the greater opportunity and research these original texts. If Bruce Lee benefited from them, you will as well.

This book is dedicated to all the brilliant minds who inspired the martial art of Bruce Lee. You deserve to be credited.

James Bishop, Ph.D.

Zen Poem

*Into a soul (kokoro) absolutely free from
thoughts and emotions,
Even the tiger finds no room to insert
its fierce claws.*

*One and the same breeze passes
Over the pines on the mountain and the oak
trees in the valley;
And why do they give different notes?*

*Some think that striking is to strike:
But striking is not to strike, nor is killing to kill.
He who strikes and he who is struck—
They are both no more than a dream that has no reality.*

*No thinking, no reflecting,—
Perfect emptiness:
Yet therein something moves,
Following its own course.*

*The eye sees it.
But no hands can take hold of it—
The moon in the stream:
This is the secret of my school.*

*Clouds and mists—
They are midair transformations:
Above them eternally shine the sun and the moon.*

*Victory is for the one.
Even before the combat.
Who has no thought of himself.
Abiding in the no-mind-ness of Great Origin.*

– D. T. SUZUKI, *Zen and Japanese Culture*, page 123

On Zen

Nirvana should be taken to mean the extinction of everything which obstructs the "real life"; at the same time, it implies "boundless expansion," and, indeed, emphasis should fall not on the image of the "drop of water which merges into the ocean," but rather on "the ocean which enters into the drop." – NANCY WILSON ROSS, *Three Ways of Asian Wisdom*, pages 113-114

The way to transcend karma lay in the proper use of the mind and the will. In Buddhist teaching, therefore, karma takes on almost the tone of opportunity, although because of the Buddha's penetrating analysis of the "illusion" of a separate self, the highest Buddhist thought does not interpret karma in a purely personal way. ... The Oneness of all life is a truth, Buddhism asserts, that can be fully realized only when false notions of a separate self—whose destiny can be considered apart from the whole—are forever annihilated. – NANCY WILSON ROSS, *Three Ways of Asian Wisdom*, pages 115, 135

Voidness is that which stands right in the middle between affirmation and negation, existence and nonexistence. The void is all-inclusive; having no opposite, there is nothing which it excludes or opposes. It is living void, because all forms come out of it, and whoever realizes the void is filled with life and power and the love of all beings. – HAJIMI NAKAMURA, quoted in Nancy Wilson Ross' *Three Ways of Asian Wisdom*, page 121

The consciousness of self is the greatest hindrance to the proper execution of all physical action. Spontaneity is lost when body muscles are hampered by an awareness of their functioning. – GERTRUDE ENELOW, *Body Dynamics: The Zen and Zest of Self-Development*, page 123

Turn yourself into a doll made of wood: it has no ego, it thinks nothing; and let the body and limbs work themselves out in accordance with the discipline they have undergone. This is the way to win. – TAJIMA NO KAMI MUNENORI, quoted in D. T. Suzuki's *Zen and Japanese Culture*, page 165

If nothing within you stays rigid, outward things will disclose themselves. Moving, be like water. Still, be like a mirror. Respond like an echo. – KUAN-YIN, quoted in *The Book of Lieh-Tzu* (translated by A.C. Graham), page 114

The tenuous, non-existent, soft and weak goes through everything; nothingness cannot be confined, the softest thing cannot be snapped. – LIEH-TZU, *The Book of Lieh-Tzu* (translated by A.C. Graham), page 33

I am moving all day and not moving at all. I am like the moon underneath the waves that ever go on rolling and rocking. – TAJIMA NO KAMI MUNENORI, quoted in D. T. Suzuki's *Zen and Japanese Culture*, page 164

In Zen there is no sense of "I am doing this," but rather an inner realization that "this is happening through me," or "it is doing this for me." The consciousness of self is the greatest hindrance to the proper execution of all physical action. Spontaneity is lost when body muscles are hampered by an awareness of their functioning." – GERTRUDE ENELOW, *Body Dynamics: The Zen and Zest of Self-Development*, page 123

The localization of the mind means its freezing. When it ceases to flow freely as it is needed, it is no more the mind in its suchness. – D. T. SUZUKI, *Essentials of Zen Buddhism*, page 452

One must transcend mere technique to acquire that "artless art" which is the by-product of the unconscious. To be immobile, in the Zen sense, does not mean to be lifeless, stiff, or motionless. It is the concentration of energy at a given focus—as at the axis of a wheel—instead of dispersal in scattered activities. – GERTRUDE ENELOW, *Body Dynamics: The Zen and Zest of Self-Development*, pages 123-124

There is no doer but the deed. There is no experiencer but the experience. Constituent parts alone roll on. This is the true and correct view. – BUDDHAGHOSA, *The Visuddhimagga*

The perfect Way is only difficult for those who pick and choose; Do not like, do not dislike; all will then be clear. Make a hair's breadth difference, and heaven and earth are set apart; If you want the truth to stand clear before you, never be for or against. The struggle between "for" and "against" is the mind's worst disease. While the deep meaning is misunderstood, it is useless to meditate on the Rest. – EDWARD CONZE, *Buddhist Texts Through the Ages*, page 295

Therefore, wisdom did not consist in trying to wrest the good from the evil but in learning to "ride" them as a cork adapts itself to the crests and troughs of the waves. – ALAN WATTS, *This is It*, page 83

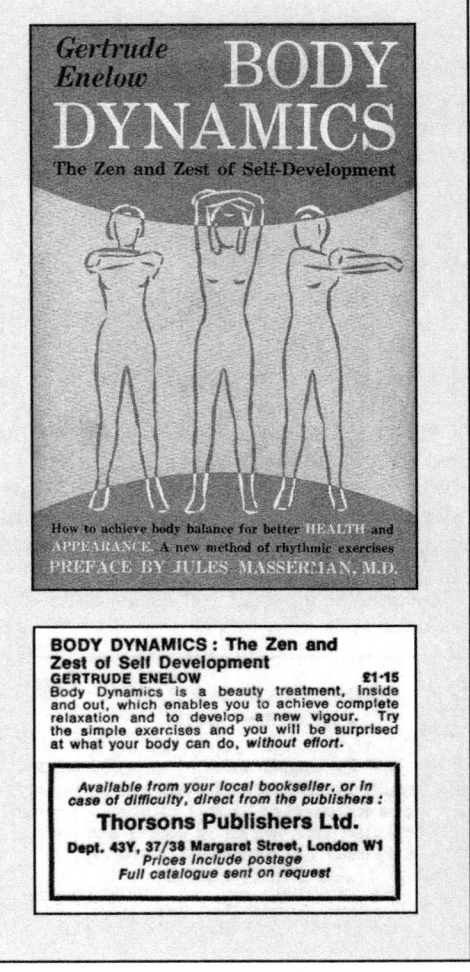

Let yourself go with the disease, be with it, keep company with it: this is the way to get rid of it. – YAGU, "Triple Treatise of the Sword" in D. T. Suzuki 's *Zen and Japanese Culture*, page 165

An assertion is Zen only when it is in itself an act and does not refer to anything that is asserted in it. – MUMON YAMADA, in D. T. Suzuki 's *Zen Buddhism: Selected Writings*, page 129

In Buddhism there is no place for using effort. Just be ordinary and nothing special. Eat your food, move your bowels, pass water, and when you're tired go and lie down. The ignorant will laugh at me, but the wise will understand. – LIN CHI, quoted in Alan Watts' *Beat Zen, Square Zen, and Zen*, page 3

Kuan Yin said: "Establish nothing in regard to oneself. Let things be what they are, move like water, rest like a mirror, respond like an echo, pass quickly like the non-existent, and be quiet as purity. Those who agree are harmonious. Those who gain, lose. Do not precede others, always follow them." – FUNG YU LAN, *A History of Chinese Philosophy, Vol. II*, page 173

Fung Yu-Lan

Professor, philosopher, native of Honan, born in 1895; graduate, National Peking University, 1918; Ph.D., Columbia, 1923; professor, National Tsing Hua University, 1927-32; dean, College of Arts, same institution, since 1933; professor and dean, National Southwest Associated University, 1938; author of *A History of Chinese Philosophy, A New Way of Life, A New Philosophy, A New Treatise on the Nature of Man, The Spirit of Chinese Philosophy.*

SOURCE: *China Handbook 1937–1945: A Comprehensive Survey of Major Developments,* page 652

Don't seek Buddhahood, for it will come to you when least expected. – PAUL WIENPAHL, *The Matter of Zen*, page 75

Give up thinking as though not giving it up. Observe the techniques as though not observing. – D. T. SUZUKI, *Zen and Japanese Culture*, page 165

There is no fixed teaching. All I can provide is an appropriate medicine for a particular ailment. – PAUL WIENPAHL, *The Matter of Zen*, page 77

Buddhism's Eight-Fold Path

This Eightfold Path is the Buddha's basic formula for deliverance from the kind of crippling invalidism that comes with having a "body-identified mind," as Gerald Heard has described mankind's general state. The eight requirements that will eliminate suffering by correcting false values and giving true knowledge of life's meaning have been summed up as follows: "(I) First, you must see clearly what is wrong. (II) Next decide to be cured. (III) You must act and (IV) speak so as to aim at being cured. (V) Your livelihood must not conflict with your therapy. (VI) That therapy must go forward at the 'staying speed,' the critical velocity that can be sustained. (VII) You must think about it incessantly, and (VIII) learn how to contemplate with the deep mind. – NANCY WILSON ROSS, *Three Ways of Asian Wisdom*, page 91

Art of the Soul

The task of art is so to state in aesthetic creation the deepest psychic and personal experiences of a human being as to enable those experiences to be intelligible and generally recognized within the total framework of an ideal world. – TOSHIMITSU HASUMI, *Zen in Japanese Art: A Way of Spiritual Experience*, page 1

Art reveals itself in psychic understanding of the inner essence of things and gives form to the relation of man with the Nothing, with the nature of the Absolute. It sees the features of the Absolute in ordinary life and gives them expression, direct, unmediated and formative. – TOSHIMITSU HASUMI, *Zen in Japanese Art: A Way of Spiritual Experience*, pages ix, xii

Art is the form-language of the human soul. We men make this form-language our own in joy and in sorrow and no less in the trivial round. Art is not just an external influence upon nature. Our own souls are what we must employ to give a new form and a new meaning to nature or the world. Constant striving after psychic and artistic expression in life—that is the be-all and the way of the art of Japan. The soul lends a new meaning to form; it seeks in artistic expression to disclose the harmony of the cosmic revelation. – TOSHIMITSU HASUMI, *Zen in Japanese Art: A Way of Spiritual Experience*, page vii

A point of tremendous importance is that for the Zen masters art is never decoration, embellishment; instead it is work of enlightenment, illumination, salvation, not in a narrow, pietistic sense, but in the sense of a flash of sudden, profound significance. Art, in other words, is a technique for acquiring liberty. The intellect having been dethroned, the artist's intuition becomes the connecting link between the self and the all. – FOSCO MARAINI, *Meeting with Japan*, page 291

All Japanese art calls for complete mastery of technique, developed by reflection within the soul of man. Outward technique by itself is not art. It is only through long training of the soul that the pupil is brought to the true inward technique. – TOSHIMITSU HASUMI, *Zen in Japanese Art: A Way of Spiritual Experience*, page xii

In art it is not merely a question of artistic dexterity, but of the artistic process within the artist. It is the 'art-less art', and its meaning is 'art of the soul'. For us Japanese the arrangement of colours, composition and line-forms means a step on the way to the absolute aesthetic world of the soul. That is 'Zen in art'. – TOSHIMITSU HASUMI, *Zen in Japanese Art: A Way of Spiritual Experience*, page xi

Rigorous technical and psychic exercises show the way into the secret of cosmic life. In the Zen of Japanese art the typical Japanese peculiarity of psychic experience becomes manifest. Everything that is formed in art is united with the human soul. The working of the soul penetrates the practical life of every day. Creation in art is the psychic unfolding of the personality, which is rooted in the NOTHING—in other words, in GOD. Its effect is a deepening of the personal dimension of the soul. By taking the way of 'Zen in art' we experience the basic ground of the cosmos, in which all existence is enclosed. – TOSHIMITSU HASUMI, *Zen in Japanese Art: A Way of Spiritual Experience*, page xii

In art it is not merely a question of artistic dexterity, but of the artistic process within the artist. It is the 'artless art', and its meaning is 'art of the soul'. ... It is the art of the soul at peace, through which—like moonlight mirrored in a deep lake—the light of eternity pours calmly down on the ground of the soul. Moon and lake, soul and heaven, earth and man fashion art for ever. ... At once philosopher, poet, painter, master of swordsmanship and the tea ceremony, of archery and flower arrangement— thus it is that the ultimate aim of the Japanese is to use his daily activity to become a pastmaster of life and so to lay hold of the art of living. Philosophers, men of learning, and masters in all branches of art must first be masters in living, for the soul creates everything. – TOSHIMITSU HASUMI, *Zen in Japanese Art: A Way of Spiritual Experience*, pages xi, 21-22, 23

All vague notions must fall before a pupil can call himself a master. The moment comes when he is alone with himself. Now he must create. – ELIZABETH S. SELDEN, *Elements of the Free Dance*, page 12

Art in the Japanese sense is the endeavour to carry over into ordinary existence the infinitely deep, inexpressible, and unknowable ground of living: it is in Japan the way to the Absolute. ... The aim of art, however, is not the one-sided promotion of spirit, soul, and senses, but the opening of all human capacities— thought, feeling, and will—to the life rhythm of the world

of nature: so will the voiceless voice be heard and the self be brought into harmony with it. The body is now a crystal from which the soul shines forth. The wind drives the clouds hither and thither. The wind is mournful and harsh, but life fluctuates, changes, and weaves its web.
— TOSHIMITSU HASUMI, *Zen in Japanese Art: A Way of Spiritual Experience*, pages 5, 88

Artistic skill, therefore, does not mean artistic perfection: it remains rather a continuing medium or reflection of some step in psychic development, the perfection of which is not to be found in form and shape, but must radiate from the human soul. — TOSHIMITSU HASUMI, *Zen in Japanese Art: A Way of Spiritual Experience*, page xii

The artistic activity of the Japanese does not consist in art itself as such: it penetrates into a deeper world in which all art-forms of things inwardly experienced flow together, and in which the harmony of soul and cosmos in the NOTHING has its outcome in reality. — TOSHIMITSU HASUMI, *Zen in Japanese Art: A Way of Spiritual Experience*, page xii

Then this deep serenity which, rising up from this body, attains the highest light, reveals itself in its own [true] form: this is the Self. So said he. This is the immortal, [this] freedom from fear: this is Brahman. And the name of Brahman is this — Reality: [and Reality is Truth]. — *The Chandogya Upanishad*

I would like at this point to indicate ten steps in the experience of truth in the DO:

1. Seeking and striving after truth. Physiological, psychological, physical, etc. Mastery of all human capacities by means of exercise and study, learning and repetition, with a view to grasping everything essential. Complete elimination of the inessential.
2. Awareness of truth. In order to become aware of truth, a definite attitude of mind is required, and this must be acquired through training. Under the guidance of the master this training consists in liberation from cosmic laws.
3. Perception of truth. Once truth is felt, it is possible by means of further training and effort to attain a definite spiritual dimension in which it is possible to perceive what truth is.
4. Understanding of truth. Man lives and works in the truth, wishes and acts within the framework of the truth. A passive retention in reality of comprehension of the truth. When the Something is oriented in the Nothing, it is true.
5. Experiencing truth. Creation out of the truth. The experience of truth is a creative process. The shapeless acquires shape, the formless form. An active mastery of truth in reality.
6. Mastering truth. The man who experiences truth creatively turns back on himself and finds the truth in himself. Consciousness of truth no longer exists. The further the understanding goes, the simpler things are.
7. Forgetting truth. With the return to and immersion in oneself, there is no truth anymore. Man finds himself as a carrier of truth in the primal consciousness.
8. Forgetting the carrier of truth. Consciousness no longer exists. In the primal consciousness the self as carrier of truth forgets and disappears.
9. Return to the primal source where truth has its roots. That is, the self and the primal consciousness, the ground of the self, disappear, and man stands over against the Nothing.
10. Repose in the Nothing.

— TOSHIMITSU HASUMI, *Zen in Japanese Art: A Way of Spiritual Experience*, page 81

Detachment refers to independence of concepts, rules and standards; not clinging or leaning; hence, the freedom of the formless to assume all forms. – VAN METER AMES, "Art for Zen and Dewey", *Proceedings of the IV International Congress of Aesthetics, Athens*, page 746

The School of Zen Buddhism may be viewed as part of the Mahayana school or entirely on its own. It uses all scriptures and is bound by none, and likewise uses any technique or means (upaya) which serves its end, which is to awaken the pupil's mind to its own enlightenment. – CHRISTMAS HUMPHREYS, *Zen Comes West*, page 21

Araki Matayemon [a great swordsman of the Tokugawa era] gave this instruction to his nephew, Watanabe Kazuma, when they were about to engage in the deadly fight with their enemy: "Let the enemy touch your skin and you cut into his flesh; let him cut into your flesh and you pierce into his bones; let him pierce into your bones and you take his life!" – D. T. SUZUKI, *Zen and Japanese Culture*, pages 73-74

The great mistake in swordsmanship is to anticipate the outcome of the engagement; you ought not to be thinking of whether it ends in victory or in defeat. Just let the Nature take its course, and your sword will strike at the right moment. – D. T. SUZUKI, *Zen and Japanese Culture*, page 177

Zen has sustained them in two ways, morally and philosophically. Morally, because Zen is a religion which teaches us not to look backward once the course is decided upon; philosophically, because it treats life and death indifferently. This not turning backward ultimately comes from the philosophical conviction; but, being a religion of the will, Zen appeals to the samurai spirit morally rather than philosophically. – D. T. SUZUKI, *Zen and Japanese Culture*, page 61

Simplicity avoids the superficial, penetrates the complex, goes to the heart of the problem and pinpoints the key factors. – WILFERD ARLAN PETERSON, *The New Book of the Art of Living*, page 50

Simplicity does not beat around the bush. It does not take winding detours. It follows a straight line to the objective. Simplicity is the shortest distance between two points. – WILFERD ARLAN PETERSON, *The New Book of the Art of Living*, page 50

The art of simplicity is simply to simplify. – WILFERD ARLAN PETERSON, *The New Book of the Art of Living*, page 50

Satori is emancipation, moral, spiritual, as well as intellectual. When I am in my isness, thoroughly purged of all intellectual sediments, I have my freedom in its primary sense. ... When the mind, now abiding in its isness—which, to use Zen verbalism, is not isness—and thus free from intellectual complexities and moralistic attachments of every description, surveys the world of the senses in all its multiplicities, it discovers in it all sorts of values hitherto hidden from sight. Here opens to the artist a world full of wonders and miracles. – D. T. SUZUKI, *Zen and Japanese Culture*, pages 16-17

Besides its direct method of reaching final faith, Zen is a religion of will-power, and will-power is what is urgently needed by the warriors, though it ought to be enlightened by intuition. – D. T. SUZUKI, *Zen and Japanese Culture*, page 63

While being trained in the art, the pupil is to be active and dynamic in every way. But in actual combat, his mind must be calm and not at all disturbed. He must feel as if nothing critical is happening. When he advances, his steps are securely on the ground, and his eyes are not glaringly fixed on the enemy as those of an insane man might be. His behavior is not in any way different from his everyday behavior. No change is taking place in his expression. Nothing betrays the fact that he is now engaged in a mortal fight. – D. T. SUZUKI, *Zen and Japanese Culture*, page 185

The sword has thus a double office to perform: to destroy anything that opposes the will of its owner and to sacrifice all the impulses that arise from the instinct of self-preservation. ... The sword comes to be identified with the annihilation of things that lie in the way of peace, justice, progress, and humanity. It stands for all that is desirable for the spiritual welfare of the world at large. It is now the embodiment of life and not of death. ... Zen speaks of the sword of life and the sword of death, and it is the work of a great Zen master to know when and how to wield either of them. Mañjuśrī carries a sword in his right hand and a sutra in his left. This may remind us of the prophet Mohammed, but the sacred sword of Mañjuśrī is not to kill any sentient beings, but our own greed, anger, and folly. It is directed toward ourselves, for when this is done the outside world, which is the reflection of what is within us, becomes also free from greed, anger, and folly. – D. T. SUZUKI, *Zen and Japanese Culture*, pages 89-90

The sword here represents the force of intuitive or instinctual directness, which unlike the intellect does not divide itself, blocking its own passageway. It marches onward without looking backward or sideways. It is like Chuang-Tzi's dissecting knife that cuts along the joints as if they were waiting to be separated. – D. T SUZUKI, *Zen and Japanese Culture*, page 90

The sword is altogether independent of all sorts of worldly interests and motivations that taint the character of its wielder. And just because of the pure-heartedness and "empty-mindedness" (mushin, wu-hsin) of the man, the sword partakes of this quality and plays its role with the utmost degree of freedom. ... This sword stands as symbol of the invisible spirit keeping the mind, body, and limbs in full activity. – D. T. SUZUKI, *Zen and Japanese Culture*, pages 181, 159

The absence of a system of stereotyped techniques. – D. T. SUZUKI, *Zen and Japanese Culture*, page 179

Nonattachment is man's original nature. [In its ordinary process], thought moves forward without a halt; past, present, and future thoughts continue as an unbroken stream. But if we can cut off this stream by an instant of thought, the Dharma-Body will be separated from the physical body, and at no time will a single thought be attached to any dharma. – HUI-NENG, quoted in *World of the Buddha* (edited by Lucien Stryk), page 338

Absence of phenomena means to be free from phenomena when in contact with them. Absence of thought means not to be carried away by thought in the process of thought. – HUI-NENG, quoted in *World of the Buddha* (edited by Lucien Stryk), page 338

Absence of thought means not to be defiled by external objects. It is to free our thoughts from external objects and not to allow dharmas to cause our thoughts to rise. – HUI-NENG, quoted in *World of the Buddha* (edited by Lucien Stryk), page 339

True thusness is the substance of thought and thought is the function of true thusness. – HUI-NENG, "Platform Sutra" in *Sources of Chinese Tradition Volume I* (edited by William Theodore de Bary), page 394

To bring the mind into sharp focus and in make it alert so that it can immediately intuit Truth, which is everywhere, the mind must he emancipated from old habits, prejudices, restrictive thought processes., and even ordinary thought itself. – WING-TSIT CHAN, "Schools of Buddhism" in *Sources of Chinese Tradition Volume I* (edited by William Theodore de Bary), page 388

In either way, the spirit and teaching of Zen is discerned in Ichiun as well as in the legendary Buddha. Both want us to scratch away all the dirt our being has accumulated even before our birth and reveal Reality in its is-ness, or in its suchness, or in its nakedness, which corresponds to the Buddhist concept of emptiness (Sunyata). – D. T. SUZUKI, *Zen and Japanese Culture*, page 179

Nan-In, a Japanese master during the Meiji era (1868-1912), received a university professor who came to inquire about Zen. Nan-in served tea. He poured his visitor's cup full, and then kept on pouring. The professor watched the overflow until he no longer could restrain himself. "It is overfull. No more will go in!" "Like this cup," Nan-In said, "you are full of your own opinions and speculations. How can I show you Zen unless you first empty your cup?" – Zen story first published by Nyogen Senzaki as featured in Paul Reps' *Zen Flesh, Zen Bones*, page 19

Organized Despair

But each man belongs to a group which claims to possess truth to the exclusion of all other groups, and these groups become religions with their explanations of man and the universe in terms of God or of an economic system, in terms of the individual or of the collective, in terms of spirit or of matter, and thus we have chaos. ... All goals apart from means are therefore an illusion and becoming is a denial of being. ... By an error repeated throughout the ages, truth, becoming a law or a faith, places obstacles, in the way of knowledge. Method, which is in its very substance ignorance, encloses it within a vicious circle which, Krishnamurti says, we should break not by seeking knowledge, but by discovering the cause of ignorance. CARLO SUARÈS, *Krishnamurti and the Unity of the Man*, pages 1-3

Paul Reps

Paul Reps was a poet, artist, and buddhist scholar. Born in Cedar City, Iowa in 1895, Reps is considered one of America's first haiku poets.

Reps spent many of his early years in Asia studying Zen buddhism. He authored a number of books, and chief among them was *Zen Flesh, Zen Bones. A Collection of Zen and Pre-Zen Writings*. A popular book that influenced a great number of people, including Bruce Lee, it provided Lee with his first exposure to the often-repeated parable about the Zen master who admonishes the Western scholar to "empty his cup".

Paul Reps passed away in 1990 at the age of 94.

But most people, instead of looking directly into the fact, cling to words and their commentaries and go on entangling themselves further and further, finally putting themselves into an inextricable snare. – D. T. SUZUKI, *Zen and Japanese Culture*, page 176

When we see a mountain, we do not see it in its suchness, but we attach to it all kinds of ideas, sometimes purely intellectual, but frequently charged with emotionality. When these envelop the mountain, it is transformed into something monstrous. This is due to our own indoctrination out of our "scholarly" learning and our vested interests, whether individual, political, social, economic, or religious. The picture thus formed is a hideous one, crooked and twisted in every possible way. Instead of living in a world presented to the Primary Nature in its nakedness, we live in an artificial, "cultured" one. The pity is that we are not conscious of the fact. – D. T. SUZUKI, *Zen and Japanese Culture*, page 175

To reach maturity does not mean to become a captive of conceptualization. It is to come to the realization of what lies in our innermost selves. This is "true knowledge" (ryochi), "sincerity" (makoto), "reverence" (kei), "'unmistakableness" (tanteki). However old a man may grow, he will not find it outworn. "Infantism" is ever fresh, energizing, and inspiring. – D. T. SUZUKI, *Zen and Japanese Culture*, pages 176-177

When there is freedom from beliefs, there is simplicity. – JIDDU KRISHNAMURTI, *The First and Last Freedom*, page 89

Wing-Tsit Chan

Wing-Tsit Chan was one of the most respected scholars of Chinese philosophy in the 20th Century. Educated at Lingnan University and Harvard, Chan taught philosophy at Columbia and Dartmouth universities.

Wing-Tsit Chan authored the book *A Source Book in Chinese Philosophy*, the contents of which Bruce Lee can be seen perusing in the most widely-circulated photo of Lee in front of his personal library.

The man who is clear and simple does not choose; what is, is. Action based on an idea is obviously the action of choice and such action is not liberating; on the contrary, it only creates further resistance, further conflict, according to that conditioned thinking. ... Life is a matter of relationship; and to understand that relationship, which is not static, there must be an awareness which is pliable, an awareness which is alertly passive, not aggressively active. – JIDDU KRISHNAMURTI, *The First and Last Freedom*, page 98

Our problem is not capacity—for capacity is not independent of relationship—but rather the understanding of relationship, which will naturally produce the capacity for quick pliability, for quick adjustment, for quick response. Relationship, surely, is the mirror in which you discover yourself. Without relationship you are not; to be is to be related. – JIDDU KRISHNAMURTI, *The First and Last Freedom*, page 104

The superficial mind may compel itself, make itself quiet; but surely such quietness is the quietness of decay, death. It is not capable of adaptability, pliability, sensitivity. So resistance is not the way. – JIDDU KRISHNAMURTI, *The First and Last Freedom*, page 160

Rituals are vain repetition which offer a marvellous and respectable escape from self-knowledge. – JIDDU KRISHNAMURTI, *Commentaries on Living, First Series*, page 24

Accumulation is self-enclosing resistance and knowledge strengthens this resistance. – JIDDU KRISHNAMURTI, *Commentaries on Living, First Series*, page 27

If you say, "There is nothing much to learn about myself because I am just a bundle of memories, ideas, experiences and traditions", then you have also stopped learning about yourself. ... The moment you have a conclusion or start examining from knowledge, you are finished, for then you are translating every living thing in terms of the old. – JIDDU KRISHNAMURTI, *Freedom from the Known*, page 24

Knowledge, surely, is always of time, whereas knowing is not of time. Knowledge is from a source, from an accumulation, from a conclusion, while knowing is a movement. A mind that is constantly in the movement of knowing, learning, has no source from which it knows. – JIDDU KRISHNAMURTI, *Talks by Krishnamurti January - June 1960: (Verbatim Report) Bombay - Banaras - New Delhi - Ojai*, page 84

Learning does not mean starting with a certain amount of knowledge and adding to it further knowledge. That is not learning at all; it is a purely mechanistic process. ... When I say, "I know myself", learning has come to an end in accumulated knowledge. Learning is never cumulative; it is a movement of knowing which has no beginning and no end. – JIDDU KRISHNAMURTI, *Talks by Krishnamurti January - June 1960: (Verbatim Report) Bombay - Banaras - New Delhi - Ojai*, page 85

You have now read a series of statements, but have you really understood? Your conditioned mind, your way of life, the whole structure of the society in which you live, prevent you from looking at a fact and being entirely free from it immediately. – JIDDU KRISHNAMURTI, *Freedom from the Known*, pages 56-57

To be free of all authority, of your own and that of another, is to die to everything of yesterday. ... The man who is not frightened of life is not frightened of being completely insecure for he understands that inwardly, psychologically, there is no security. When there is no security there is an endless movement and then life and death are the same. – JIDDU KRISHNAMURTI, *Freedom from the Known*, page 19, 77

If you say, "I am free", then you are not free. It is like a man saying, "I am happy". The moment he says, "I am happy" he is living in a memory of something that has gone. ... To come upon it the mind has to learn to look at life, which is a vast movement, without the bondage of time, for freedom lies beyond the field of consciousness. ... To be free of all authority, of your own and that of another, is to die to everything of yesterday. – JIDDU KRISHNAMURTI, *Freedom from the Known*, page 71, 20

Freedom from the known is death, and then you are living. ... To find out actually what takes place when you die you must die. This isn't a joke. You must die—not physically but psychologically, inwardly, die to the things you have cherished and to the things you are bitter about. If you have died to one of your pleasures, the smallest or the greatest, naturally, without any enforcement or argument, then you will know what it means to die. – JIDDU KRISHNAMURTI, *Freedom from the Known*, page 78, 77

It is only when you do not respond to a challenge with your whole being that there is a conflict, a struggle, and this brings confusion and pleasure or pain. And the struggle breeds memory. That memory is added to all the time by other memories, and it is those memories which respond. Anything that is the result of memory is old and therefore never free. There is no such thing as freedom of thought. It is sheer nonsense. – JIDDU KRISHNAMURTI, *Freedom from the Known*, page 36

Secondly, Zen discipline is simple, direct, self-reliant, self-denying; its ascetic tendency goes well with the fighting spirit. The fighter is to be always single-minded with one object in view; to fight, looking neither backward nor sidewise. To go straight forward in order to crush the enemy is all that is necessary for him. He is therefore not to be encumbered in any possible way, be it physical, emotional, or intellectual. – D. T. SUZUKI, *Zen and Japanese Culture*, page 62

If you want to understand the actual you must give your whole attention, all your energy, to it. That attention and energy are distracted when you create a fictitious, ideal world. So can you completely banish the ideal? The man who is really serious, with the urge to find out what truth is, what love is, has no concept at all. He lives only in what is. – JIDDU KRISHNAMURTI, *Freedom from the Known*, page 56

Freedom from the Known (1969)

Krishnamurti shows how people can free themselves radically and immediately from the tyranny of the expected -- opening the door to transforming society and relationships. *(from the publisher)*

So, to go into the question of what love is we must first free it from the encrustation of centuries, put away all ideals and ideologies of what it should or should not be. To divide anything into what should be and what is, is the most deceptive way of dealing with life. – JIDDU KRISHNAMURTI, *Freedom from the Known*, pages 80-81

And no one can teach you how to be attentive. If any system teaches you how to be attentive, then you are attentive to the system and that is not attention. – JIDDU KRISHNAMURTI, *Freedom from the Known*, page 116

The specialist, the psychologist, the analyst, have divided fear into deep and superficial layers, but if you follow what the psychologist says or what I say, you are understanding our theories, our dogmas, our knowledge, you are not understanding yourself. – JIDDU KRISHNAMURTI, *Freedom from the Known*, page 45

There is only total fear, but how can the mind which thinks in fragments observe this total picture? – JIDDU KRISHNAMURTI, *Freedom from the Known*, page 45

So, experience does not free the mind, and learning through experience is only a process of forming new patterns based on one's old conditioning. I think it is very important to understand this, because as we grow older, we get more and more entrenched in our experience, hoping thereby to learn; but what we learn is dictated by the background, which means that through the experience by which we learn there is never freedom but only the modification of conditioning. – JIDDU KRISHNAMURTI, *Think on These Things*, page 160

Fundamentally, discipline implies some kind of conformity, does it not? It is conformity to an ideal, to an authority; it is the cultivation of resistance, which of necessity breeds opposition. – JIDDU KRISHNAMURTI, *Commentaries on Living, Second Series*, page 48

Mere isolation in an enclosing idea is not a release from conflict. ... When you are in a receptive state of mind, things can be easily understood; you are listening when your real attention is given to something. But unfortunately, most of us listen through a screen of resistance. We are screened with prejudices, whether religious or spiritual, psychological or scientific; or with our daily worries, desires and fears. And with these for a screen, we listen. Therefore, we listen really to our own noise, to our own sound, not to what is being said. – JIDDU KRISHNAMURTI, *Freedom from the Known*, pages 29, 21

Ideas have become far more important to us than action—ideas so cleverly expressed in books by the intellectuals in every field. The more cunning, the more subtle, those ideas are the more we worship them and the books that contain them. We are those books, we are those ideas, so heavily conditioned are we by them. We are forever discussing ideas and ideals and dialectically offering opinions. – JIDDU KRISHNAMURTI, *Freedom from the Known*, page 100

Truth cannot be given to you by somebody. You have to discover it; and to discover, there must be a state of mind in which there is direct perception. There is no direct perception when there is a resistance, a safeguard, a protection. Understanding comes through being aware of what is. – JIDDU KRISHNAMURTI, *Freedom from the Known*, page 20

It needs an extraordinarily astute mind, an extraordinarily pliable heart, to be aware of and to follow what is; because what *is* is constantly moving, constantly undergoing a transformation, and if the mind is tethered to belief, to knowledge, it ceases to pursue, it ceases to follow the swift movement of what is. What *is* is not static, surely—it is constantly moving, as you will see if you observe it very closely. – JIDDU KRISHNAMURTI, *Freedom from the Known*, page 21

Whatever one's opinion about the advisability of making hooking and swinging part of one's style, there cannot be the least argument about the necessity of acquiring perfect defence against it. Nearly all modern boxers hook and swing a great deal, indeed many of the strongest natural fighters do practically nothing else. – NORMAN CLARK, *How to Box*, page 93

How can there be ways, methods, systems by which to arrive at something that is living? To that which is static, fixed, dead, there can be a way, a definite path, but not to that which is living. If you want to understand your wife, your neighbour, your friend, there is no 'way' to do it; there is no system by which to understand a living human being. Similarly, you cannot go to that which is living, dynamic, through any way or method. But you reduce reality, God, or what name you will, to a static thing, and then invent methods by which to reach it. – JIDDU KRISHNAMURTI, *Talks by Krishnamurti January - June 1960: (Verbatim Report) Bombay - Banaras - New Delhi - Ojai*, page 32

Truth has no path, and that is the beauty of truth, it is living. A dead thing has a path to it because it is static, but when you see that truth is something living, moving, which has no resting place, which is in no temple, mosque or church, which no religion, no teacher, no philosopher, nobody can lead you to—then you will also see that this living thing is what you actually are— your anger, your brutality, your violence, your despair, the agony and sorrow you live in. In the understanding of all this is the truth, and you can understand it only if you know how to look at those things in your life. And you cannot look through an ideology, through a screen of words, through hopes and fears. – JIDDU KRISHNAMURTI, *Freedom from the Known*, page 15

Actually, there is no such thing as bodhi wisdom. What the Buddha talked about in that connection was an adaptation of means to the end of men, like pretending yellow leaves are gold coins in order to stop the children crying. ... Thus, to avoid creating a new karma involves avoiding spiritual cultivation. That being so, the true cultivation is to not cultivate. Hence this kind of cultivation is the cultivation of non-cultivating. – FUNG YU-LAN, *The Spirit of Chinese Philosophy*, page 162

To avoid creating a new karma is not to refrain from doing anything at all, but to have no deliberate mind in whatever one does. As Ma Tsu put it, "The intrinsic nature of man is already enough. Not to be clamped to either good or evil, this is all that a man engaged in spiritual cultivation needs to do. To cleave to the good and to eschew evil, and to regard all things as unreal and to enter into contemplation, all these are creaturely activities." ... To be without a deliberate mind is to have no thoughts. – FUNG YU-LAN, *The Spirit of Chinese Philosophy*, pages 162, 163

Acceptance, denial and conviction prevent understanding. To understand, surely, there must be a state of attention in which there is no sense of comparison or condemnation, no waiting for a further development of the thing we are talking about in order to agree or disagree. There is an abeyance or suspension of all opinion, of all sense of condemnation or comparison; you are just listening to find out. Your approach is one of inquiry, which means that you don't start from a conclusion; therefore, you are in a state of attention, which is really listening. – JIDDU KRISHNAMURTI, *Talks by Krishnamurti January - June 1960: (Verbatim Report) Bombay - Banaras - New Delhi - Ojai*, page 83

We are concerned with understanding the mind; and in understanding there is no condemnation, no demand for a pattern of action. You are merely observing; and observation is denied when you concern yourself with a pattern of action, or merely explain the inevitability of a slavish life. – JIDDU KRISHNAMURTI, *Talks by Krishnamurti January - June 1960: (Verbatim Report) Bombay - Banaras - New Delhi - Ojai*, page 4

We may have political freedom but inwardly we are not free and therefore there is no space. No virtue, no quality that is worthwhile, can function or grow without this vast space within oneself. And space and silence are necessary because it is only when the mind is alone, uninfluenced, untrained, not held by infinite varieties of experience, that it can come upon something totally new. – JIDDU KRISHNAMURTI, *Freedom from the Known*, page 106

There is an awareness without choice, without any demand, an awareness in which there is no anxiety; and in that state of mind there is perception. It is this perception alone that will resolve all our problems. – JIDDU KRISHNAMURTI, *Talks by Krishnamurti January - June 1960: (Verbatim Report) Bombay - Banaras - New Delhi - Ojai*, page 86

To understand what is knowledge and go beyond the partial, the limited, to experience that which is creative, requires, not just a moment of perception, but a continuous awareness, a continuous state of inquiry in which there is no conclusion—and this, after all, is intelligence. – JIDDU KRISHNAMURTI, *Talks by Krishnamurti January - June 1960: (Verbatim Report) Bombay - Banaras - New Delhi - Ojai*, page 83

The problems of the world are so colossal, so very complex, that to understand and so to resolve them one must approach them in a very simple and direct manner; and simplicity, directness, do not depend on outward circumstances nor on our particular prejudices and moods. – JIDDU KRISHNAMURTI, *The First and Last Freedom*, page 42

The understanding of oneself is not a result, a culmination; it is seeing oneself from moment to moment in the mirror of relationship—one's relationship to property, to things, to people and to ideas. – JIDDU KRISHNAMURTI, *The First and Last Freedom*, page 48

In order to act rightly, there must be right thinking; to think rightly, there must be self-knowledge; and self-knowledge can come about only through relationship, not through isolation. – JIDDU KRISHNAMURTI, *Krishnamurti's Talks in India 1948 (Verbatim Report) Series II - Bangalore*, page 84

To know oneself is to study oneself in action, which is relationship. – JIDDU KRISHNAMURTI, *The First and Last Freedom*, page 32

If you want to understand the actual you must give your whole attention, all your energy, to it. That attention and energy are distracted when you create a fictitious, ideal world. So can you completely banish the ideal? The man who is really serious, with the urge to find out what truth is, what love is, has no concept at all. He lives only in what is. – JIDDU KRISHNAMURTI, *Freedom from the Known*, page 56

Whatever the mind does to free itself will always be within the field of time. Any effort the mind makes will further limit the mind, because effort implies the struggle towards a goal; and when you have a goal, a purpose, an end in view, you have placed a limit on the mind; and it is with such a mind that you are trying to meditate. – JIDDU KRISHNAMURTI, *Talks by Krishnamurti January - June 1960: (Verbatim Report) Bombay - Banaras - New Delhi - Ojai*, page 29

This evening I see something totally new, and that newness is experienced by the mind; but tomorrow that experience becomes mechanical, because I want to repeat the sensation, the pleasure of it. I establish a process, I set up a method through which I seek to recapture that newness; so it becomes mechanical. Everything the mind touches, inevitably becomes mechanical, non-creative. – JIDDU KRISHNAMURTI, *Talks by Krishnamurti January - June 1960: (Verbatim Report) Bombay - Banaras - New Delhi - Ojai*, page 30

We shall find the truth when we examine the problem. The problem is never apart from the answer; the problem is the answer. If I examine the problem, if I am sympathetic, sensitive to the problem, if I look into it, explore it, I begin to understand it; and the understanding of the problem is the dissolution of the problem. – JIDDU KRISHNAMURTI, *Talks by Krishnamurti January - June 1960: (Verbatim Report) Bombay - Banaras - New Delhi - Ojai*, page 89

The capacity to delve into what is comes into being when we observe what is with undivided attention. – JIDDU KRISHNAMURTI, *Talks by Krishnamurti January - June 1960: (Verbatim Report) Bombay - Banaras - New Delhi - Ojai*, page 84

True thusness is without thought; it cannot be known through conception and thought. – SHEN-HUI, "Elucidating the Doctrine" in *Sources of Chinese Tradition Volume I* (edited by William Theodore de Bary), page 426

All thought is partial, it can never be total. Thought is the response of memory, and memory is always partial, because memory is the result of experience; so thought is the reaction of a mind which is conditioned by experience. All thinking, all experience, all knowledge is inevitably partial; therefore, thought cannot solve the many problems that we have. – JIDDU KRISHNAMURTI, *Talks by Krishnamurti January - June 1960: (Verbatim Report) Bombay - Banaras - New Delhi - Ojai*, page 84

The mind is originally without activity; the Way is always without thought. – SHEN-HUI, "Elucidating the Doctrine" in *Sources of Chinese Tradition Volume I* (edited by William Theodore de Bary), page 397

Insight means realizing that one's original nature is not created. – SHEN-HUI, "Elucidating the Doctrine" in *Sources of Chinese Tradition Volume I* (edited by William Theodore de Bary), page 398

There will be calmness when one is free from external objects and is not perturbed. – HUI-NENG in *Sources of Chinese Tradition Volume I* (edited by William Theodore de Bary), page 395

Being tranquil means not having been created. ... Not being created means not having any illusion or delusion. – SHEN-HUI, "Elucidating the Doctrine" in *Sources of Chinese Tradition Volume I* (edited by William Theodore de Bary), pages 399, 400

There is no thought except that of the true thusness. Thusness does not move, but its motion and function are inexhaustible. – SHEN-HUI, "Elucidating the Doctrine" in *Sources of Chinese Tradition Volume I* (edited by William Theodore de Bary), page 396

To meditate means to realize the imperturbability of one's original nature. Meditation means to be free from all phenomena and calmness means to be internally unperturbed. – HUI-NENG, in *Sources of Chinese Tradition Volume I* (edited by William Theodore de Bary), page 394

Meditation, surely, can never be a process of concentration, because the highest form of thinking is negative thinking. Positive thinking is destructive to inquiry, to discovery. I am thinking aloud, negatively. Through negation there is creation. Negation is not the opposite of the positive, but a state in which there is neither the positive nor its reaction as the negative. It is a state of complete emptiness; and it is only when the mind is completely empty, in this sense, that there is creation. – JIDDU KRISHNAMURTI, *Talks by Krishnamurti January - June 1960: (Verbatim Report) Bombay - Banaras - New Delhi - Ojai*, page 31

Concentration is a form of exclusion; and where there is exclusion, there is a thinker who excludes. It is the thinker, the excluder, the one who concentrates, that creates contradiction, because then there is a centre from which there can be a deviation, a distraction. – JIDDU KRISHNAMURTI, *Talks by Krishnamurti January - June 1960: (Verbatim Report) Bombay - Banaras - New Delhi - Ojai*, page 31

There is a state of action, a state of experiencing, without the experiencer and the experience. This sounds rather philosophical, but it is really quite simple. – JIDDU KRISHNAMURTI, *The First and Last Freedom*, page 51

Concentration is exclusion; attention, which is total awareness, excludes nothing. It seems to me that most of us are not aware, not only of what we are talking about but of our environment, the colours around us, the people, the shape of the trees, the clouds, the movement of water. – JIDDU KRISHNAMURTI, *Freedom from the Known*, page 31

So the problem is, surely, to free the mind totally, so that it is in a state of awareness which has no border, no frontier. ... The state of attention, which is not concentration, has no frontier; it is a giving of your whole being to something, without exclusion. – JIDDU KRISHNAMURTI, *Talks by Krishnamurti January - June 1960: (Verbatim Report) Bombay - Banaras - New Delhi - Ojai*, pages 7, 30

Concentration is a narrowing down of the mind. To narrow down the mind may be very effective in the case of a school-boy in a class; but we are concerned with the total process of living, and to concentrate exclusively on any particular aspect of life, belittles life. – JIDDU KRISHNAMURTI, *Talks by Krishnamurti January - June 1960: (Verbatim Report) Bombay - Banaras - New Delhi - Ojai*, pages 31-32

Love is something that is new, fresh, alive. It has no yesterday and no tomorrow. It is beyond the turmoil of thought. It is only the innocent mind which knows what love is, and the innocent mind can live in the world which is not innocent. – JIDDU KRISHNAMURTI, *Freedom from the Known*, page 89

But we do not ask. We want to be told. One of the most curious things in the structure of our psyche is that we all want to be told because we are the result of the propaganda of ten thousand years. – JIDDU KRISHNAMURTI, *Freedom from the Known*, page 121

Do you use the opposite as a means of avoiding the actual which you don't know how to deal with? Or is it because you have been told by thousands of years of propaganda that you must have an ideal - the opposite of 'what is' - in order to cope with the present? When you have an ideal you think it helps you to get rid of 'what is', but it never does. ... You have a concept of what you should be and how you should act, and all the time you are in fact acting quite differently; so you see that principles, beliefs and ideals must inevitably lead to hypocrisy and a dishonest life. – JIDDU KRISHNAMURTI, *Freedom from the Known*, pages 65-66

My mind does not want to be disturbed; it does not want to question, to be made uncertain, so it establishes a pattern of conduct, of thought, a pattern of relationship to man and to nature, as well as to possessions, things. ... The mind invents symbols and becomes a slave to the symbols; and then the symbols become far more important than the action of living. – JIDDU KRISHNAMURTI, *Talks by Krishnamurti January - June 1960: (Verbatim Report) Bombay - Banaras - New Delhi - Ojai*, pages 28-29

While, from one point of view, Zen has no method, from another it has a definite technique of meditation. It is against this background of definite technique that the "method of no-method" has its value as a surprising contrast. The success of Zen lies in its freedom both to use technique and to dispense with it; it is not bound to any one-sided procedure. – ALAN WATTS, *Zen*, page 32

We accept a standard of behaviour as part of our tradition as Hindus or Muslims or Christians or whatever we happen to be. We look to someone to tell us what is right or wrong behaviour, what is right or wrong thought, and in following this pattern our conduct and our thinking become mechanical, our responses automatic. ... We are second-hand people. We have lived on what we have been told, either guided by our inclinations, our tendencies, or compelled to accept by circumstances and environment. We are the result of all kinds of influences and there is nothing new in us, nothing that we have discovered for ourselves; nothing original, pristine, clear. – JIDDU KRISHNAMURTI, *Freedom from the Known*, pages 9-10

The self is a complex entity, moving, living, struggling, wanting, denying, with pressures and stresses and influences of all sorts continually at work on it. So you will discover for yourself that this is not the way; you will understand that the only way to look at yourself is totally, immediately, without time; and you can see the totality of yourself only when the mind is not fragmented. What you see in totality is the truth. – JIDDU KRISHNAMURTI, *Freedom from the Known*, page 30

Jiddu Krishnamurti

Jiddu Krishnamurti was born into poverty in the Indian city of Madanappalle on May 11, 1895.

In 1909, the then 13-year-old Krishnamurti made the acquaintance of Charles Leadbeater, a leader in the religious movement known as Theosophy. Leadbeater claimed to sense an aura around Krishnamurti and began to suspect that the boy was a vessel for Theosophical deity Lord Maitreya, whom Theosophists believed had previously been incarnated in the person of Jesus Christ. With his parents' permission, Leadbeater and the Theosophical Society took guardianship of Jiddu Krishnamurti with the intention to prepare him for his role as the great World Teacher. A new organization, the Order of the Star in the East, was formed with the sole purpose of facilitating Krishnamurti's education and grooming.

Krishnamurti was relocated to England to be educated in the Western fashion. In England, he was heralded by Theosophists as their coming World Teacher, although he made a poor student in Western academics.

In 1922, Krishnamurti, then 27 years of age, relocated to Ojai, California. On August 17, 1922, Krishnamurti reported experiencing a sharp pain at the back of his neck. He fell into a state of delirium mixed with periods of unconsciousness where he claimed to have a mystical experience; the symptoms continued nightly for approximately two months, during which he claimed to have gained a greater spiritual awakening.

When his brother Nitya died in 1925, Krishnamurti, who had been told that his brother was essential to Krishnamurti's purpose as the World Teacher, began to question the truth of Theosophy. His philosophy and talks began to evolve and take on a new direction.

On August 3, 1929, the Order of the Star in the East gathered at a camp in the city of Ommen in the Netherlands to make official Jiddu Krishnamurti's ascension to the role of World Teacher and the commanding figure of the Order. Upon accepting his role, Krishnamurti shocked the attendees and (when the news spread) the entire Theosophical movement by immediately dissolving the Order of the Star in the East and declaring that he was no incarnated deity. Further, he admonished the audience for their blind devotion to religious institutions and adherence to religious doctrine. "I maintain that truth is a pathless land," said Krishnamurti, "and you cannot approach it by any path whatsoever, by any religion, by any sect. That is my point of view, and I adhere to that absolutely and unconditionally. Truth, being limitless, unconditioned, unapproachable by any path whatsoever, cannot be organized; nor should any organization be formed to lead or coerce people along a particular path."

Krishnamurti spent the remaining decades of his life as a celebrated philosopher, author, and speaker, carrying his message of personal liberation to millions of people, including being a monumental influence on the beliefs of Bruce Lee, who first discovered the philosophy of Krishnamurti in a California bookstore in 1966. Bruce Lee may even have realized the opportunity to see and speak with Krishnamurti. An entry in Lee's daytimer diary, dated March 7, 1971, indicated his intent to attend a talk by Krishnamurti that morning at the Santa Monica Civic Auditorium. Whether he actually attended is unknown.

It becomes clearer and clearer that every neurosis conceals a universal human problem—the problem of ripening. In its deepest sense ripening means the same thing both for the sound and the unsound, that is, the progressive integration of the individual with his being, his essence, wherein he takes part in the great Being. – KARLFRIED GRAF VON DURCKHEIM, *Hara: The Vital Centre of Man*, page 12

A point of tremendous importance is that, for the Zen masters, art is never decoration, embellishment; instead it is work of enlightenment, illumination, salvation, not in a narrow, pietistic sense, but in the sense of a flash of sudden, profound significance. Art, in other words, is a technique for acquiring liberty. The intellect having been dethroned, the artist's intuition becomes the connecting link between the self and the all. – FOSCO MARAINI, *Meeting with Japan*, page 291

Experience is an impediment to truth, for experience is of time, it is the outcome of the past; and how can a mind which is the result of experience, of time, understand the timeless? The truth of experience does not depend on personal idiosyncrasies and fancies; the truth of it is perceived only when there is awareness without condemnation, justification, or any form of identification. – JIDDU KRISHNAMURTI, *Commentaries on Living, First Series*, page 93-94

Detachment refers to independence of concepts, rules, and standards; not clinging or leaning; hence, the freedom of the formless to assume all forms. – VAN METER AMES, "Art for Zen and Dewey", *Proceedings of the IV International Congress of Aesthetics, Athens*, page 746

The School of Zen Buddhism may be viewed as part of the Mahayana school or entirely on its own. It uses all scriptures and is bound by none, and likewise uses any technique or means (upaya) which serves its end, which is to awaken the pupil's mind to its own enlightenment. – CHRISTMAS HUMPHREYS, *Zen Comes West*, page 21

Partial culture runs to the ornate; extreme culture to simplicity. – CHRISTIAN NESTELL BOVEE, *A Dictionary of Thoughts: Being a Cyclopedia of Laconic Quotations from the Best Authors of the World, Both Ancient and Modern* (edited by Tryon Edwards), page 111

How is it possible then to free ourselves from the psychological structure of society, which is to free ourselves from the essence of conflict? It is not difficult to trim and lop off certain branches of conflict, but we are asking ourselves whether it is possible to live in complete inward and therefore outward tranquility? – JIDDU KRISHNAMURTI, *Freedom from the Known*, page 61

So, I must enquire into what it means to see totally. As long as I am looking at life from a particular point of view or from a particular experience I have cherished, or from some particular knowledge I have gathered, which is my background, which is the 'me', I cannot see totally. I have discovered intellectually, verbally, through analysis, the cause of my dependence, but whatever thought investigates must inevitably be fragmentary, so I can see the totality of something only when thought does not interfere. – JIDDU KRISHNAMURTI, *Freedom from the Known*, page 62

Let us put it another way. We are always comparing what we are with what we should be. The should-be is a projection of what we think we ought to be. Contradiction exists when there is comparison, not only with something or somebody, but with what you were yesterday, and hence there is conflict between what has been and what is. There is *what is* only when there is no comparison at all, and to live with what is, is to be peaceful. – JIDDU KRISHNAMURTI, *Freedom from the Known*, page 63

Truth is not something dictated by your pleasure or pain, or by your conditioning as a Hindu or whatever religion you belong to. The religious mind is a state of mind in which there is no fear and therefore no belief whatsoever but only what is—what actually is. – JIDDU KRISHNAMURTI, *Freedom from the Known*, page 119

The sword used by men of this school therefore, no ordinary sword with a form, or at least with a definitely designated form. Being swordsmen, they no doubt carry a sword in their hands when encountering an actual opponent, but the sword is a sword of formless form. When an enemy stands before it, therefore, he does not know how to cope with it, he cannot trace its movements, and before he can adjust himself, he is already beaten down. – D. T. SUZUKI, *Zen and Japanese Culture*, page 201

Odagiri Ichiun, or rather Hariya Sekiun, who was Ichiun's teacher and the founder of the school, called it "The Sword of No-abiding Mind" (Mujushin-ken). This phrase is taken from the Mahayana-Buddhist Vimalakirti Sutra (Yu ma Kyo), one of the texts very much used by Zen-men. The sutra describes the ultimate source of all things as "No-abode." "No-abode" or "having no abiding place anywhere" means that the ultimate source of all things is beyond human understanding, beyond the categories of time and space. As it thus transcends all modes of relativity, it is called "having no abode" to which any possible predications are applicable. The sword used by men of this school is, therefore, no ordinary sword with a form, or at least with a definitely designated form. – D. T. SUZUKI, *Zen and Japanese Culture*, page 201

Psychologically stated, the sword now symbolizes the Unconscious in the person of the swordsman. He then moves as a kind of automaton. He is no more himself. He has given himself up to an influence outside his everyday consciousness, which is no other than his own deeply buried Unconscious, whose presence he was never hitherto aware of. – D. T. SUZUKI, *Zen and Japanese Culture*, page 209

The human being is not a local entity. He is everywhere. If the individual merely acts in a particular corner of the vast field of life, then his action is totally unrelated to the whole. So, one has to bear in mind that we are talking of the whole not the part, because in the greater the lesser is, but in the lesser the greater is not. – JIDDU KRISHNAMURTI, *Freedom from the Known*, page 12

Hui-neng's first two lines, on the contrary point out that what the "First Principle" expresses is really inexpressible, and his last two lines say that for reaching it there can be no spiritual cultivation. No cultivation does not really mean the absence of any kind of cultivation. What it signifies is a "cultivation by means of non-cultivation." These differences between Shen-hsiu and Hui-neng represent differences between the northern branch of Ch'anism (which later became discredited), and the southern branch. Thus, it was asserted by most subsequent Ch'anists that the way to express the First Principle is not to say anything about it, that is, "to state through non-statement"; likewise they maintained that the way to cultivate spiritual cultivation is not to cultivate, that is, "to cultivate through non-cultivation." ... To practice cultivation through cultivation is to act with conscious mind, that is to say, to practice assertive activity. Such activity lies within the sphere of the things of life and death, and therefore is itself a thing subject to generation and destruction. – WILLIAM BRIGGS, *Anthology of Zen*, pages 86, 88

You have now started by denying something absolutely false—the traditional approach—but if you deny it as a reaction, you will have created another pattern in which you will be trapped; if you tell yourself intellectually that this denial is a very good idea but do nothing about it, you cannot go any further. – JIDDU KRISHNAMURTI, *Freedom from the Known*, page 11-12

PRELIMINARIES

To become different from what we are, we must have some awareness of what we are.

– ERIC HOFFER,
The Passionate State of Mind,
page 93

Training

Training is one of the most neglected phases of athletics. Too much time is given to the development of skill and too little to the development of the individual for participation. The body is treated as if it were an object and subject to definite rules and regulations. Nothing could be further from the truth. Training deals not with an object, but with the human spirit and human emotions. It takes intellect and judgment to handle such delicate qualities as these. – EDWIN HAISLET, *Boxing*, page 100

Training is the *psychological* and *physiological* conditioning of an individual preparing for intense neural and muscular reaction. It implies discipline of the mind and power and endurance of the body. It means skill. It is all these things working together in harmony. – EDWIN HAISLET, *Boxing*, page 100

Training means not only knowledge of the things which will build the body, but also knowledge of the things which will tear down or injure the body. Improper training will result in injuries. Training, then, is concerned with the prevention of injuries as well as first-aid to injuries. – EDWIN HAISLET, *Boxing*, page 100

BOXING BY EDWIN HAISLET

The book *Boxing* by Edwin L. Haislet (sometimes referred to as *Boxing: A Self-Instruction Manual*) was first released in 1940 by A. S. Barnes & Company, a major publisher of sports reference books in the mid-20th Century. *Boxing* became the best-selling title in the company's "Barnes Sports Library" series. By the time of Haislet's retirement from academia in 1976, the book was in its 20th printing.

The 120-page book by the Golden Gloves boxing coach covers the important fundamental points of stance and footwork as well as striking and defense. It is illustrated with drawings based on the photography of Phil Brain Sr., Haislet's colleague at the University of Minnesota and the school's tennis coach.

Celebrated fighting and martial arts analyst Jack Slack described the book *Boxing* as the "bible of striking" and "one of the best boxing manuals I have ever read."

Bruce Lee also agreed with that sentiment. No other book on fighting in Lee's collection is responsible for as many items found in the *Tao of Jeet Kune Do* as Haislet's book. The small book is the true source for 140 passages and images found between the covers of Bruce Lee's posthumous 1975 book.

To learn more about the author of *Boxing*, Edwin L. Haislet, read the biography of Haislet included in this book beginning on page 80.

WHO WROTE THE TAO?

Supplementary Training

Bob Hoffman's Daily Dozen

First Series - Daily Six
(Stretching Exercises)

1. [Forward] Bend
2. Twist
3. Stoop
4. Turn
5. Bend
6. [Cat] Stretch

Second Series - Daily Six
(Strength & Muscle Building Exercises)

7. [Palms Up] Curl
8. Pull
9. Press
10. Row
11. [Dead Weight] Lift
12. Squat

– BOB HOFFMAN, *Bob Hoffman's Daily Dozen*, page 7

Power Training

1. Press lockout
2. Press start
3. Rise on toes
4. Pull
5. Squat
6. Shrug
7. Deadlift
8. Quarter squat
9. Frog kick

– BOB HOFFMAN, *Functional Isometric Contraction System*, pages 21, 28

Warming Up

The process which elicits the acute physiological changes that prepare the organism for strenuous physical performance is known as "warming up". – LAURENCE ENGLEMOHR MOREHOUSE and PHILIP J. RASH, *Sports Medicine for Trainers*, page 24

To gain the greatest benefit, warming up procedures should imitate as closely as possible the movements to be used in the event. Warming up with a heavier implement, or using two bats or clubs, will impair coordination. – LAURENCE ENGLEMOHR MOREHOUSE and PHILIP J. RASH, *Sports Medicine for Trainers*, page 25

Warming up improves performance in vigorous activities by two essential means. First, a rehearsal of the skill before competition commences, fixes in the athlete's neuromuscular coordinating system the exact nature of the impending task. It also heightens his kinesthetic senses. Second, the rise in body temperature facilitates the biochemical reactions supplying energy for muscular contractions. Elevated body temperature also shortens the periods of muscular relaxation and aids in reducing stiffness. As a result of these two processes there is an improvement in accuracy, strength, and speed of movement, and an increase in tissue elasticity, which lessens the liability to injury. – LAURENCE ENGLEMOHR MOREHOUSE and PHILIP J. RASH, *Sports Medicine for Trainers*, page 24

TAO FAST FACTS

Much of the material that Bruce Lee intentionally prepared for *Tao of Jeet Kune Do* was published as the 1976 *Bruce Lee's Fighting Method* series by Mito Uyehara.

It is axiomatic that no baseball pitcher use his arm violently until he warms it up carefully. The same principle is equally applicable to any muscles that are to be used so vigorously, but the principle is not so well followed in some activities. In spite of great precautions, pulled or strained muscles are not unusual in track, and plague many fall football training camps. – JOHN DOBSON LAWTHER, *Psychology of Coaching*, page 276

The duration of the warm-up period varies with the event. In ballet the dancers spend two hours before the performance, commencing with very light movements and gradually increasing the intensity and range of motions until the moment before their appearance. This, they feel, reduces the risk of a pulled muscle which would destroy the perfection of their movements. – LAURENCE ENGLEMOHR MCREHOUSE and PHILIP J. RASH, *Sports Medicine for Trainers*, page 25-26

The athlete of more advanced years tends to warm up more slowly and for a longer time. This fact may be due to greater need for a longer warming-up period, or it may be because an athlete tends to get "smarter" as he gets older. – JOHN DOBSON LAWTHER, *Psychology of Coaching*, page 277

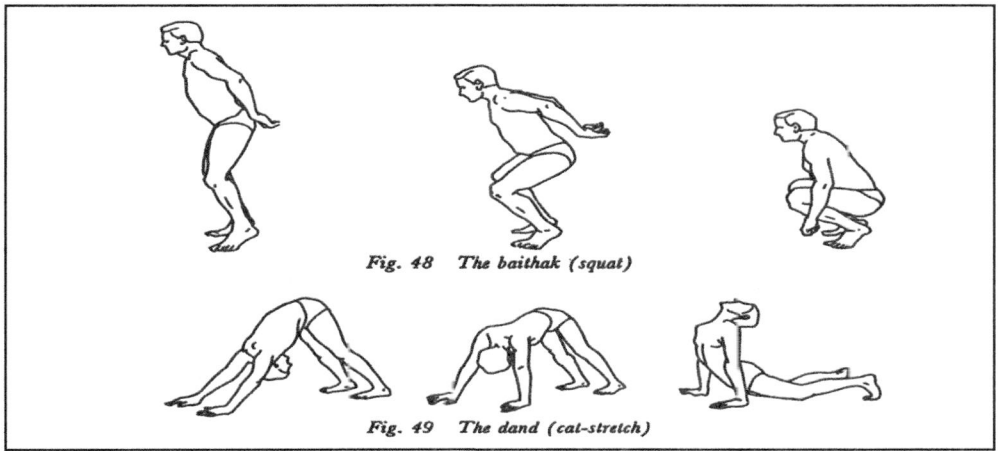

Fig. 48 The baithak (squat)

Fig. 49 The dand (cat-stretch)

Indian Wrestling Exercises – ROBERT W. SMITH and DONN DRAEGER, *Asian Fighting Arts*, page 148

On-Guard Position

Proper posture is a matter of effective interior organization of the body which can be achieved only by long and well-disciplined practice. – ROBERT G. BLANCHARD, *The Mechanics of Judo: Analytical Studies of Selected Standing Techniques*, page 21

[The On-Guard Position] – The body in this position should be so poised that all of its muscles can act with the greatest speed and ease. As all fencing movements develop from the guard, it follows that this position requires a pose which ensures complete muscular freedom. – LUIGI BARBASETTI, *The Art of the Foil: With a Short History of Fencing*, page 12

The fundamental boxing position is that position most favorable to the mechanical execution of the techniques and skills which make up boxing. It allows complete relaxation yet at the same time gives a muscle tonus most favorable to quick reaction time. – EDWIN HAISLET, *Boxing*, page 1

Coleman Roberts Griffith

Coleman Roberts Griffith (1893-1966) is often referred to as the father of sport psychology in America. Griffith earned his doctorate in experimental psychology in 1920 and was one of the first academics to establish a research center to study the psychological factors in sports. Ahead of his time, Griffith was unheralded during his life but found a new audience with the emergence of sports psychology as a distinct field in the 1960s.

Proper stance or correct posturing does three things:

- It ensures a position of the body and of its several members which is most favorable mechanically for the next move to be made. The stance of the track man on his marks favors in a mechanical way a quick start. The stance of the golfer favors an accurate swing at the ball. The stance of the forward in basketball favors in a mechanical way the balance and equilibrium of his body.
- Stance favors the maintenance of what we may call a "poker body," that is, a body which reveals no more of its intended movements than a poker face reveals the cards held by the player. A "poker body" is of particular value in football where the linesmen must give absolutely no hint of the play that is coming over their position. Neither may the backfield man give any hint of the direction of his run. It is a well-known law in psychology that the intended movements of a person are easily reflected in a corresponding bodily posture. If a man is planning to move to the right, he will have an involuntary tendency to lean in that direction. If a boxer plans to feint with his left and follow up with a right to the pit of the stomach, his eyes will have an involuntary tendency to flicker toward the opponent's abdomen. Stance means that the body is tensed just enough to conceal these movements which might betray a man. Too much stance, that is, a body which is too tense, stands in the way of quick reaction. Too little stance, that is, a body which is too much relaxed, reveals involuntary movement and also stands in the way of quick action.
- This leads to the third use of stance, *viz.*, putting the body under that particular tension or at that degree of tonus which will be most favorable to quick reaction and to high coordination. We are, as a matter of fact, never wholly relaxed, even when we go to sleep, unless we have given ourselves long training in that respect. An infant does relax-so completely that it feels as though it would fall apart in our arms were it not for the sack-like skin that holds it together. Men can approach this degree of relaxation by long and patient practice and it is a state in which rest is most beneficial; but it is a state that does not favor quick action. In ordinary life, the muscles of the body are always under partial contraction or always at a certain level of tonus. Proper stance means the distribution of tonus in such a way that actual movement of a coordinated group of muscles will come without delay and without inaccuracies.

– COLEMAN ROBERTS GRIFFITHS,
Psychology of Coaching: A Study of Coaching Methods from the Point of View of Psychology, pages 53-54

Charles Louis de Beaumont

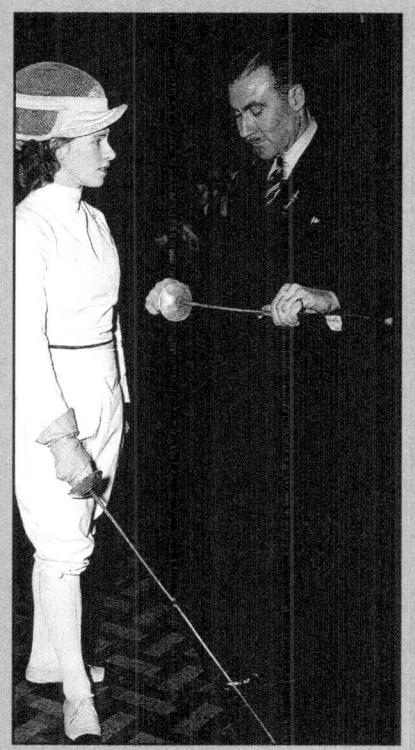

Charles Louis de Beaumont was born in Liverpool in 1902 to Louis, a French academic working in Great Britain and his London-born wife, Kathleen. Beaumont's surname was Klein at birth, but his father, fearing the growing anti-German sentiment leading into the first World War, later changed the family name to Beaumont in 1913.

Charles Louis de Beaumont was the most important figure in British fencing for almost 40 years. Beaumont served as the captain of seven British Olympic fencing teams and also served as the president of the Amateur Fencing Association.

His books *Fencing: Ancient Art and Modern Sport* and *Teach Yourself Fencing* are considered modern classics in the sport of fencing and were very influential to Bruce Lee during the development of Jeet Kune Do. The two books combined were the true source of 68 passages in the *Tao of Jeet Kune Do*.

Charles Louis de Beaumont succumbed to cancer at his home in London on July 7, 1972. At a memorial for Beaumont three weeks later, his colleague Emrys Lloyd said this of the fencer:

"But it is not for his personal performance as a fencer that Charles will be best remembered in British fencing, but by the services that he gave to fencing for forty years. To say that his services were unique would be true, but it would only be half the tale. He not only gave to fencing more than any other has given, but he gave his heart and his soul - and a large part of his life. In doing so he forewent other pleasures that he would have liked to be able to enjoy more often - riding hunting and travelling for private pleasure; but Charles did what he liked and he liked what he did, and we can be certain, and glad, that he enjoyed the work he did for fencing to the full."

The orthodox on-guard position must be varied slightly to suit the muscular structure of each individual fencer. The position adopted should be the one which is found to give the maximum ease and relaxation, combined with smoothness of movement. – CHARLES LOUIS DE BEAUMONT, *Fencing: Ancient Art and Modern Sport*, page 32

If you practice the physical skills of this art diligently and have the proper spiritual attitude, you will perfect it. – CHARLES V. GRUZANSKI, *Spike and Chain: Japanese Fighting Arts*, page 96

The Head

In boxing, the head is treated as if it were a part of the trunk with no independent action of its own. It should be carried forward, with the chin pinned down to the breast-bone. This position must never vary no matter how the body shifts. If the body turns, the head turns. – EDWIN HAISLET, *Boxing*, page 5

The chin is not "tucked" behind the left shoulder except in an extreme defensive position. "Tucking" the chin into the left shoulder turns the neck into an unnatural position, takes away the support of the muscles, and prevents straight bone alignment. It also tenses the left shoulder and arm, preventing free action and causing fatigue. – EDWIN HAISLET, Boxing, page 5

With the chin dropped directly forward and pinned tight to the breast-bone the muscles and bone structure are in the best possible alignment, and only the top of the head is presented to the opponent making it impossible to hit a man on the point of the chin. – EDWIN HAISLET, Boxing, page 5

> Carry the shoulder and arm relaxed and ready at all times. – EDWIN HAISLET, Boxing, page 4
>
> The entire arm and shoulder must be loose and relaxed so that the boxer will be able to snap or whip out the jabs in rapier-like thrusts. – JOHN J. Walsh, Boxing Simplified, page 24
>
> Carry the left hand about shoulder height and off the left shoulder to the left as far as possible without raising the left elbow. – EDWIN HAISLET, Boxing, page 4

The preference for a low-line position with absence of blade is easily explained. When we discussed the various forms of attack we made a point of stressing the fact that many offensive actions were preceded by attacks on the blade. Quite rightly, fencers have found that it is none too easy to attack the blade when it is lowered into the low line. By adopting this form of defensive tactic, the opponent has less opportunity to beat, or take the blade. If his offensive game is based on these preparatory movements, he is severely handicapped, and partly checked. – ROGER CROSNIER, Fencing with the Electric Foil, page 63

John J. Walsh

John J. Walsh was a professor and boxing coach for the University of Wisconsin. He coached there from 1934 to 1960. As coach, he led his team to eight NCAA boxing championships. In recognition of his unpralleled success, the NCAA named the team championship trophy in his honor. His book, Boxing Simplified, is the source of 23 passages in the Tao of Jeet Kune Do.

Walsh had a fierce and acrimonious rivalry with fellow coach Edwin Haislet. He retired as a coach in 1960, after the death of one of his students following a NCAA boxing match which also resulted in the NCAA ending support of collegiate boxing.

Walsh died in Madison, Wisconsin on November 1, 2001 at the age of 89.

The Rear Arm and Hand

Place the right elbow directly down and in front of the short ribs, holding the right band open with palm toward the opponent and directly in front of the right shoulder. Keep the right hand forward in line with the left shoulder. The arm should be relaxed and easy, ready to attack or defend. – EDWIN HAISLET, Boxing, page 5

The Trunk

The position of the trunk is controlled primarily by the position of the left foot and leg. If the left foot and leg is in the correct position the trunk automatically assumes the proper position. The one important thing about the trunk is that it should form a straight line with the left leg. As the left foot and leg is turned inward, the body rotates to the right, which presents a narrow target to the opponent. If, however, the left foot and leg is rotated outward, the body is squared toward the opponent presenting a large target. For defensive purposes the narrow target is advantageous, while the square position lends itself better to attack. – EDWIN HAISLET, Boxing, page 4

John Dobson Lawther

John Dobson Lawther (1899-1996) was a football and basketball coach and professor, first at Westminster College and later at Pennsylvania State University. Lawther was also a fellow of the American College of Sports Medicine.

Lawther's book, *Psychology of Coaching*, is the true source of 49 entries in the *Tao of Jeet Kune Do*.

Stance

The semi-crouch, which you have been using, is the best stance for fist-fighting for the following reasons: (a) Your weight is forward just enough to stimulate explosive straight punching; (b) it is forward enough to prevent your being knocked off balance or floored easily; (c) nevertheless, the weight is not forward so far as to interfere with your footwork – and footwork is important in keeping you at long range in a fist-fight; (d) you are at all times in a comfortably balanced position from which you can attack, counter, or defend--without preliminary movement. – JACK DEMPSEY, *Championship Fighting: Explosive Punching and Aggressive Defense*, page 65

The pattern of bent knees, crouched trunk, forward center of gravity, and partially flexed arms has already been mentioned as characteristic of "readiness" in many sports. – JOHN DOBSON LAWTHER, *Psychology of Coaching*, page 295

Most fencing manuals recommend an equal division of the weight of the body on both legs. We consider this injurious in practice, for when the right foot is moved forward, the right leg should be hampered as little as possible. However, when the right leg has to carry a large portion of the body weight, it will be necessary to transfer that weight to the left leg before starting the lunge. This movement involves a delay and also warns your opponent. Both factors are bound to reduce the chances of eventual success. – LUIGI BARBASETTI, *The Art of the Foil: With a Short History of Fencing*, page 14

Raising the left heel ever so little, you cock the leg ready to pull the trigger and go into action. You take full advantage of one of the mightiest springs in all creation, the arch of the foot, which in the lunge releases its tremendous power through the pressure exerted on the ground by the ball of the foot itself. – ALDO NADI, *On Fencing*, page 51

The primary purpose of boxing is hitting. Therefore, the use of the fundamental position is to obtain the most favorable position for hitting. – EDWIN HAISLET, *Boxing*, page 2

To hit effectively it is necessary to shift the weight constantly from one leg to the other. This means perfect control of body balance. Balance is the most important consideration of the fundamental position. – EDWIN HAISLET, *Boxing*, page 2

The body in this position should be so poised that all of its muscles can act with the greatest speed and ease. – LUIGI BARBASETTI, *The Art of the Foil: With a Short History of Fencing*, page 12

You don't look like the old cut of John L. Sullivan on the barroom wall. Your chest is not blown up. You are all back, elbows, forearms, fists and forehead. You look more on the order of a cat with his back hunched up and ready to spring, except that you are relaxed. Your opponent hasn't much to shoot at. Your chin is tucked between your shoulders. Your elbows protect your sides. You are partially contracted in the middle. Still, you are in position to move around freely and to hit with either hand. – FRANK GILMER, *Push Yourself: A Book for Amateur Boxers and Boxing Fans*, pages 13-14

All punches are thrown from the on-guard position. The boxer must assume the on-guard position again at the finish of each punch with all possible rapidity. – JOHN J. WALSH, *Boxing Simplified*, page 22

Frank Gilmer

Frank Bostick Gilmer was born on May 31, 1906 in Charlottesville, Virginia. He studied law at the University of Virginia, where he was also a member of the university boxing team from 1925 to 1928, eventually becoming captain. He won the Southern College conference featherweight title in 1929 and the conference lightweight championship in 1930. Gilmer had a short and largely undistinguished stint as a professional fighter.

After college, Gilmer moved to Libertyville, Illinois where he began working as an attorney for the Chicago law firm of Winston, Strawn, and Shaw. He would remain with the law firm for 46 years.

While working as an attorney, Frank Gilmer continued his affiliation with boxing. He became a referee for the National Collegiate Athletic association and the Illinois Athletic commission, and in 1938 became a judge for the annual Golden Gloves and Catholic Youth organization tournaments. In 1943 Gilmer transitioned to professional referee, officiating a total of 39 professional bouts. He also served as the boxing coach of the Libertyville Boys Club for 13 years.

In 1956, at the age of 50, Gilmer was appointed chairman of the Illinois Athletic Com-

mission (which supervised professional boxing and wrestling) by then Governor William Stratton. Gilmer's appointment came at a time when a great deal of criticism was being leveled at the sport for its connection to graft and organized crime. At a news conference announcing the appointment, Gilmer told the press he wanted to "build the sport of boxing back in public opinion." He further added: "I would like the people to believe again it is a valuable and necessary sport particularly in these times of prosperity and soft living."

Frank Gilmer was appointed to the role to build trust in the sport. "Frank Gilmer's integrity stands out like a blackberry in a bowl of milk," said Illinois Supreme Court justice George W Bristow. Yet despite Frank Gilmer defending Illinois boxing as "the cleanest of any in the country", his tenure as chairman was dogged by allegations of fight fixing and cheating in the state.

Gilmer wrote two books on boxing: *Push Yourself: A Book for Amateur Boxers and Boxing Fans* (1941) and *How to Judge Boxing* (1960), both of which were owned by Bruce Lee. *Push Yourself* was the true source of 35 passages in the *Tao of Jeet Kune Do*.

Gilmer said, "boxing's greatest need is for competent teachers of the sport. The average boxer today has never really been taught sufficient boxing techniques."

Frank Gilmer died on April 8, 1978 at the age of 71.

Since in traditional painting the artist was limited by the use of colors and held to restricting rules and measurements, he could never fully reveal spiritual reality. – CHANG CHUNG-YUAN, *Creativity and Taoism*, pages 218-219

Progressive Weapons Charts

The straight left is the safest blow in boxing, because of the advanced position of the left arm and because, in following through the arm delivery, the body is still farther swung out of range. The follow through also carries your right farther back, from whence it can be snapped forward with added momentum and force. The straight left is the swiftest full-arm blow that can be delivered from the fundamental stance because it has the shortest distance to travel—it is more than half-way there before it starts. – PHILADELPHIA JACK O'BRIEN, *Boxing*, page 31

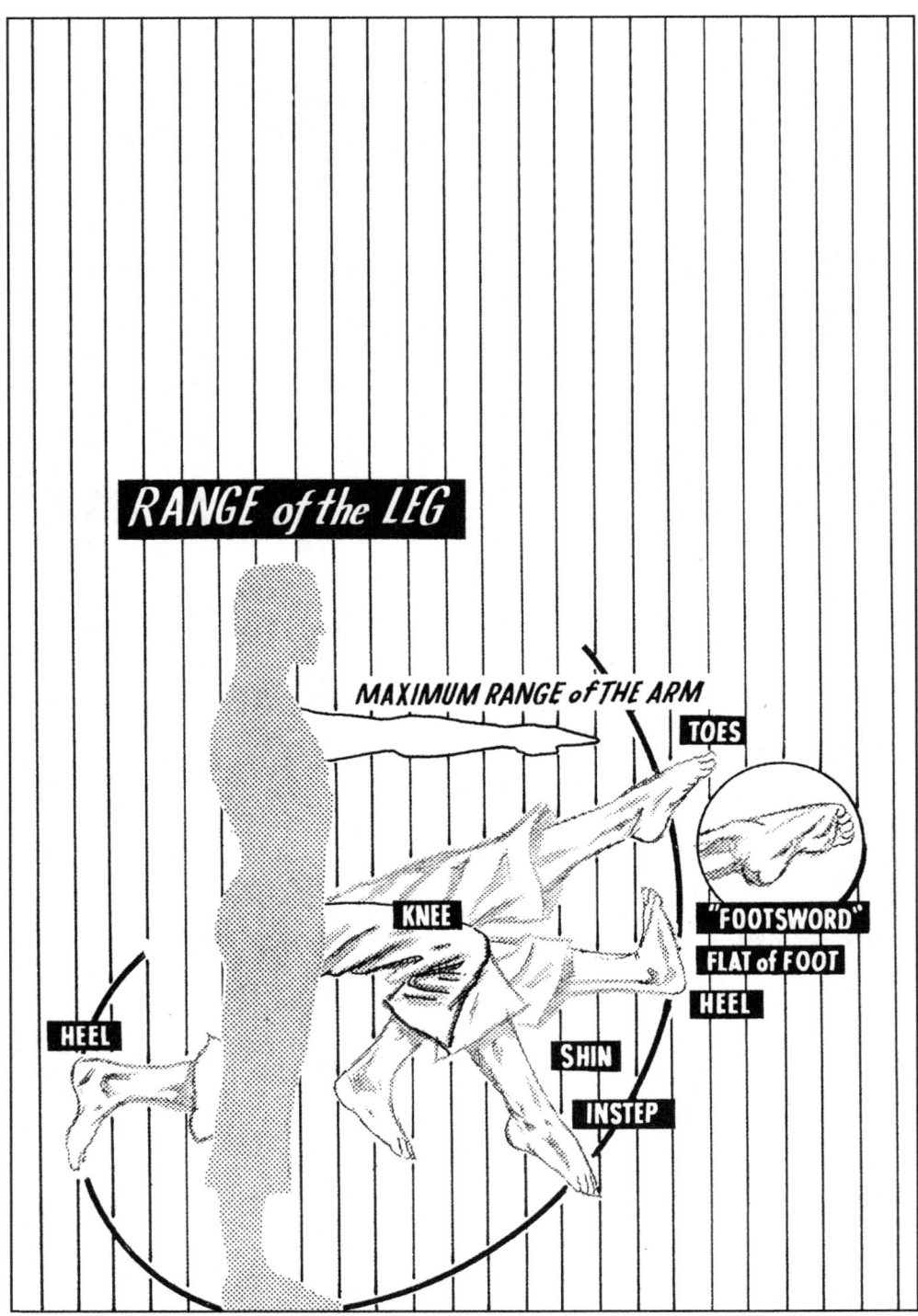

— ED PARKER, *Secrets of Chinese Karate*, page 121

THE LITERARY SOURCEBOOK OF THE TAO OF JEET KUNE DO

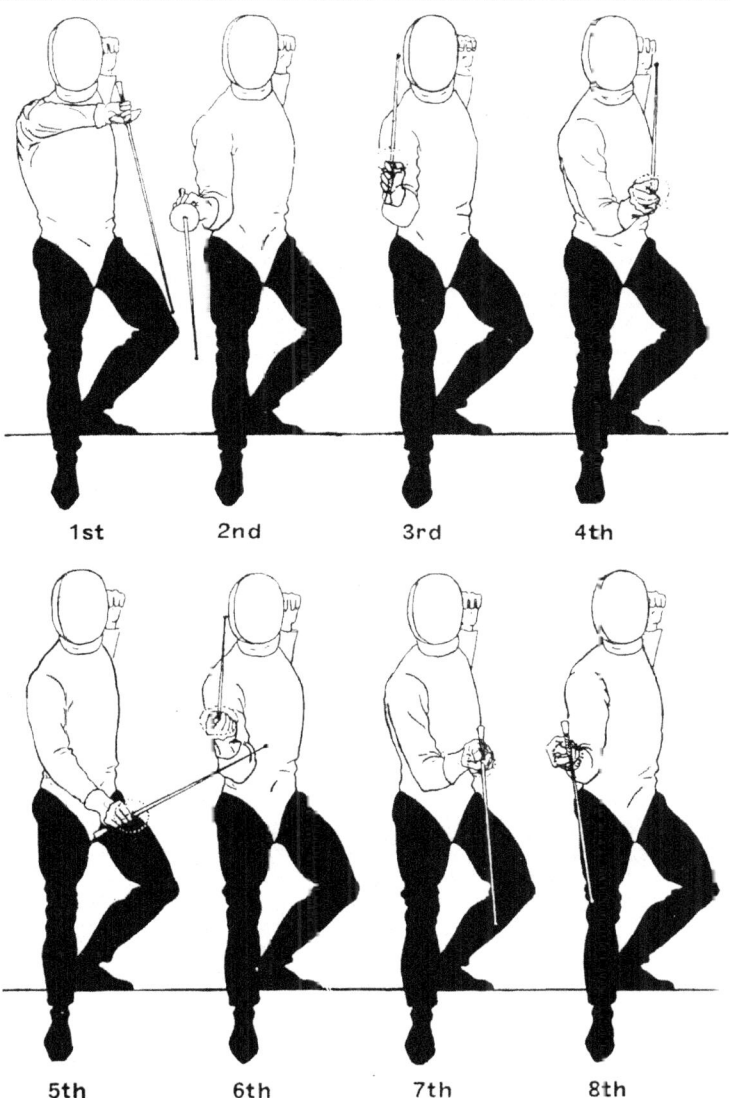

1st 2nd 3rd 4th

5th 6th 7th 8th

TAO FAST FACTS

The Eight Basic Defensive Positions, seen on pages 37-39 of the *Tao of Jeet Kune Do*, appear to be based upon the eight classical parries in fencing. This example illustration was taken from page 35 of the book *Fundamentals of Foil Fencing* by Joseph Vince. It is unclear whether this illustration was used as the source of Bruce Lee's own illustration, but it is included here for the education of the reader. Joseph Vince's book was included in Bruce Lee's personal collection of fencing books.

D. T. Suzuki

Suzuki Daisetsu Teitarō was a Japanese Buddhist monk, scholar, and philosopher. Born on October 18, 1870 in Honda-machi, Kanazawa, Ishikawa Prefecture in Japan, Suzuki was descended from an ancestral line of samurai. He and his family were left impoverished after the death of his father, and the existential questions born of his hardships led him to seek answers in religion and philosophy.

Suzuki studied at Waseda University and University of Tokyo. While a student at Tokyo University, he began studying Zen Buddhism at the Buddhist temple of Engaku-ji under the tutelage of Zen master Imakita Kōsen and later Shaku Sōen. It is said that Suzuki, unable to afford the train fare, would walk all night after classes to attend morning meditation at the Zen temple. Eventually withdrawing from the university, D. T. Suzuki dedicated all of his time to Shaku Sōen and the temple.

It was Suzuki's translation of Shaku Sōen's address for the Parliament of Religions conference in Chicago that caught the attention of Paul Carus, a German-American philosopher and scholar. When Carus inquired about translating Eastern texts for a Western audience, Shaku Sōen recommended D. T. Suzuki for the job. By 1897, Suzuki came to live with Carus in the United States, where their first collaboration was a translation of the Chinese classic, the *Tao Te Ching*. In 1907, Suzuki also published his first English-language book, *Outlines of Mahāyāna Buddhism*. This book launched a lifetime endeavor devoted to sharing the ideas of Eastern philosophy and religion with the West.

By 1909, D. T. Suzuki was back in Japan and teaching at Gakushuin University.

In 1911, Suzuki married an American woman, Beatrice Erskine Lane. His wife was a theosophist, and eventually Suzuki became a practicing theosophist as well. Suzuki also continued his studies in Zen with Master Shaku Sōen.

When Shaku Sōen died in 1919, the married couple relocated to Kyoto. Within a year, D. T. Suzuki was appointed Professor of Buddhist Philosophy at the Otani University. A year later he founded the scholarly journal *Eastern Buddhist*. During his pro-

fessional teaching career, D. T. Suzuki also had visiting professor assignments at Oxford University and Columbia University.

In 1936, D. T. Suzuki returned to the United States and Great Britain for a speaking tour. It was during this time that he met Christmas Humphreys, who managed the Buddhist Lodge in London, and Humphreys' twenty-year-old student – Alan Watts.

Suzuki gained worldwide recognition for his series of essays on Zen Buddhism. D. T. Suzuki's view on Zen Buddhism differed from a number of his peers. Suzuki argued that Zen Buddhism reflected a great deal of philosophy drawn from the Chinese Taoism influences to which the early Chan Buddhists were exposed.

D. T. Suzuki authored a number of books on Zen Buddhism and Eastern philosophy. Among his best-known works were the three-volume *Essays in Zen Buddhism*, *Studies in Zen Buddhism*, *Manual of Zen Buddhism*, *Zen Buddhism and Psychoanalysis* (with Erich Fromm and Richard De Martino), and *Zen and Japanese Culture*. The latter book was one of the most influential books in Bruce Lee's library, accounting for a significant portion of Lee's personal philosophy and the true source of over 50 passages found in the *Tao of Jeet Kune Do*.

"Zen is not something to understand in the intellectual sense," said Suzuki in 1964. "Zen is life itself. When you live it, when you are it yourself, you will at once realize it, see it, and know what it is."

D. T. Suzuki died on July 12, 1966 in Kamakura Japan at the age of 95. His legacy is that of the man most responsible for the spread of Zen Buddhism in the Western world. Psychiatrist Carl Jung praised Suzuki's efforts to bring Zen to the West, writing: "Suzuki's works on Zen Buddhism are among the best contributions to the knowledge of living Buddhism. We cannot be sufficiently grateful to the author, first for the fact of his having brought Zen closer to Western understanding, and secondly for the manner in which he has achieved this task."

WHO WROTE THE TAO?

八打
THE EIGHT ALLOWABLE TARGETS

每部位皆屬次要, 雖不致命, 亦必重傷, 如遇強手, 非此不足以致勝, 然不可輕予施用, 以傷好生之德, 惟吾同道慎之。

These are all secondary targets. Although not life-threatening, they are sure to cause injury. If you encounter an attacker who is highly skilled, these will be sufficient to defeat him. But you must not employ them rashly or you may do injury to your own life-sparing virtue. I hope you will be mindful of this point.

(一打)眉頭雙睛
1. the spot between the eyebrows
(二打)唇上人中
2. the Renzhong acupoint above the upper lip
(三打)穿腮耳門
3. the hollow between cheek and earlobe
(四打)背後骨縫
4. the spine
(五打)脅內肺腑
5. the lungs underneath the upper ribs
(六打)撩陰高骨
6. the pelvic bone
(七打)鶴膝虎頭
7. the soft tissue just below the kneecap
(八打)破骨千斤
8. the shins

八不打
THE EIGHT FORBIDDEN TARGETS

是皆致命之處, 苟非性命相搏, 幸毋施用, 若對方不念人命之為重, 亦祗招之而已。

All of these targets are for life-threatening situations [and are thus the primary targets]. If you are not fighting for your life, I hope you will not employ them. Only use them if your attacker clearly does not consider human life to be of any value.

(一不打)太陽為首
1. the temples
(二不打)正中鎖喉
2. the windpipe
(三不打)中心兩壁
3. the solar plexus
(四不打)兩肋太極
4. the false ribs
(五不打)海底撩陰
5. the groin
(六不打)兩腎對心
6. the kidneys
(七不打)尾閭風府
7. the tailbone
(八不打)兩耳扇風
8. the ears

– Wong Hon Fan; Guangyu Luo, *Praying Mantis Book #01: Secrets of the Mantis Boxing Art* 螳螂拳術闡秘, page 23-24

TAO FAST FACTS

Wong Hon Fan 黃漢勛 was a Hong Kong-based practitioner of Praying Mantis gung fu, often referred to as the "Mantis King". He was one of the chief figures of the martial arts revitalization movement in China during the 20th Century. A prolific writer, he authored more than 30 books on Praying Mantis. His books were a source of inspiration for Bruce Lee, and elements of the books can be seen above and in Lee's *Tao of Gung Fu*.

Wong Hon Fan passed away in 1973, the same year as Bruce Lee.

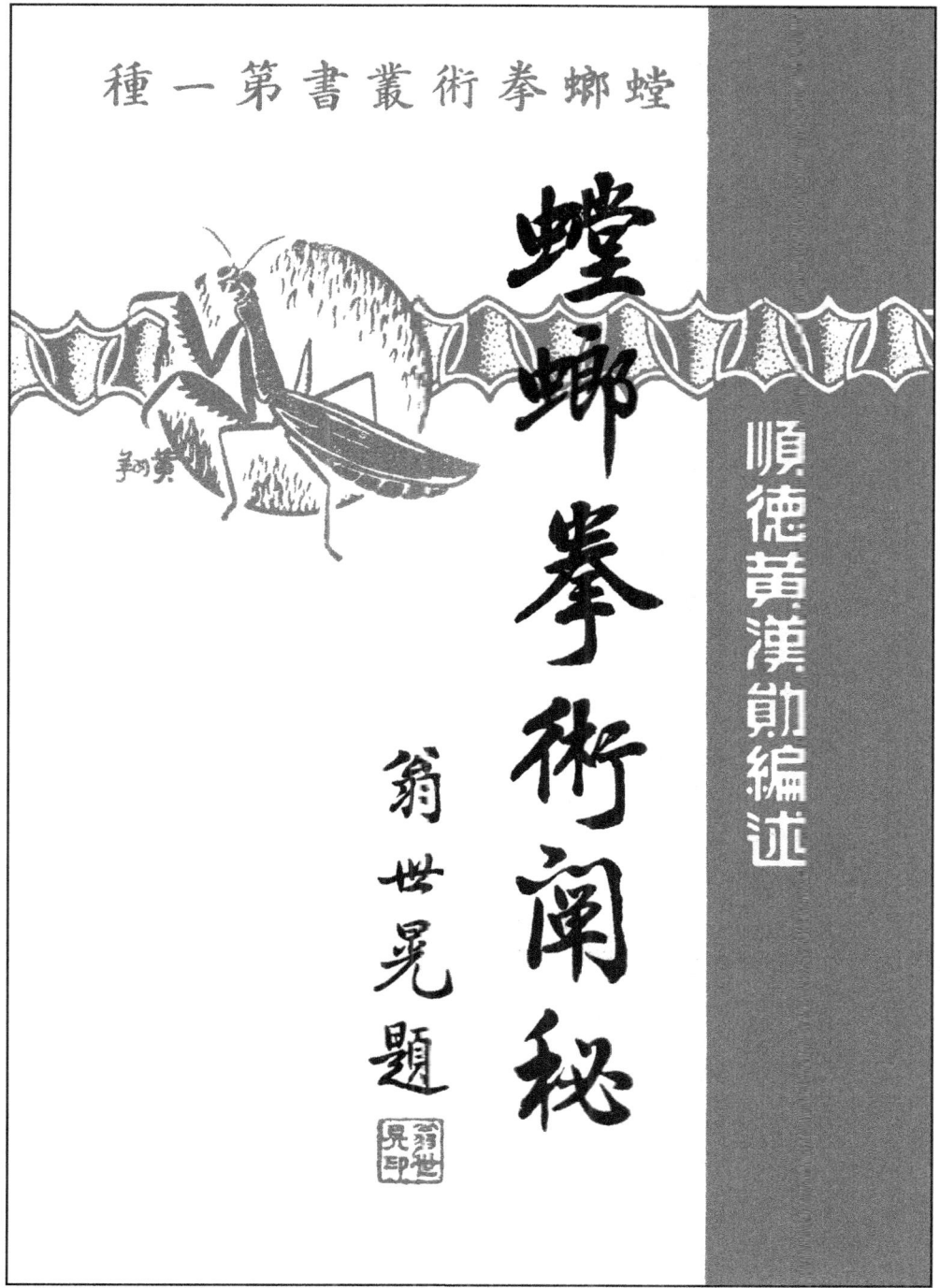

Wong Hon Fan and Guangyu Luo's *Praying Mantis Book #01: Secrets of the Mantis Boxing Art* 螳螂拳術闡秘, the first in a series of over two dozen booklets on Praying Mantis gung fu.

QUALITIES

Coordination

Coordination is, by all means, the most important consideration in any study of proficiency in sports and athletics. Coordination is the quality which enables the individual to integrate all the powers and capacities of his whole organism into an effective doing of the act in which he is engaged. It is the basis of all skill in every kind of complex physical activity. – JESSE FEIRING WILLIAMS, M.D. and EUGENE WHITE NIXON, M.A., *The Athlete in the Making*, page 24

Before movement can take place there must be a change of muscular tension on both sides of the joint that is to be moved. The effectiveness with which this muscular teamwork can be accomplished is one of the factors that determines limits of speed, endurance, power, agility and accuracy in all athletic performances. – LAURENCE ENGLEMOHR MOREHOUSE and PHILIP J. RASH, *Sports Medicine for Trainers*, page 31

In static or slow resistive activities, such as executing a handstand or supporting a heavy barbell, the muscles on both sides of the joints act strongly to fix the body in the desired position. When rapid motion takes place, as in running or throwing, the muscles closing the joints shorten and those on the opposite side lengthen to permit the movement. There is still tension on both sides, but on the lengthening side, it is considerably reduced. – LAURENCE ENGLEMOHR MOREHOUSE and PHILIP J. RASH, *Sports Medicine for Trainers*, page 31

Any excessive tension in the lengthening muscles acts as a brake and thereby slows and weakens the action. Such antagonistic tension increases the energy cost of muscular work, resulting in early fatigue. When a new task with a demand that is different in intensity of load, rate, repetition, or duration is undertaken, an entirely new pattern of "neurophysiological adjustment" must be acquired. Thus, the fatigue experienced in new activities is not just from using different muscles but is also due to the braking caused by improper coordination. – LAURENCE ENGLEMOHR MOREHOUSE and PHILIP J. RASH, *Sports Medicine for Trainers*, page 31

The outstanding characteristic of the expert athlete is his ease of movement, even during maximal effort. The novice is characterized by his tenseness, wasted motion, and excess effort. That rare person, the "natural athlete," seems to be endowed with the ability to undertake any sport activity, whether he is experienced in it or not, with ease. The ease is his ability to perform with minimal antagonistic tension. It is more present in some athletes than in others but can be improved by all. – LAURENCE ENGLEMOHR MOREHOUSE and PHILIP J. RASH, *Sports Medicine for Trainers*, page 31

The fencer whose movements seem awkward, who never seems to find the proper distance, is always being timed, never "out-guesses" his opponent, and always gives warning of his intentions before they become serious, is suffering chiefly from a lack of coordination. The well-coordinated fencer, and all good fencers must have coordination, does everything smoothly and gracefully. He seems to glide in and out of distance with the minimum effort and a maximum of deception. His timing is usually good because his own movements are so rhythmical that they tend to establish complementary rhythm on the part of his opponent, which rhythm he can break to his own advantage because of his perfect control of his own muscles. He seems to out-guess his opponent because he usually takes the initiative and to a large extent forces the reactions of his opponent, and above all, he does everything with decision because he has confidence in himself and makes his movements with a purpose rather than with a doubting hope. – JULIO MARTINEZ CASTELLÓ, *The Theory and Practice of Fencing*, pages 59-60

Muscles have no power to guide themselves, but that the manner in which they act, and consequently the effectiveness of our performances, depends absolutely upon how the nervous system guides the muscles involved in the act. If I reach for the gravy and upset the water glass, the mishap may be attributed to the failure of my nervous system to guide my muscles properly, rather than to any failure to see the glass. If I step on my partner's expensive dancing slippers, it is hardly to be supposed that I am merely brutal by nature, or that I intend to discourage further social intercourse with this particular individual; rather the fault lies with a nervous system which sends impulses to the wrong muscles, or sends them a fraction of a second too soon or too late, or sends them in improper sequence or in poorly apportioned intensity. – JESSE FEIRING WILLIAMS, M.D. and EUGENE WHITE NIXON, M.A., *The Athlete in the Making*, page 28

This means that my nervous system *has been trained* to the point where it sends impulses to certain muscles causing these particular muscles to contact at exactly the proper hundredth of a second, at the same time shutting off impulses to other antagonistic muscles, thus allowing them to relax. It means that these impulses come in just the exact intensity required, and that they stop coming at the exact fraction of a second when they are no longer needed. – JESSE FEIRING WILLIAMS, M.D. and EUGENE WHITE NIXON, M.A., *The Athlete in the Making*, page 33

Therefore, the learning of coordination is a matter of training the nervous system, and not a question of training muscles. … Now this transition from totally uncoordinated muscular effort to skill of the highest perfection is a process of developing connections in the nervous system. The psychologists and biologists tell us that the billions of elements in the nervous system are not in direct connection with each other, but that the fibers of one nerve cell intertwine with those of other cells in such close proximity that impulses can pass from one to others by a process of induction. This point at which the impulse passes from one nerve cell to another is called the "synapse." The synapse theory explains why the baby who displayed the totally uncoordinated responses to the sight of the ball eventually becomes the big-league ball player. – JESSE FEIRING WILLIAMS, M.D. and EUGENE WHITE NIXON, M.A., *The Athlete in the Making*, pages 77, 78

Of the three great laws of learning probably the most important for sports and athletics is the *Law of Exercise*. One aspect of this law, the *Law of Use*, tells us that learning is a matter of forming connections in the nervous system by practice, and that each performance of an act strengthens the connections involved, and makes the next performance easier, more certain, and more readily done. On the contrary the *Law of Disuse* tells us that disuse tends to weaken any connections that have been formed and makes doing of the act more difficult and uncertain. … In the first place the teacher or learner must realize that we can attain skill only by actually doing the thing we are trying to learn. … An absolute essential to effective teaching is the realization that no knowledge or skill can be poured into the learner, but that we learn solely by doing, or reacting. … If we remember that learning of skills is a matter of forming pathways and connections in the nervous system it is easy to understand that the individual with the more "plastic" nervous system will more readily acquire the connections that are the basis of skill. … The question involved is whether this is a more efficient and economical method of learning boxing than to begin boxing from the first. – JESSE FEIRING WILLIAMS, M.D. and EUGENE WHITE NIXON, M.A., *The Athlete in the Making*, pages 89, 89-90, 90, 91-92, 100

The *Law of Readiness* tells us that the more "ready" the individual is to respond to a stimulus the more satisfaction he finds in the response, and the more "unready" he is the more annoying he finds it to be forced to act. ... To become a champion or near champion requires a condition of readiness that causes the individual to approach with pleasure even the most tedious practice sessions. The individual in this state of readiness, given reasonable teaching and encouragement, and time to practice, is very certain to be heard from. – JESSE FEIRING WILLIAMS, M.D. and EUGENE WHITE NIXON, M.A., *The Athlete in the Making*, pages 81-82, 82-83

IMPORTANT: If the athlete tries to continue practicing finely skilled movements after he becomes fatigued, he begins to substitute gross motions for fine ones and generalized efforts for specific ones. Wrong movements tend to supervene, and the athlete's progress is set back. Thus, the athlete practices fine skills only while he is fresh. When he becomes fatigued he shifts to tasks employing gross movements designed principally to develop endurance. – LAURENCE ENGLEMOHR MOREHOUSE, PH.D. and PHILIP J. RASH, *Scientific Basis of Athletic Training*, page 28

Precision

Accuracy means precision of movement and generally is used in the sense of exactness in projection of a force. – JOHN DOBSON LAWTHER, *Psychology of Coaching*, page 235

Precision is made up of controlled hand and foot movements and technique. These movements should eventually be executed with a minimum of strength and exertion yet must achieve the desired result. Precision can only be attained through a considerable amount of practice and training on the part of *both the beginner and the experienced fencer*. – JULIUS PALFFY-ALPAR, *Sword and Masque*, page 40

Accuracy means precision of movement, and generally is used in the sense of exactness in projection of a force. A rather common theory is that skill is best acquired by learning accuracy first, before the skill act is attempted with much power or speed. – JOHN DOBSON LAWTHER, *Psychology of Coaching*, page 235

A mirror is a definite aid to achieving precision. If the salle has a mirror available, a constant check on posture, hand positions, and fencing movements is a great aid. – JULIUS PALFFY-ALPAR, *Sword and Masque*, page 40

Power

To be accurate, the throwing and striking skills should be executed from a body base that possesses enough strength to maintain adequacy of balance during the action. – JOHN DOBSON LAWTHER, *Psychology of Coaching*, page 258

The use of momentum is discovered and incorporated with the mechanical advantages, neural impulses are sent to the working muscles so as to bring a sufficient number of fibers into action at precisely the right time, while impulses into the antagonistic muscles are reduced to lessen resistance-all acting to improve efficiency and to make the best use of available power. – LAURENCE ENGLEMOHR MOREHOUSE, PH.D. and PHILIP J. RASH, *Scientific Basis of Athletic Training*, page 27-28

In approaching an unfamiliar task, the athlete tends to overmobilize his muscular forces, exerting more effort than required. During a few repetitions the neuromuscular coordinating system learns exactly how much effort is needed. – LAURENCE ENGLEMOHR MOREHOUSE, PH.D.

and PHILIP J. RASH, *Scientific Basis of Athletic Training*, page 27

In sports, one thinks of the powerful athlete not as the strong athlete only but as the one who can exert his great strength quickly. The smaller man who can swing faster may hit as hard, or as far, as the heavier man who swings slowly. ... Since power equals force times speed, if the athlete learns to make faster movements he increases his power even though the contractile pulling strength of his muscles (as measured on a dynamometer) remains unchanged. – JOHN DOBSON LAWTHER, *Psychology of Coaching*, page 231

The athlete who is building muscles through such exercises should be very sure to work adequately on speed and flexibility at the same time; otherwise he is apt to defeat his own purpose of improving his all-round athletic efficiency. ... Combined with adequate speed and endurance, high levels of strength lead to excellence in most sports. One might think of the analogy of chasing a rabbit with a low-geared truck, or of the bull with its colossal strength futilely pursuing the matador. – JOHN DOBSON LAWTHER, *Psychology of Coaching*, pages 260, 257

Endurance

Endurance is developed by *hard* and *continuous* exercise which exceeds the "steady" physiological state and produces near exhaustion for the time being. Considerable respiratory and muscular distress should develop. THOMAS K. CURETON quoted in John Dobson Lawther's *Psychology of Coaching*, page 271

Although special exercises are valuable to strengthen weak muscles to improve endurance, performance of the event is the best way to train for the event. – LAURENCE ENGLEMOHR MOREHOUSE and PHILIP J. RASH, *Sports Medicine for Trainers*, pages 23-24

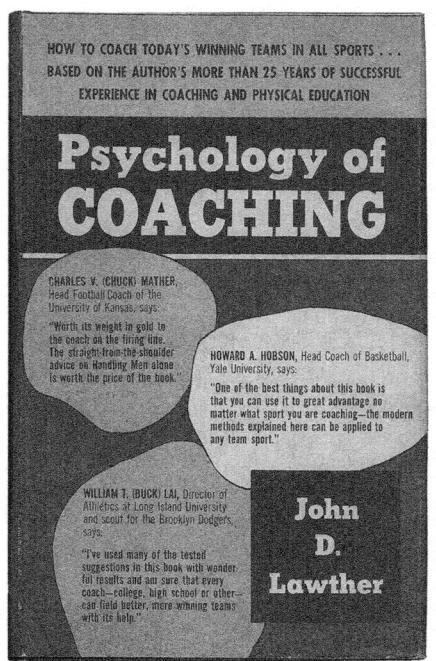

Most beginning athletes are unwilling to drive themselves hard enough. They should punish themselves, and then rest adequately, only to increase the output of effort after the rest. ... The athlete must learn "to punish himself" in order to attain high levels. Long hours of work made up of many short, high-speed efforts interspersed with periods of milder activity seems to be the best endurance-training procedure. – JOHN DOBSON LAWTHER, *Psychology of Coaching*, page 271

Four hypotheses have been advanced in recent years by champions of extra-endurance sports. The first is the one already mentioned of endurance training being best acquired through a rather extensive succession of sprints interspersed with easier running. The second hypothesis is that endurance is specific to the rate of speed for which one is trained. ... A third hypothesis is that runners so trained can insert changes of pace in their distance running, changes that employ different movements and, to some degree, different muscle fibers. ... The fourth hypothesis is that extreme endurance training should include much more (longer) work than what has been customary in America. ... That such "Spartan" training exists and that it has paid off in championships is evident. – JOHN DOBSON LAWTHER, *Psychology of Coaching*, pages 272-273

Exercise for endurance development should be gradually and carefully increased. Since the rate of increase should not be too rapid, the time span for development must be adequate. Six weeks seem to be a scanty minimum for sports that require considerable endurance, and six weeks are really only the beginning. An athlete is merely in shape to begin real work and perhaps try some competition. The peak of achievement will be approached in years. – JOHN DOBSON LAWTHER, *Psychology of Coaching*, page 271

It is rather evident that endurance is lost rapidly if one ceases to work at its maintenance. – JOHN DOBSON LAWTHER, *Psychology of Coaching*, page 275

Balance

To hit effectively it is necessary to shift the weight constantly from one leg to the other. This means perfect control of body balance. Balance is the most important consideration of the fundamental position. – EDWIN HAISLET, *Boxing*, page 2

Balance is achieved only through correct body alignment. The feet, the legs, the trunk, the head are all important in creating and maintaining a balanced position. The arms are important only because they are the vehicles of body force. They only give expression to body force when the body is in proper alignment. A position of the hands and arms which facilitates easy body expression is important. The foot position is the most important phase of balance. Keeping the feet in proper relation to each other as well as to the body helps to maintain correct body alignment. – EDWIN HAISLET, *Boxing*, page 2

Too wide a stance prevents proper body alignment, destroying balance but obtaining solidity and power at the cost of speed and efficient movement. A short stance prevents balance as it does not give a basis from which to work. Speed results but at a loss of power and balance. – EDWIN HAISLET, *Boxing*, page 2

The secret of the proper stance is to keep the feet always directly under the body which means that the feet should be a medium distance apart. Either the weight is balanced over both legs or the weight is carried slightly forward over a straight left leg with the left side of the body forming a straight line from the left heel to the tip of the left shoulder. This position permits relaxation, speed, balance, and easy movement as well as a mechanical advantage, making possible tremendous power. – EDWIN HAISLET, *Boxing*, page 2

In general, for athletic contests, preparatory stance will include a coiled or semi-crouched posture and a lowered and forward center of gravity. The defensive center behind the football line, the infielder in baseball waiting as the ball is pitched, or the tennis player ready to receive the serve, are examples. With the bending of the knee, the center of gravity moves forward a little to be practically over the balls of the feet. ... For general readiness, the heels usually remain just touching the ground even after the knees bend. The knee bending with the heels remaining close to the ground has the effect of making the angle smaller between the top of the foot and the shin. This decrease in the angle at the instep permits a longer arc of rotation, hence a greater distance of application of force when one spring or pushes from the feet. Slight ground contact of the heel aids in balance and decreases tension. – JOHN DOBSON LAWTHER, *Psychology of Coaching*, page 226

Remember: always leave a space between your feet; never get your feet crossed. – FRANK GILMER, *Push Yourself: A Book for Amateur Boxers and Boxing Fans*, page 16

By never getting your feet crossed you are always braced and not likely to be pushed off balance or knocked down because of bad footwork. – FRANK GILMER, *Push Yourself: A Book for Amateur Boxers and Boxing Fans*, page 16

"Postural Habits":
1. Lower center of gravity
2. Lateral width to the base
3. Weight on the balls of the feet
4. Knees rarely straight even in running, and
5. A center of gravity kept under delicate and rapid control, are characteristic habits of athletes in games that require sudden and frequent changes of direction. These postural habits are characteristic of readiness in motion as well as readiness of static posture.
   – JOHN DOBSON LAWTHER, *Psychology of Coaching*, page 227

John Dobson Lawther, 1942

These postural habits are characteristic of readiness in motion as well as readiness of static posture. The athlete displays these static and phasic motor habits before and immediately after each act, in preparation for the next act. When sudden movement may be necessary the good athlete is rarely caught with a straight knee or with other completely straightened joint angles. From such bent-knee preparatory running has come the well-known statement that "the good athlete always runs as if his pants needed pressing." – JOHN DOBSON LAWTHER, *Psychology of Coaching*, page 227

Balance in athletics is the control of one's center of gravity plus the control and utilization of body slants and of unstable equilibrium, hence gravity pull, to facilitate movement. One student defined balance in athletic sports as "being able to throw one's center of gravity beyond the base of support, chase it, and never let it get away." – JOHN DOBSON LAWTHER, *Psychology of Coaching*, page 297

The short step, the glide as contrasted with the hop or cross-step, the wider base, the lower center of gravity, the toed-out foot-position, all are devices to keep the center of gravity under more precise control. ... When it is necessary to run rapidly, they try to take small enough steps so that the center of gravity is rarely out of control. – JOHN DOBSON LAWTHER, *Psychology of Coaching*, pages 297, 227

Body slants in a preparatory position are counterbalanced with extended arm, leg, or both. – JOHN DOBSON LAWTHER, *Psychology of Coaching*, page 297

Man is either at rest or in motion. He is therefore constantly governed by mechanical principles: the principles of statics or stability when he is at rest and the principles of dynamics or motion when he is moving. Not infrequently, he is subject to both types of principles at the same time. Animate bodies, unlike inanimate ones, must make quick transitions from one state to the other in order to adjust to the forces acting upon them. They also frequently need to be stable in one part of their body in order to give or receive impetus successfully with another. This in-between state might well be called balance-in-motion, or dynamic balance. – KATHARINE F. WELLS, *Kinesiology: The Scientific Basis of Human Motion*, page 66

As can be readily seen, the fencer's center of gravity changes constantly, varying with his own actions and those of his opponent's. – JULIUS PALFFY-ALPAR, *Sword and Masque*, page 42

– JULIUS PALFFY-ALPAR, *Sword and Masque*, page 49

Balance, a very important factor in fencing, must be under control at all times so that the fencer will not be slow in executing his movements or lose his control in the middle of an action. – JULIUS PALFFY-ALPAR, *Sword and Masque*, page 41

If a fencer prepares for an attack, the center of gravity should imperceptibly be shifted to the front foot in order to allow the back leg and foot freedom for the shortest, fastest, and most explosive lunge or flèche. – JULIUS PALFFY-ALPAR, *Sword and Masque*, page 41

In preparing a parry, the center of gravity should be shifted slightly to the rear foot so that the distance is increased and more time is allowed for the parry and riposte movements. – JULIUS PALFFY-ALPAR, *Sword and Masque*, page 41

Training Aids

The finest exercise for the development of a sense of balance is undoubtedly skipping. Not ordinary haphazard skipping, but the real thing. First, skip on one foot, holding the other in front of you; then skip on the other. After that skip on alternate feet with each revolution of the rope - not so simple as it may appear - and work up to the highest possible speed. Keep the skipping going for three minutes the duration of a round - then rest for a minute and skip for another three minutes. Three rounds of skipping in a variety of ways will form the opening for a good workout. – JIM DRISCOLL, *The Straight Left and How to Cultivate It*, page 41

Philadelphia Jack O'Brien

Joseph Francis Hagan, better known professionally as Philadelphia Jack O'Brien, was born on January 17, 1878 in Philadelphia, Pennsylvania, the son of Irish immigrants from Londonderry. Although groomed to join his father in his contracting business, O'Brien bucked his parents' expectations and quietly pursued his dreams of becoming a prizefighter. In an effort to hide his activities from his parents, he fought in amateur tournaments using the last name of a neighborhood friend. Thus, boxer Jack O'Brien was born. To distinguish himself from another fighter with the same name from New York, O'Brien later added his hometown of "Philadelphia" to his name.

Eventually, his parents caught on to what O'Brien was doing. After coming home with a black eye, his father, Patrick Hagan, remarked sarcastically: "You must have had your face where O'Brien's was supposed to be."

O'Brien initially started his professional career as a lightweight, but as he matured and gained mass he transitioned to heavyweight. In 1900 he traveled to England to box some of England's best boxers, knocking out England's heavyweight title holder in 11 rounds. He acted as his own press agent, sending cable reports of the bouts to American newspapers back home. When he embarked on his voyage to England, only his sisters came to see him off. When he returned, he was shocked to discover he had become a boxing sensation, greeted at the port by the mayor of Philadelphia and 10,000 fans.

During his sojourn in England, Philadelphia Jack O'Brien picked up a taste for English menswear and English prose. He came back with 18 trunks of gentleman's clothing. He thereafter was known for his manner of dress, often sporting a top hat and frock coat.

Much of his career in the following years was comprised of fights that were more exhibition bouts than real competitions. Often, he would rehearse with his opponents prior to a fight, in order to guarantee a good show. He negotiated from promoters 75% of the gate receipts, and by 1904 was worth an estimated $80,000 (adjusted for inflation, that would be about $2,500,000 today).

In 1905, Philadelphia Jack O'Brien fought an aging Bob Fitzsimmons for the world light heavyweight title. He gave Fitzsimmons 13 punishing rounds before Fitzsimmons finally collapsed. O'Brien's time as the champ was short-lived, as he abandoned the heavyweight title when he refused to defend it. He retired in 1910 at the age of 36 with a professional boxing record of 192 fights, with 92 wins and six losses, 13 draws, five no contests, and 76 no decisions. After retirement, he collaborated with S. E. Bilik of the University of Illinois on a boxing book, simply titled *Boxing*. In his later years, O'Brien owned and operated a gym in New York City.

Philadelphia Jack O'Brien died on November 12, 1942 in New York City at the age of 64.

O'Brien's book on boxing made an impression on Bruce Lee. It is the true source of 13 passages from the *Tao of Jeet Kune Do*.

JOSEPH F. A. HAGAN, better known as Philadelphia Jack O'Brien, is pictured (left) as a gentleman concert violinist, and (right) as light-heavyweight boxing champion of the world. He died today in New York City.

Good Form

Economy of motion. "Good form" is supposed to achieve best results with a minimum of lost motion and a minimum of wasted energy. – JOHN DOBSON LAWTHER, *Psychology of Coaching*, page 286

This is another way of saying that the physically educated person knows how to conserve energy by using the least possible amount of energy to achieve a given result, eliminating the unnecessary motions and muscle contractions which fatigue him without accomplishing any useful purpose. – ELEANOR METHENY, *Body Dynamics*, page 53

The ability to relax at will is acquired in the same manner that any other neuromuscular skill is learned. It must first be experienced and the "feeling" of it perceived; then it must be practiced until the feeling can be reproduced whenever desired. The first step, then, is to acquire the kinesthetic perception, or the feeling, of relaxation. The second step is to practice until this feeling can be reproduced at will. The third step is to reproduce that feeling voluntarily in in potentially tension-creating situations. – ELEANOR METHENY, *Body Dynamics*, page 59

The ability to feel this contraction and relaxation, to know what a muscle is doing, is called "kinesthetic perception." his kinesthetic perception is also important to balanced and efficient movement, for unless the individual senses or feels the rightness or wrongness of a movement, he has no basis for correcting it or for trying to establish it as a habitual pattern. Kinesthetic perception is developed by consciously placing the body and its parts in a given position and "getting the feel" of it. This feeling of balance or imbalance, grace or awkwardness, serves as a constant guide to the body as it moves. – ELEANOR METHENY, *Body Dynamics*, page 96

WHO WROTE THE TAO?

Kinesthetic perception should be developed to such a degree that the body is uncomfortable unless it performs each motion with a minimum of effort to produce maximum results.
– ELEANOR METHENY, *Body Dynamics*, page 97

While working up each stroke, the pupil will have to pass through five stages. The first four will be undergone in collaboration with the master, while the fifth can be accomplished either with the master or with a fellow trainee.

> STAGE 1. Technical readaptation to the requirements of the electric foil.
> STAGE 2. Building up precision, rhythm, synchronization, while augmenting speed progressively.
> STAGE 3. Timing and the ability to seize an opportunity when offered.
> STAGE 4. Preparation to fighting conditions.
> STAGE 5. Application under fighting conditions.

– ROGER CROSNIER, *Fencing with the Electric Foil*, pages 80-81

Relaxation is a physical state, but it is controlled by the mental state. It is acquired by the conscious effort to control the thought as well as the action pattern. It takes perception, practice, and willingness to train the mind into new habits of thinking and the body into new habits of action. – ELEANOR METHENY, *Body Dynamics*, page 69

Relaxation refers to degree of tension of the musculature. The rule in sports is to try to have no more tension in the acting muscles than is necessary to perform the act; and to have as low a degree of tension in the antagonists to the contracting muscles as possible and still maintain any necessary inhibitory control. – JOHN DOBSON LAWTHER, *Psychology of Coaching*, page 297

Muscles are always in a slight state of tension, and this is as they should be. But when they begin to "tighten up" too much we find our speed and skill being handicapped. The main difficulty in such cases lies in the over tension of the antagonistic muscles. – JESSE FEIRING WILLIAMS, M.D. and EUGENE WHITE NIXON, M.A., *The Athlete in the Making*, page 107

A lower degree of tension in the acting muscles means less energy usage. It is evident that tense antagonistic muscles, opposing those acting, would cause the athlete to waste energy in working against himself. Moreover, precision and exactness in skill performance are upset by stiffness or resistance to the movement. – JOHN DOBSON LAWTHER, *Psychology of Coaching*, page 297

In coordinated, graceful, and efficient movement, the opposing muscles must be able to relax and lengthen readily and easily. – ELEANOR METHENY, *Body Dynamics*, page 96

But after all relaxation in sports depends upon the cultivation of mental poise and emotional control. The player who is angry, fearful, or too anxious will lack this quality, and his performance will not be his best. – JESSE FEIRING WILLIAMS, M.D. and EUGENE WHITE NIXON, M.A., *The Athlete in the Making*, page 108

The difference in such cases is a matter of relaxation. To relax in sports does not mean to become careless or indifferent. The relaxation desired is relaxation of muscles rather than of mind or attention. – JESSE FEIRING WILLIAMS, M.D. and EUGENE WHITE NIXON, M.A., *The Athlete in the Making*, page 107

It means that he expends mental and physical energy constructively, conserving it when it does not contribute to the solution of the problem and spending it freely when it does. – ELEANOR METHENY, *Body Dynamics*, page 68

Energy saved by sound mechanics of form can be utilized in the longer persistence or the more forceful expression of the skill. – JOHN DOBSON LAWTHER, *Psychology of Coaching*, page 287

The older athlete tends to become more conscious of this latter aspect of form – form as a means of energy conservation. ... The great athlete saves energy because his extra skill makes each motion more effective, he makes fewer needless motions, and his conditioned body uses less energy per movement. – JOHN DOBSON LAWTHER, *Psychology of Coaching*, page 287

Always train in good form. Form is as important in boxing as in any other sport. Learn to move easily and smoothly. ... Coordinate your footwork and hitting so that they work together in perfect time. To do this from the beginning and to loosen your muscles start your workout with shadow boxing. ... At first be concerned entirely with proper form; later, when you automatically do things right, concentrate on working hard. Shadow boxing will make you look like a boxer quicker than anything else you can do. – FRANK GILMER, *Push Yourself: A Book for Amateur Boxers and Boxing Fans*, page 70

The mastery of these fundamentals and their progressive application is the secret of learning boxing. There is no mysterious short-cut procedure whereby skill in boxing may be acquired. – CLARENCE E. KENNEDY, *Boxing Simplified*, page ii

The drill maneuvers are executed from one side of the body, and at the outset it should be borne in mind that in most cases the same tactics for each maneuver must be drilled on the opposite side of the body for the proper balance in efficiency. – CLARENCE E. KENNEDY, *Boxing Simplified*, page ii

Economy of Motion

Motion economy. There is a best way to perform any task, and it is the job of the coach in athletics and the time-and-motion specialist in industry to find it. A few of the principles that have been found to be of importance in improving performance are as follows:

1. Momentum should be employed to overcome resistance.
2. Momentum should be reduced to a minimum if it must be overcome by muscular effort.
3. Continuous curved motions require less effort than straight line motions involving sudden and sharp changes in direction.
4. When the initiating muscles are unopposed, allowing free and smooth motion, the movements are faster, easier, and more accurate than restricted or controlled movements.
5. Work arranged to permit an easy and natural rhythm is conducive to smooth and automatic performance.
6. Hesitation or the temporary and often minute cessation of motion should be eliminated from the performance.

– LAURENCE ENGLEMOHR MOREHOUSE
and PHILIP J. RASH,
The Physiology of Exercise, page 83

When changing your style from one round to the next to keep your opponent guessing, it is well to remember not to change your basic form. By changing style, I mean switching plans, changing from body punching to head punching, or perhaps advancing more slowly, changing from a rushing attack to a waiting game. Your form remains the same. – BARNEY ROSS, *Fundamentals of Boxing*, pages 55-56

But what is correct form? Again, teachers and learners alike often arrive at a wrong answer to this question. Good form in sports may be defined as the particular technique which enables the individual to attain maximum efficiency in the activity. – JESSE FEIRING WILLIAMS, M.D. and EUGENE WHITE NIXON, M.A., *The Athlete in the Making*, page 95

Balance is vital to good form. Whether it is a jab or a hook that you are throwing, you will not have sustained power unless balance and perfect timing give you enough leverage. – BARNEY ROSS, *Fundamentals of Boxing*, pages 54-55

Keep relaxed at all times. This cardinal rule of every sport applies particularly to boxing. If you tighten up, you lose the flexibility and timing which are so important to successful boxers. Remember this, above all things. – BARNEY ROSS, *Fundamentals of Boxing*, page 29

Vision Awareness

The learning of great speed in visual recognition is a basic beginning for hitting a baseball curve, returning a twisting service in tennis, or catching batted balls curved by the wind or curved by extra spin on the ball. ... The goalie practice is the type needed. It includes short, concentrated, daily practices in seeing quickly. – JOHN DOBSON LAWTHER, *Psychology of Coaching*, pages 217, 218

High levels of perceptual speed are the product of learning, not of inheritance. Almost any boy can acquire great speed of perception through practice in speeding up his perception. – JOHN DOBSON LAWTHER, *Psychology of Coaching*, page 218

A boy who is a little slow in reaction time, or in speed of running, may compensate for this slowness. He may learn to recognize the situation quickly that he has more time to field the ball, intercept the pass, return the serve, or deflect the puck. – JOHN DOBSON LAWTHER, *Psychology of Coaching*, page 218

Fewer choices, faster action. The speed of perception is somewhat affected by the distribution of the observer's attention. When the cue to be recognized is likely to be one of several, each of which requires a different response, the time is lengthened. ... Choice reactions take longer than simple reactions. If there is only one case to which it is proper to throw the fielded ball, the action is faster. The more possible choices, the slower in getting under way the action tends to be. If the choices are too complex, the player is confused and remains undecided, doing nothing. – JOHN DOBSON LAWTHER, *Psychology of Coaching*, page 218

As soon as possible, however, an athlete's awareness is shifted from small details to larger ones, and finally to the whole action, without a thought given to any single part. After an outstanding performance, the highly skilled athlete has absolutely no recollection of the exact manner in which he performed the feat-and this is as it should be. – LAURENCE ENGLEMOHR MOREHOUSE and PHILIP J. RASH, *Sports Medicine for Trainers*, pages 99-100

Attention habits. Habits of attending properly in order to distinguish cues more quickly may be established. A habit of diffusing the attention over a wider area helps the offensive passer to see openings more quickly. – JOHN DOBSON LAWTHER, *Psychology of Coaching*, page 220

For most rapid perception, attention must be at its maximum focus on the thing to be perceived. – JOHN DOBSON LAWTHER, *Psychology of Coaching*, page 222

Experiments indicate that if the cue to act can be made auditory instead of visual, the athlete's response is more rapid. ... If the cue is so simple as to permit a focus of attention on response, the focus of attention on movement produces faster action than the focus on hearing or seeing the cue; in short, when the cue to act can be received incidentally, the athlete should concentrate his attention on making the first movements. ... Auditory cues, when occurring close to the athlete, are responded to more quickly than visual cues. – JOHN DOBSON LAWTHER, *Psychology of Coaching*, pages 221, 222

Team skills should be taught so that one's own team will have as few choice-reactions to make as possible, and so that the opponents will be confronted with a variety of possible responses. – JOHN DOBSON LAWTHER, *Psychology of Coaching*, page 221

Athletes in team games are continually trying to force the opponent into the slower, choice-reaction situation; for example, a defensive man in basketball tries to place himself at the exact distance that leaves the opponent in doubt as to whether it is better to try to shoot or dribble by. – JOHN DOBSON LAWTHER, *Psychology of Coaching*, page 219

Fakes and feints are athletic devices to direct the opponents' attention and preliminary action in the wrong direction if possible, and to make a little hesitation by the opponent necessary before he can be sure of his cue to act. Of course, an additional advantage is gained if the opponent can be induced to make a preliminary motion in an inappropriate direction. – JOHN DOBSON LAWTHER, *Psychology of Coaching*, page 219

The offensive opponent who can throw or kick only from one side permits the defensive opponent the faster action of a one-sided focus of attention. – JOHN DOBSON LAWTHER, *Psychology of Coaching*, page 220

A person reacts to a quick motion towards his eyes by instinctively blinking. A fencer hit on the mask by a headcut will also automatically blink at the moment of the hit. The opponent, if aware that the fencer closes his eyes when threatened, may provoke this reaction and utilize the moment of blindness for a hit. – JULIUS PALFFY-ALPAR, *Sword and Masque*, page 43

Central vision means that the eyes and attention are fixed on one point. In *peripheral vision*, however, although the eyes are fixed on one point, the attention is expanded to a larger field. Central vision may be thought of as being sharp and clear, while peripheral vision is more diffuse. – JULIUS PALFFY-ALPAR, *Sword and Masque*, page 45

The master helps the student learn to expand his attention over the entire area by making full use of his peripheral vision. The following is a simple exercise to develop this type of vision. The master extends his index finger and instructs the student to concentrate on the point of the finger. He then brings the index finger of his other hand into the student's field of view and slowly describes letters and numerals with it. The student should be able to expand his attention sufficiently to recognize the figures without changing the focus of his eyes. The field of vision is enlarged by distance and diminished at close range. – JULIUS PALFFY-ALPAR, *Sword and Masque*, page 46

The field of vision is enlarged by distance and diminished at close range. Also, it is generally easier to follow the opponent's footwork than his point or hand since the foot moves relatively slow compared to the more rapidly moving hand or point. – JULIUS PALFFY-ALPAR, *Sword and Masque*, page 46

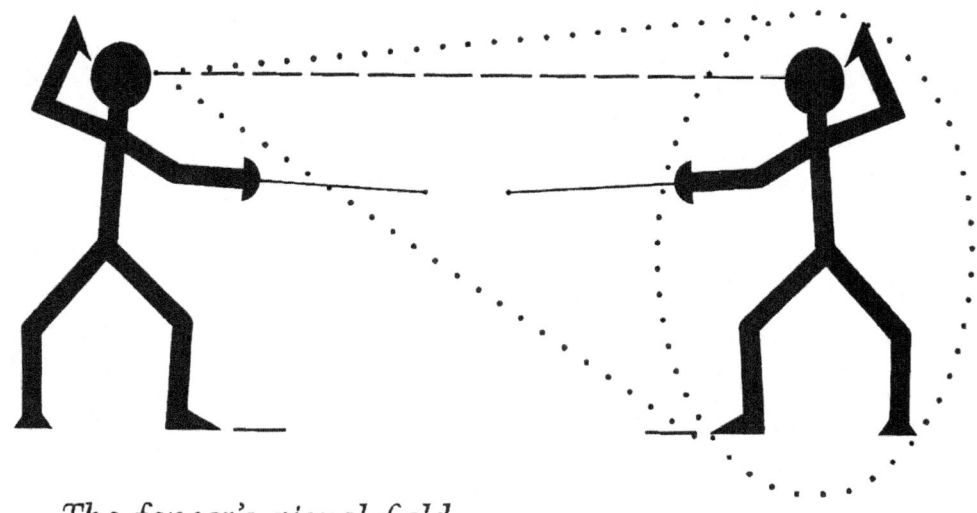

The fencer's visual field.

– JULIUS PALFFY-ALPAR, *Sword and Masque*, page 46

Speed

Let us pinpoint the athletic qualities most desirable in a fencer. They are: (a) Mobility; (b) the physical ability to lengthen movements of arm and legs, in other words to increase reach; (c) spring and resilience; (d) resistance to fatigue, i.e., stamina; (e) physical and mental alertness; (f) imagination and anticipation. – ROGER CROSNIER, *Fencing with the Electric Foil*, page 18

Since the key to attaining speed is muscular elasticity, exercises which increase skill and flexibility of both hand and footwork are indispensable building blocks for the fencer. – JULIUS PALFFY-ALPAR, *Sword and Masque*, page 41

Good form will improve speed. Good physical condition makes the individual faster, as does a certain amount of emotional stimulation, while poor condition or illness makes him slower. – JESSE FEIRING WILLIAMS, M.D. and EUGENE WHITE NIXON, M.A., *The Athlete in the Making*, page 117

Another thing, don't carry out your shadow boxing and at the same time hold a running commentary with an admirer who may be watching you. Keep your mind on the job, imagine that your worst enemy, if you happen to have one, is there in front of you and go out to give him all you have got. Use your imagination to the utmost, try and anticipate the moves your phantom rival will endeavour to put across and work yourself up into a real fighting frame of mind. – JIM DRISCOLL, *The Straight Left and How to Cultivate It*, page 49

One of the greatest adjustments the novice athlete must make to competition is to overcome the natural tendency to try too hard - to hurry, strain, press and try to run the whole race, or play the whole game at once. ... As the athlete forces himself to give everything he has to the performance, his mental demands exceed his physical capacities. The result may be described as *generalized*, rather than *specific*, effort. Overall tension and unnecessary muscular contractions act as brakes, reducing speed and dissipating energy. The body performs better when the athlete lets it go than when he tries to drive it. When the athlete is running as fast as he can, he should not feel as though he ought to be running faster. – LAURENCE ENGLEMOHR MOREHOUSE and PHILIP J. RASH, *Sports Medicine for Trainers*, page 36

TAO FAST FACTS

The *Tao of Jeet Kune Do* contains a reference to "offensive passer" on page 55. A curious use of terminology given that the *Tao of Jeet Kune Do* is a book about martial art, but the term actually refers to quarterbacks in the sport of American football. The passage containing the reference comes from page 220 of John Dobson Lawther's *Psychology of Coaching*.

Work methods to increase speed. The preliminary warming-up to reduce viscosity, increase elasticity and flexibility, and tune the system to a higher physiological tempo (heart rate, blood flow and pressure, respiratory adjustment), adds to possible speed. The preliminary muscular tonus and partial contraction, a suitable stance and an attention focus add to speed possibility. The reduction of stimuli-reception to rapid perceptual habits and the reduction of the resultant movements to fast-reacting habit patterns also make greater speed possible. – JOHN DOBSON LAWTHER, *Psychology of Coaching*, page 229

After momentum in a throwing or striking movement has been generated by longer radius and a long arc of swing, the speed may be increased by suddenly shortening the radius. This effect is seen in the "pull-in" at the last of the arc in the hammer throw, in the backward thrust against the forward leg by the batter in baseball, and so on. The snapping of a towel or a whip are common examples of the same principle. – JOHN DOBSON LAWTHER, *Psychology of Coaching*, pages 229-230

The Secrets of Judo: A Text for Instructors and Students

by Jiichi Watanabe and Lindy Avakian

The whiplike or coil-spring action of the human body in its throwing and striking movement-patterns is a remarkable phenomenon. The movement of the body may start with the push by the toes, continue with the straightening of the knees and the trunk, add the shoulder rotation, the upper arm swing, and culminate in a forearm, wrist, and finger snap. The timing is such that each segment adds its speed to that of the others. The shorter lever principle is used to accentuate many of the particular speeds of this uncoil or whip. The rotation of each segment around its particular joint-fulcrum is made at high speed for that particular part; but this segment rate is accelerated tremendously because of the fact that it rotates around a fulcrum already highly accelerated. – JOHN DOBSON LAWTHER, *Psychology of Coaching*, page 231

All the accumulated speeds of the body are present at the elbow when the forearm snaps over this fast-moving elbow-fulcrum to release the ball. Most of the distance throwing or striking acts illustrate these speed principles. One does not "hit with his feet" but he does start the momentum with his feet. ... An important aspect of this multiple action of acceleration is the introduction of *each segment movement as late as is possible* in order to take full advantage of the peak acceleration of its fulcrum. The arm is kept so far behind that the chest muscles pulling against it are tensed and stretched. The final wrist snap is postponed until the last instant before release or, in striking, before contact. In golf, for example, the arms are approximately over the ball by the time the wrist snap is started. In baseball, the batter snaps his wrists just as he hits the ball. In football, the punter puts the last snap into his knee and foot as, or a shade after, he makes contact with the ball. ... It is this last-moment acceleration that is meant by such coach directions as "block through the man" in football, or "punch through the man" in boxing. *The principle is to preserve the maximum acceleration up to the last instant of contact.* This concept is sometimes confused with the idea of a full, free, uninhibited motion of body inertia after the contact is over. The first principle, of maintaining increasing acceleration as long as there is contact, is sound. The second principle is sound only when such relaxing follow-through will not interfere with speed of the next act. – JOHN DOBSON LAWTHER, *Psychology of Coaching*, pages 231-232

Speed is a complex aspect of behavior. I includes time of recognizing and time of reacting. The more complex the situation to which one reacts, the slower one is likely to be. – JOHN DOBSON LAWTHER, *Psychology of Coaching*, page 233

The athlete can accelerate his speed by learning proper attention focus and suitable preparatory sets and postures. The rate at which he can contract his muscles is an important aspect in his relative speed. – JOHN DOBSON LAWTHER, *Psychology of Coaching*, page 234

Certain physical principles govern speed shortened radius for quicker action, onger arc for imparting greater momentum, centering weight for speed in rotation, and multiplying speed by sequential but overlapping and concurrent movements. The question an individual athlete must answer is what kind of speed is most effective for his particular work method. – JOHN DOBSON LAWTHER, *Psychology of Coaching*, page 234

It's not how fast it travels but how soon it gets there that counts. – JOHN DOBSON LAWTHER, *Psychology of Coaching*, page 216

Timing

In fencing, speed and timing are complementary, and speed in delivering a stroke will lose most of its effectiveness unless the stroke is properly timed. – CHARLES LOUIS DE BEAUMONT, *Fencing: Ancient Art and Modern Sport*, page 193

Reaction Time

In excitation and message transfer, a time gap, like a physical solid, occurs between the stimulus and the contraction of the muscles. This time gap is called reaction time. – JIICHI WATANABE and LINDY AVAKIAN, *The Secrets of Judo: A Text for Instructors and Students*, page 28

Reaction time may be defined in two ways. It may be defined as the time that elapses from the occurrence of the stimulus, or cue to act, to the beginning of the muscle movement, or as the time from the occurrence of the stimulus to the completion of a simple muscular contraction. – JOHN DOBSON LAWTHER, *Psychology of Coaching*, page 223

TAO FAST FACTS

Although the exact source remains unclear, the types of speed described on page 56 of the *Tao of Jeet Kune Do* (perceptual speed, mental speed, initiation speed, performance speed, and alteration speed) appear to be taken from terminology most commonly used in the performance science applied to the sport of tennis.

If the perception is a simple thing like hearing a gun or seeing a dropped flag, the amount of possible improvement of perceptual speed is less. The techniques of preparatory movements can be improved so that response time is shortened. As mentioned above, the direction of one's attention to the motor act can shorten the response time. The remaining factor, under the second definition, is that of muscle contraction speed. – JOHN DOBSON LAWTHER, *Psychology of Coaching*, page 223

In each of the cases just cited the "speed" displayed in getting into action depends therefore upon three considerations:

1. The time required for the stimulus of the sight of the ball, or the blow starting, or the sound of the gun, to reach the brain
2. Plus the time required for the brain to relay the impulse through the proper nerve fibers to the proper muscles
3. Plus the time required for the muscles to get into action after receiving the impulse

This combined period of time is known technically as the "reaction time." – JESSE FEIRING WILLIAMS, M.D. and EUGENE WHITE NIXON, M.A., *The Athlete in the Making*, pages 37-38

The following are typical situations or conditions in which the time required for reaction becomes longer:

1. When one is not trained in judo.
2. When one's mind or body is fatigued.
3. When one is absent-minded.
4. When one is emotionally upset.

– JIICHI WATANABE and LINDY AVAKIAN,
The Secrets of Judo: A Text for Instructors and Students, page 31

Next let us consider how you can lengthen the reaction time of your opponent:

- When stimuli are combined, the reaction time becomes longer. If your opponent knows that you can apply hane-goshi from both sides, he must be ready for an attack from both sides. Therefore, his reaction time becomes longer.
- When your opponent inhales, his reaction time is longer than when he exhales. We can exert a stronger force when we exhale than when we inhale. While inhaling, your opponent will find it difficult to defend himself against your attack, whether he be a master or a beginner in judo.
- When your opponent focuses his attention on one movement, his reaction time to another stimulus becomes long.
- The moment your opponent is off balance in any direction, his reaction time becomes longer.

– JIICHI WATANABE and LINDY AVAKIAN,
The Secrets of Judo: A Text for Instructors and Students, page 32

Warming up, physiological condition, and degree of motivation, all affect reaction time slightly. To a large degree, reaction time seems to be unaffected by training. – JOHN DOBSON LAWTHER, *Psychology of Coaching*, page 223

Movement Time

A period of fencing time *(temps d'escrime)* is the time taken by a fencer to perform one single fencing movement with the arm, the blade, or the foot. – CHARLES LOUIS DE BEAUMONT, *Teach Yourself Fencing*, page 51

It is in no way related to time as measured by fractions of a second because fencers vary in the time they take to execute a fencing movement. – CHARLES LOUIS DE BEAUMONT, *Teach Yourself Fencing*, page 51

Making an unexpected attack or the removal of the blade as the opponent is about to engage it are examples of actions executed in time. – JULIUS PALFFY-ALPAR, *Sword and Masque*, page 94

It is not necessary to execute an action in time with a quick or violent motion. A movement that starts from rest without obvious preparation and proceeds *smoothly without hesitation* may be so unexpected that it succeeds in hitting the opponent before he is alerted. – JULIUS PALFFY-ALPAR, *Sword and Masque*, page 109

He must minimize this danger [of counter-attack], either by causing his opponent to lose a period of fencing-time, or by protecting himself against a stop-hit while he is gaining distance. ... Simple attacks are undoubtedly difficult to bring off and have a better chance of success when they are preceded by an attack on the blade which will produce some form of reaction, and permit a period of time to be gained. But, whether or not these simple attacks are preceded by a preparation, they are dependent on great point accuracy and the fact that they are driven home confidently and with speed. – ROGER CROSNIER, *Fencing with the Epee*, pages 57, 51

The fencer soon discovers that an action, although technically perfect, can be frustrated by the opponent's preventive hits, which take the right of way over to the opponent's side. Therefore, it is essential to time the attack at exactly the right moment when the opponent cannot avoid being hit. – JULIUS PALFFY-ALPAR, *Sword and Masque*, page 44

Timing in fencing means the ability to recognize the opportunity and seize the right moment for an action. Timing can be analyzed through its physical, physiological and psychological aspects.

1. The hit may land when the opponent is in the midst of making a movement himself (during the course of a movement).
2. The hit may land in the fluctuating cyclic events of tension.
3. A hit may be made may be made when the opponent is not paying attention, when his concentration flags, or when he is preoccupied with his own plans.

– JULIUS PALFFY-ALPAR, *Sword and Masque*, page 44-45

This perfect moment may be either seized instinctively or provoked consciously. The opponent may be induced to do something specific or to attack a given target (as in the case of a second intention attack on counter-time). The opportunity for a good time-hit in most cases lasts only for an instant. Good fencers must sense rather than perceive their chance to strike. – JULIUS PALFFY-ALPAR, *Sword and Masque*, page 45

Keeping the proper distance from the master who moves backward and forward is the first exercise which refines the student's reactions. Another early timing exercise consists of having the student make a thrust with a lunge at the moment when the master changes positions or takes his blade away from engagement. ... The *evasive thrust* is a simple attack in time against the opponent's attempt at engagement. The movement is similar to the disengage attack, but the point must be removed before the opponent touches the blade. The evasive thrust must be practiced against the simple, semi-circular, and circular engagements.
– JULIUS PALFFY-ALPAR, *Sword and Masque*, pages 94, 95

Whether or no a boxer possesses a knockout punch depends fundamentally on two things – *leverage* and *timing*. Timing is an integral part of leverage, but the reverse is not the case. ... Good timing on its own is sufficient to give the striker dynamic power behind his punches.
– PETER MCINNES, *Tackle Boxing This Way*, pages 25, 26

Timing one's blows in boxing means the art of hitting the rival as he comes forward, or perhaps is lured into coming forward through a clever piece of feinting. – PETER MCINNES, *Tackle Boxing This Way*, page 26

He seems to out-guess his opponent because he usually takes the initiative and to a large extent forces the reactions of his opponent, and above all, he does everything with decision because he has confidence in himself and makes his movements with a purpose rather than with a doubting hope.
– JULIO MARTINEZ CASTELLÓ, *Theory and Practice of Fencing*, page 59

Broken Rhythm

Ordinarily, two fencers of equal ability can follow each other's movements, and unless there is a considerable difference in speed they should stalemate each other. The movements of the attacking and defending blades work almost in rhythm with each other, and although there is a slight advantage in the initiative of the attack, it must also be backed by superior speed in order to land successfully. However, when this rhythm is broken, speed is no longer the primary element in the success of the attack or counter-attack of the man who has broken the rhythm. If the rhythm has been well established, there is a tendency to continue in the sequence of the movement. In other words, each man is *motor-set* to continue the sequence of the movements. The man who can break this rhythm by a slight hesitation or an unexpected movement can now score an attack or counter attack with only moderate speed; for his opponent is motor-set to continue with the previous rhythm, and before he can adjust himself to the change, he has been hit. That is why the touch on time is usually such a pretty touch, for it seems to catch its victim flat-footed. – JULIO MARTINEZ CASTELLÓ, *Theory and Practice of Fencing*, pages 56-57

Timing has to be felt and mastered as a psychological problem even more than as a fencing problem, for the breaking of the rhythm relies on the fact that *the victim is going to continue for a fraction of a second in the sequence of movements which has suddenly been interrupted.*
– JULIO MARTINEZ CASTELLÓ, *Theory and Practice of Fencing*, page 57

Sometimes, timing involves attacking with many threatening movements, and if the defender accepts this rhythm and attempts to parry these various threats, then a slight hesitation will break the rhythm and provide the opportune moment to launch the final attack. On other occasions when your opponent is in the midst of making an advance or threatening movements on his own account, you may succeed in breaking the rhythm by at first apparently reacting as he expects, and then by suddenly launching a counter attack when he thinks you should be following his feint, you should land, for he is motor-set to continue with his threats, and cannot adjust himself to the necessity of parrying until after you have scored. ... In general, however, timing means that you initiate your attack or movement when your opponent has started preparation of an attack. Thus, timing becomes a question of taking advantage of the slight interval before he can readjust himself to make a parry. – JULIO MARTINEZ CASTELLÓ, *Theory and Practice of Fencing*, pages 57, 58

Tao of Jeet Kune Do - **Personal Impacts**

I grew up in West Belfast at the height of the troubles and I gained much strength from Bruce lee's philosophical interpretations. When experiencing anxiety as a result of trauma, my response was to fight it, challenge it, but this attitude only provided more fuel to my anxious state. The following quote was to be a guide for me to understand and overcome my anxieties:

> "Let yourself go with the disease, be with it, keep company with it - this is the way to be rid of it."

Acceptance was the true key of my recovery from alcohol and addiction. For the past 12 years, I have travelled the world competing in sword tournaments and raising money for charity. I have no doubt in my mind that Bruce Lee was of great support through difficult times.

Aidan Cochrane
Belfast, Northern Ireland

Cadence

This regulating of one's speed to correspond with that of the adversary s known as cadence. – ROGER CROSNIER, *Fencing with the Foil*, page 246

A correctly judged cadence permits the calm control of every stroke. This control, in its turn, will allow the sabreur to select, with more ease, the movements of offence and defence which will bring about a hit. – ROGER CROSNIER *Fencing with the Foil*, page 186

As in the case of the incorrect choice of stroke, here again the attacker, by his excessive speed, has parried himself. – ROGER CROSNIER, *Fencing with the Foil*, page 247

Ideally a fencer *should seek* to impose his cadence on an opponent. This may be achieved by *intentionally varying the cadence of his movements*. For example, he can deliberately establish a certain rhythm in his feints in a composite attack, until the defender is induced to follow that cadence. – CHARLES LOUIS DE BEAUMONT, *Fencing: Ancient Art and Modern Sport*, pages 199-200

By obtaining this edge of speed on the adversary he is being led. In other words, it is he who, continually, will have to try to catch up. If one has a sufficient margin of speed in hand, it is possible to maintain this advantage, which is known as "imposing the cadence". To do so must have a moral effect on the opponent, who, finding himself subjected to his adversary's will in this important factor of speed, cannot fail to suffer in his confidence. It will affect the regularity of his execution and the quality of his accuracy. A correctly judged cadence permits the calm control of every stroke. This control, in its turn, will allow the sabreur to select, with more ease, the movements of offence and defence which will bring about a hit. – ROGER CROSNIER, *Fencing with the Sabre*, page 186

Sequences of actions being shorter at sabre than at foil and epee, changes of cadence are not seen quite so often as at other weapons. If at foil, for example, fencers are willing to follow, and seek, long exchanges or rallies in order to effect a change of cadence, to catch the opponent unprepared, such tactics at sabre are more usually applied to offensive actions. In most cases, they are prepared by a series of false attacks, and feints, executed at a normal rhythm. The preparation has the effect of lulling the opponent into a false sense of preparedness. It accustoms his reactions to a cadence other than that which will be used for the attack itself. Then the movements comprising the attack are *suddenly accelerated* and more likely to find him lagging behind. – ROGER CROSNIER, *Fencing with the Sabre*, pages 187-88

A very effective change of cadence is to *slow down*, instead of speed up, the final action of a compound attack or riposte. The defender, moving up or across to the line he believes to be that of the final action, does not find the contact he expects. Instinctively, he leaves that line for another in the hope of finding the blade, opening up his target to the slowly delivered cut. This form of delivery is known as attacking, or riposting, in *broken-time*, and is very often successful. – ROGER CROSNIER, *Fencing with the Sabre*, page 188

Speed, applied *at the opportune moment*, together with the correctly judged cadence in the execution of the movement, will go a long way towards ensuring the success of a stroke. – ROGER CROSNIER, *Fencing with the Sabre*, page 186

Tempo

The success of a fencing action depends on whether we perform it at the right time or not. We must surprise our opponent and catch the moment of his helplessness! – JOHN KARDOSS, *Sabre Fencing: History, Theory, Practice*, page 59

That little *fragment of time* which is the most suitable in which to accomplish effective fencing action is called in fencing terminology *"tempo"*. – JOHN KARDOSS, *Sabre Fencing: History, Theory, Practice*, page 59

From a *psychological point of view*, the moment of surprise, and from the *physical point of view*, the moment of helplessness, are the right moments to attack. This is the true conception of tempo - *choosing the exact psychological and physical moment of weakness in an opponent*. – JOHN KARDOSS, *Sabre Fencing: History, Theory, Practice*, page 59

There are also tempo opportunities when the opponent makes conscious movement, thus when he steps forward, makes an invitation, goes into a bind, etc. In such and similar cases the moment for attack is *when he is executing the movement, because until he finishes it, he cannot change to the reverse.* This is the real amount of helplessness. – JOHN KARDOSS, Sabre Fencing: History, Theory, Practice, page 59

We should bear in mind in every action that the peak of the art of fencing is *tempo*, but at the same time be careful that the adversary does not mislead us by giving false tempo opportunities. – JOHN KARDOSS, Sabre Fencing: History, Theory, Practice, page 76

When for each stroke a pupil knows:

HOW-it is done;
WHY-it is done;
WHEN-it is done;

and finally, can apply the answer to each question successfully, then he knows the stroke perfectly and can proceed to another. – ROGER CROSNIER, Fencing with the Foil, page 244

– THOMAS INCH, Boxing: Secret of the Knock-Out page 115

Stop-Hit

Finally, a valuable tactical movement, which is facilitated at epee by the wide measure, is to attack the opponent on his preparation of attack. – CHARLES LOUIS DE BEAUMONT, Fencing: Ancient Art and Modern Sport, page 133

A time-hit is a stop-hit which *anticipates*, and *intercepts*, the final line of the attack, and is delivered in such a way that the executant is covered. ... Delivered on the 'final' of the attack it cannot gain time and permits no margin of error in either timing, or the correct anticipation of the form which the attack will take. – ROGER CROSNIER, Fencing with the Epee, pages 146, 47

The stop-hit is a counter-offensive movement which must, by hitting the attacker, arrest him in the development of his attack and fulfill the implication of its name. ... We may state that an attacker who prepares his attack by first stepping forward, by changing his engagement, or by beating his opponent's blade, is liable to be stop-hit by a fencer who with a direct or indirect counter-offensive movement stop-hits him. – ROGER CROSNIER, Fencing with the Foil, page 157

WHO WROTE THE TAO?

A compound attack badly executed, e.g.:

(a) with a bent arm;
(b) with wide badly directed blade actions;
(c) by feinting in the on-guard position and lunging with a second disengagement,

could allow the stop-hit to land on the first of any of these movements composing the attack, which is being made in two or more periods of fencing time. To make the stop-hit legitimate the point would have to land:

(a) while the arm was bent and before it stretched;
(b) on the first feint of the badly directed point;
(c) on the first feint of the attack executed in two-time.

Without fearing to mention strokes which have not been described before, we can mention those whose appellation will allow the student to understand their meaning, so that we may state that an attacker who prepares his attack by first stepping forward, by changing his engagement, or by beating his opponent's blade, is liable to be stop-hit by a fencer who with a direct or indirect counter-offensive movement stop-hits him. – ROGER CROSNIER, *Fencing with the Foil*, page 158

Let us repeat that the stop-hit is obviously an excellent means of defence against an opponent who attacks wildly, with insufficient care to covering, or who comes too close. – ROGER CROSNIER, *Fencing with the Epee*, page 47

Correct appreciation of time and distance is essential to the making of an effective stop hit which, while usually made with a straight thrust, may also be made with a disengagement or counterdisengagement. – CHARLES LOUIS DE BEAUMONT, *Fencing: Ancient Art and Modern Sport*, page 88

It is often necessary to angulate the wrist in order to dominate the opponent's blade. – CHARLES LOUIS DE BEAUMONT, *Teach Yourself Fencing*, page 54

In each of the examples which have been given, the student must understand that, if he delivers his stop-hit when the last movement of the attack is being executed, then it will not be awarded to him. He will find that in order to make sure that his action does land in time, it is advisable to lean forward as if to meet the attacker. – ROGER CROSNIER, *Fencing with the Foil*, page 159

Although we have, in the several examples which precede this, covered most of the conditions favourable to the stop-hit, it would be as well to impress on the student, that such a stroke is more often useful and successful against preparations with a step forward, where the margin of time allowing for success is greater than with attacks not preceded by them. We can therefore, say, that generally the stop-hit is the stroke chosen to deal with preparations with a step forward. – ROGER CROSNIER, *Fencing with the Foil*, page 160

The epeeist must train himself to be constantly prepared to make a stop hit during the course of any movement of a phrase. The successful introduction of a stop hit not only enables many valuable hits to be scored but has a devastating moral effect on a forceful and confident opponent. ... It is therefore essential that the epeeist should develop opportunism and train himself to place his stop hits with speed and accuracy and from a variety of angles. – CHARLES

LOUIS DE BEAUMONT, *Fencing: Ancient Art and Modern Sport*, page 121

Counter-Time

Many of the older epeeists maintained that it was dangerous and, therefore, foolish to attack without, first of all, having gained control of the opponent's blade. To put this theory into practice, these exponents of the dueling-sword, amongst whom Philippe Cattiau, of France, was the recognized king, used every means at their disposal, patiently and systematically to draw the stop-hit. It brought the adversary's blade within their reach and gave them the opportunity of gaining control of it. – ROGER CROSNIER, *Fencing with the Epee*, page 74

The second-intention attack is, as its name implies, a *premeditated* movement, generally used against a fencer who has formed the habit of continually attempting stop hits or who attacks into the attack, that is to say one who launches an attack as soon as his opponent makes any offensive movement. – CHARLES LOUIS DE BEAUMONT, *Fencing: Ancient Art and Modern Sport*, page 91

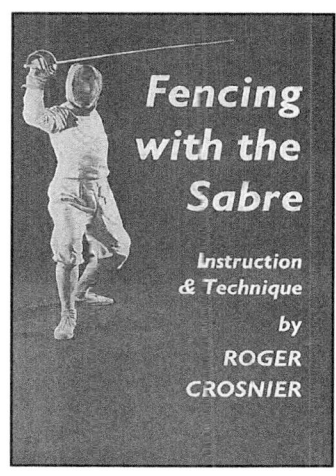

Counter-time is the action of drawing the opponent's stop-hit, or time-hit, parrying it and riposting from it. It is an action of second intention. ... The difficulty in being successful at bringing off this action of second intention which is counter-time, lies not so much in drawing the stop-cut, as in correctly timing the parry which deflects it. The speed of the opponent's reactions will have to be found and his cadence judged. – ROGER CROSNIER, *Fencing with the Sabre*, pages 163-164

Distance must be judged correctly to minimize the danger of being hit while still being within reach of the opponent in order to land the final movement of the counter-time sequence, which is the riposte. – ROGER CROSNIER, *Fencing with the Sabre*, page 164

The success of a counter-time movement largely depends on concealing one's real intentions and inducing the opponent to make his stop hit or stop hit in opposition with conviction, so that he has little opportunity to recover when it is parried before the riposte lands. – CHARLES LOUIS DE BEAUMONT, *Fencing: Ancient Art and Modern Sport*, page 91

A stop hit may be drawn in a variety of ways, such as by The stop hit may be drawn in a variety of ways: by use of invitations, by intentionally uncovered feints, by making false attacks with a half-lunge or merely by stepping forward. – CHARLES LOUIS DE BEAUMONT, *Fencing: Ancient Art and Modern Sport*, page 91

It will be wise to riposte with opposition of blade so as not to be hit by the continuation of the stop-hit. – ROGER CROSNIER, *Fencing with the Epee*, page 74

If the opponent realises that a second intention attack is being prepared, he may make his stop hit merely as a feint in order to parry the expected riposte and score with a counter-riposte. Indeed a second intention attack may be drawn by making it appear that one had a predilection for the stop hit: whenever the opponent makes any offensive movement. – CHARLES LOUIS DE BEAUMONT, *Teach Yourself Fencing*, pages 54-55

Attacks and ripostes, however well designed and executed, will generally fail unless they are delivered at the right moment and at the right speed. ... A simple example of the right choice of time is provided by an attack by disengagement. From the normal on-guard position at foil, a disengagement can be parried by a lateral movement of the sword-hand which travels a matter of a few inches, while the attacker's point has to travel several feet to reach the target. Under these conditions the fastest attack should be parried by even a slow defensive movement, and this disparity in time will be aggravated if the attack is directed towards a side of the target towards which the defender's blade is already moving to close the line. – CHARLES LOUIS DE BEAUMONT, *Fencing: Ancient Art and Modern Sport*, page 199

It is obvious that the attack should be timed to move towards a part of the target from which the opponent's blade is moving away, that is *into an opening rather than a closing line,* if it is to have the best chance of overcoming the disadvantage of time and distance to which it is always subject. – CHARLES LOUIS DE BEAUMONT, *Fencing: Ancient Art and Modern Sport*, page 199

Similarly, an excellent moment to launch an attack is when an opponent is himself preparing an attack. His attention and blade movements will then be momentarily concentrated more on attack than defence. – CHARLES LOUIS DE BEAUMONT, *Fencing: Ancient Art and Modern Sport*, page 199

An attack on preparation is often effective against a fencer who maintains a particularly accurate fencing measure and who is difficult to reach because he keeps just out of lunging distance whatever offensive movement is made. The attack can often be made after the opponent has been drawn within distance and induced to prepare an attack by a short step back. – CHARLES LOUIS DE BEAUMONT, *Fencing: Ancient Art and Modern Sport*, page 101

An attack on preparation must not be confused with an attack into an attack. The former is made during the preparation and before the opponent's attack begins, and secures the right of way under the rules governing foil fencing. The attack into the attack will not have this priority, because it is in fact a counter-offensive movement and is subject to the rules governing the stop hit which have already been mentioned. A very exact choice of distance and careful timing is required if the attack on preparation is not only to obtain priority in time over the opponent's attack, but so to appear to the judges. – CHARLES LOUIS DE BEAUMONT, *Fencing: Ancient Art and Modern Sport*, page 103

Attitude

The state of the athlete's mind as he faces his event determines the degree of excess tension he will carry into the event. The athlete free from excess tension as he awaits his performance is typically self-confident. He has what is commonly known as "a winning attitude." He sees himself as master of the athletic situation confronting him. To many athletes, being a champion is a matter of "psychological necessity." Fed by previous successes and having completely rationalized previous failure, he feels himself a Triton among minnows. – LAURENCE ENGLEMOHR MOREHOUSE and PHILIP J. RASH, *Sports Medicine for Trainers*, page 33

As an event approaches, the athlete often notices a feeling of weakness in his midsection. He may complain of "butterflies in his stomach." His viscera are churning with nervous excitement; he feels nauseated and may vomit; his heart pounds, he may feel a throbbing in his throat; he may experience pain in his lower back. The experienced athlete recognizes these sensations not as an inner weakness, but as an inner surplus. The coach and trainer know that these signs indicate a preparedness for violent activity. In fact, the athlete who expresses a feeling of euphoria before an event is probably in a poor state of readiness. Many athletes call it "adrenalburger," a condition affected by adrenomedullary activity, augmented by the stimulating effect of the competitive situation. The explanation for this probably lies in the function of the medulla of the adrenal gland, the activity of which is augmented by the stimulating effect of the competitive situation. – LAURENCE ENGLEMOHR MOREHOUSE and PHILIP J. RASH, *Sports Medicine for Trainers*, page 35

Experience shows that an athlete who forces himself to the limit can keep going as long as necessary. This means that ordinary effort will not tap or release the tremendous store of reserve power latent in the human body. Extraordinary effort, highly emotionalized conditions or a true determination to win at all costs will release this extra energy. Therefore, an athlete is actually as tired as he feels and, if he is determined to win, he can keep on almost indefinitely to achieve his objective. The attitude, "You can win if you want to badly enough," means that the will to win is constant. No amount of punishment, no amount of effort, no condition is too "tough" to take in order to win. Such an attitude can be developed only if winning is closely tied to the boy's ideals and dreams. – EDWIN HAISLET in *The 1947 Official National Collegiate Athletic Association Boxing Guide* (edited by Carl P. Schott), page 14

He must learn to perform at top speed all the time, not to coast with the idea he can "open up" when the time comes. The real competitor is the one who gives all he has at all times. The result is that he works close to his capacity and in doing so forms an attitude of giving all he has. In order to create this state, a boy must be driven longer and harder than he would normally continue. – EDWIN HAISLET in *The 1947 Official National Collegiate Athletic Association Boxing Guide* (edited by Carl P. Schott), page 14-15

Peter McInnes

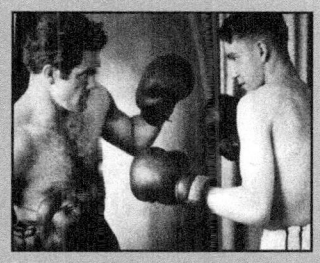

Peter McInnes was an amateur boxer and historian. Born in 1926 in Hampshire, England, he was the son of the mayor of Bournemouth, where he lived most of his life.

He studied law at Cambridge. While serving as an officer in the Army, he competed in hundreds of amateur boxing competitions. His most notable fight may have been with one of the Kray Twins, a pair of notorious British gangsters.

McInnes later became a journalist and television commentator covering the sport of boxing. He also dabbled in boxing promotion. One of his books, *Tackle Boxing This Way*, is the source of 17 passages in the *Tao of Jeet Kune Do*.

Peter McInnes was a childhood friend of boxing champion Freddie Mills, and they remained friends until Mills' death in 1965. He would later claim that Freddie Mills' death by gunshot, ruled a suicide, was murder committed by the Krays. "My belief, and it is also the belief of his thousands of friends, fans and admirers," said McInnes, "is that he was murdered by racketeers when he refused to continue paying protection money which was being extorted on his London nightclub."

Peter McInnes died in February of 2007 at the age of 80.

TOOLS

Before I studied Zen – mountains were mountains, and trees were trees.
While I was studying Zen – mountains were no longer just mountains, and trees were no longer just trees.
When my studying of Zen had ceased – mountains were once more mountains, and trees were once more trees!

– Zen Buddhist statement,
as recounted in Jeffrey Swann's
Toehold on Zen, page 101

It is a correct maxim that a good offense is the best defense. A good offense consists of leads, false moves and counterpunches supported by mobility, endurance and generalship. The false moves are called feints. – FRANK GILMER, *Push Yourself: A Book for Amateur Boxers and Boxing Fans*, page 17

A good boxer is able to beat his opponent to the punch with lightning-fast leads, to draw out his opponent's counter-punches with feints in such a way as to make the counter-punches miss, thereby leaving the opponent out of position and an easy mark for a counterpunch of the boxer doing the leading. – FRANK GILMER, *Push Yourself: A Book for Amateur Boxers and Boxing Fans*, pages 17-18

It is this ability to outsmart an opponent and outmaneuver him that is the skill and science of the sport of boxing. To have this ability you must understand hitting and the different types of blows and when and where they are best put into use. As the result of long practice, you must become able to get your full weight and strength into each punch. You must deliver the proper blow at the proper time as automatically as a driver shifts the gears of his car into second. – FRANK GILMER, *Push Yourself: A Book for Amateur Boxers and Boxing Fans* page 18

When you have developed hitting into something automatic it will become instantaneous and your mind will be free to plan your battle as the fight progresses and new situations arise. You can reach this point of development if you are willing to do the necessary training. That training grind is the most valuable thing boxing has to offer. The rest is velvet. – FRANK GILMER, *Push Yourself: A Book for Amateur Boxers and Boxing Fans*, page 18

John Kardoss

John Kardoss was born on April 12, 1910 in Budapest Hungary. As a college student, he was the fencing champion of Hungarian University. Kardoss was a major proponent of the Hungarian method of fencing.

After college, Kardoss became director of five theaters. Kardoss served in the Royal Hungarian Army as an officer during World War II. As part of his duties, he organized sabotage measures against the Germans and aided in the escape of allied war prisoners. After the war, he managed a series of theatres.

In the 1950s, Kardoss moved to Australia and earned his Australian citizenship. He taught fencing at Sydney University and to the Australian Navy and Army. He was also a public lecturer and the drama critic for the *Sydney Sun*.

He authored a book on sabre fencing in 1955. *Sabre Fencing: History, Theory, Practice* was the first book on the subject written in English. The book is the true source of 10 passages in the *Tao of Jeet Kune Do*.

In 1963, he was appointed as director of the office of cultural affairs at Long Island University in New York. He died in New York on July 9, 1969 at the age of 59.

The elements of attack are all techniques which are used to carry attack by strategy. They are the devices and skills of the finished boxer. Requiring speed, deception, timing, and judgment, they are the tools of the master craftsman who blends them into perfect attack. – EDWIN HAISLET, *Boxing*, page 65

Attack by deception is the attack of the master. The master boxer has at his command techniques to bewilder and confuse the opponent, thereby creating many openings. He feints his opponent into "knots." He combines hitting with feinting in such a manner that both appear to be the same. He draws bis opponent to him *forcing whatever leads he desires*. Through defensive hitting and judicious movement, he keeps his *opponent off balance*. The master boxer has the ability to get in close and understands the value of infighting. He has so perfected the "shift" that it is used for attack as well as defense. Finally, he is the master of counter fighting for be knows *when to attack and when to allow attack*. ... Scientific attack then is no simple matter but requires years of study and practice for Its successful use. – EDWIN HAISLET, *Boxing*, page 65

Four Basic Methods of Attack

Leading

The master of attack must know the value of a straight lead. He must know what is liable to happen on any lead. He realizes that for every lead there is an opening, and for every opening, a counter, and for every counter a block. These things he understands but he also knows how and when to lead with comparative safety. – EDWIN HAISLET, *Boxing*, page 66

Leading with the left hand, guarding with the right while moving to the left, makes negligible any opening that ordinarily results from a straight left lead. – EDWIN HAISLET, *Boxing*, page 66

Feinting

Feinting is characteristic of the expert boxer. It requires using the eyes, the hands, the body, and the legs in a single effort to deceive an opponent. These movements are really decoys and if the opponent attempts to adjust his defense, the expert takes advantage of the openings created. Feinting is also used to ascertain what the opponent's reactions will be to each movement. – EDWIN HAISLET, *Boxing*, page 66

COMING SOON...
Tao of Jeet Kune Do
by Bruce Lee
The martial arts book of the century!
Entirely written & illustrated by Bruce Lee!

This is the book that has been talked and whispered about for several years. It took time to gather Bruce's notes and drawings and arrange them with the seven volumes into a single, massive book. But here it is, the most comprehensive work ever written on the martial arts and written by the most famous martial artist that ever lived! Bruce discusses the principles, observations and training that make Jeet Kune Do. His own sketches and finished drawings illustrate the work throughout. Now, with his wife Linda Lee's authorization, Ohara presents it to the public, impressively bound and artistically crafted.
Send a self-addressed envelope & receive your copy now.

ABOVE: Ohara Publications' 1975 advertisement announcing the release of the *Tao of Jeet Kune Do*.

Feinting creates only momentary openings. To be able to take advantage of the openings created means instant reflex action, or foreknowledge of what openings will be created by certain feints. Such familiarity presupposes practice, for only through the actual practicing of many feints against many kinds of opponents may a general reaction tendency be determined. … In boxing, as in football, an opening should be "set up." Once an opening is created by a certain feint, that opening should not be used until a clean sure blow will result. … A good boxer knows what openings will result before he feints and makes use of this knowledge and initiates his follow-up action almost before the opening results. Whenever two boxers of equal speed, strength, and skill are matched, the one who is the master of the feint will be the winner. – EDWIN HAISLET, *Boxing*, page 66

The essential elements in feinting are rapidity, change, deception and precision, followed by clean crisp blows. Feints used too often in the same way will enable the opponent to time them for a counter-attack thus defeating their very purpose. – EDWIN HAISLET, *Boxing*, page 66

Feints against the unskilled are not as necessary as against the skilled. Many different combinations of feints should be practiced until they are natural movements. – EDWIN HAISLET, *Boxing*, page 66

Drawing

Drawing is closely allied to feinting. Whereas in feinting an opening is created, in drawing some part of the body is left unprotected in order that a particular blow will be led by the opponent thus developing an opportunity to use a specific counter. – EDWIN HAISLET, *Boxing*, page 67

Feinting is only a part of drawing. Drawing uses the method of strategy, and the method of crowding or forcing. Being able to advance while apparently open to attack, but ready to counter if successful, is a phase of boxing that few ever develop. Many boxers refuse to lead. Then to be able to draw or force a lead becomes very important. – EDWIN HAISLET, *Boxing*, page 67

Infighting

Infighting is the art of boxing at close range. Not only does it take skill to get in close, but it takes skill to stay there. To get inside, it is necessary to slip, weave, duck, draw, or feint. – EDWIN HAISLET, *Boxing*, page 67

Keeping in mind our earlier remarks that, because of the large target, epee is a careful game, it will be readily understood that each hit must be painstakingly and patiently prepared. – ROGER CROSNIER, *Fencing with the Epee*, page 85

Valuable as is such advance information, one should still approach each unknown opponent with caution. It is generally fatal to start a bout with a set plan, for instance on the basis that so and so always attacks, or never ripostes direct. – CHARLES LOUIS DE BEAUMONT, *Fencing: Ancient Art and Modern Sport*, page 198

Jim Driscoll

"Peerless" Jim Driscoll is unquestionably one of finest boxers that Great Britain has ever produced. Skillful technique, stoic endurance, and a superb straight left kept him at the very top of his game for more than 15 years. With a career record of 63-4-6 with 39 knockouts, Driscoll etched his place rightfully in the annals of the professional world of pugilism.

One of five children, Jim Driscoll was born into poverty on December 15, 1880 in the docks area of Cardiff. After losing his father at an early age, it was imperative that Jim learned how to handle himself. Stories are told of how the young paperboy would wrap his fists with newspaper and offer to spar with his workmates, and, to make a few extra shillings, would stand with his hands behind his back goading people to hit him. To their astonishment, they would always miss.

As with many Welsh boxers of his time, Jim began his career in the fairground boxing booths, which were commonplace in Wales. The booths would provide all sizes and shapes of opponents and would be the perfect grounding for any would-be champion. A master of defense, Jim Driscoll could hold his own with the very cream of the time, many of whom were frustrated by his effortless ability to slip and weave their best punches, before he himself would demonstrate the correct way to land a punch. Jim Driscoll was the master of the straight left.

In 1906, following a loss to Harry Mansfield in a highly disputed points decision, Driscoll fought reigning champion Joe Bowker for the British featherweight. The fight went the full 15 rounds with Driscoll defeating Bowker on points. The following year they met again, after Jim gave up his title, and this time Bowker went down in the seventeenth round making Driscoll a two-time British Champion. In the year 1908 Jim took the Empire title from Charles Griffin over 15 rounds and exacted revenge by defeating Harry Mansfield in the sixth round.

Then America beckoned. Driscoll was fiercely patriotic and defensive of British boxers at a time when American and French fighters dominated the sport. The United States was keen to see the Welshman about whom they had heard so much. His reputation

had preceded him. Driscoll beat the very best that America could offer. His skill in the ring, defense, and superior boxing ability wowed the Americans. With lightning fast hands and feet, he could fight at full pace all evening if need be and was surely but methodically fighting his way to the champ - Abe Atell.

Papers of the day gave Driscoll all 10 rounds against Atell. As usual, Driscoll utilized his stiff left jab and Atell, although going the distance, was swollen and bruised.

Unfortunately, this was the era of the no-decision in America, where a fight was considered a draw if one boxer was not knocked out. This rule prevented Driscoll from being declared a world champion. An almost immediate call for a rematch was on the cards, but Driscoll had already boarded a passenger ship back home to Wales to meet a promise to take part in an annual charity boxing event for Nazareth House Orphanage in Cardiff - a cause close to his heart. "I never break a promise," Driscoll claimed.

Jim Driscoll returned to a hero's welcome. Following a knockout win against Arthur Hayes, he went on to fight and beat Spike Robson for the British title. The coveted Lonsdale belt adorned his waist for the third time, which secured his ownership of the belt. But Driscoll was now pushing 30 years old, and following a brief return to America to fight Pal Moore - in which Driscoll was defeated on points in the sixth round - he returned to Cardiff to fight Freddie Welsh. A brutal, somewhat dirty fight, Welsh covered his body continuously - not allowing Driscoll any chance to work the inside. Driscoll, frustrated by the tactics, was eventually disqualified for head butting in the tenth round - finally bringing an end to a disappointing bout.

Driscoll went on to beat Spike Robson again to retain his British title and then onto

Frenchman Jean Poesy, whom he defeated for the European title. Driscoll's final fight before the First World War began was against Owen Moran - a staggering 20 round draw.

Driscoll had a six-year hiatus due to the Great War. He was 40 years old and already in poor health. His final bout was against Frenchman Charles Ledoux. The bout lasted 17 rounds. He looked grey and frail but when the bell rang it was still very much "Peerless" Jim Driscoll flying from the corner. For 15 rounds he held his own until a surprise body shot sent him reeling - only to be saved by the bell. It was the beginning of the end. Driscoll was finished - the towel was thrown in by his corner during the following round.

After his retirement from the fight game in the early Twenties, Jim Driscoll published several books on the methodology of boxing. Unlike the other books of the time, these were far more scientific in their approach to the sport while coupled with a much more comfortable, conversational read.

Following a long battle with tuberculosis, Jim Driscoll passed away on January 30, 1925. He was buried in Cathay's Cemetery in the very heart of Cardiff. Driscoll's funeral remains one of the largest outpourings of emotion the city has ever seen. More than 100,000 people lined the coffin's journey from Newtown to its final resting place. The headstone was provided by the Sisters of Nazareth House in honor of his long-standing charitable work for the orphanage. To this day, the nuns continue to adorn his graveside

with fresh daffodils. A statue was erected in 1997 near Central Boys Boxing Club where he trained, and if you are ever driving through the dock area of the city, chances are that you will at some point drive along Jim Driscoll Way. Fitting tributes to one of Cardiff's favourite sons.

The final bell may have struck for "Peerless" Jim Driscoll many years ago, but his achievements, skill and above all dedication to his craft continue to ring true a century later.

– Dean Routledge
Excerpted from
The Textbook of Boxing: The Deluxe Edition by Jim Driscoll
Published in 2008 by Promethean Press

PATRICK STRONG ON THE TAO OF JEET KUNE DO

Patrick Strong
Actor, personal trainer, original student of Bruce Lee

Once you understand a few principles you can look to Bruce Lee's notes in the *Tao of Jeet Kune Do*. The problem is that Bruce was simply taking notes, rather than writing a book. He wasn't writing a thesis or a book that would have explained the concepts in far greater method and detail. Beware, the *Tao of Jeet Kune Do* is incredibly incomplete.

However, there is value in the *Tao of Jeet Kune Do* for those who understand the roots of Bruce's methodology. Understanding those roots is the key to understanding Bruce Lee, if you are so inclined. Where do you get that understanding? You get it through research and your own self-examination.

Bruce used this analogy to explain it: "Pretend that a young man wants to learn to fight, and I let him fight one of my students, instructing him to fight the best way that he can and with everything he's got. At this point, he knows very little about fighting. When he fights, he just fights from his instincts: punching, kicking, elbowing, whatever. He is 'innocent'. [Bruce used this word, "innocent". It is a key word.]

"Now I teach him a new way to stand, move, punch, kick. He can hardly walk let alone fight. And when I tell him to fight, he is far worse off than before. Nothing seems to work. Everything is mechanical. He is trying to use the way. He is limited.

"And yet, he continues to train until, one day, everything becomes natural once again. Only, the way he stands, walks, punches, kicks, and uses his elbows are very much different. His movement is more efficient. He is faster and more powerful. He is no longer 'stuck' in his movement." Once again, he is "innocent".

To be "innocent" is to use no way as the way. To be "innocent" is to have no limitation.

Kicking

The Patagonian Purr-Kick:

A knee cannot have the mobility of the head. ... The direct kick is the quickest, most powerful, and hardest to block. ... Since many boxers retain most of the weight on their rear leg it is often necessary to bypass the lead leg and go through with an attack to the rear knee. This is so because kicking a knee which bears no weight is fairly fruitless. Generally, the more weight on the leg, the more damage you can do to the knee. — JOHN F. GILBEY (Robert W. Smith), *Secret Fighting Arts of the World*, pages 101, 102

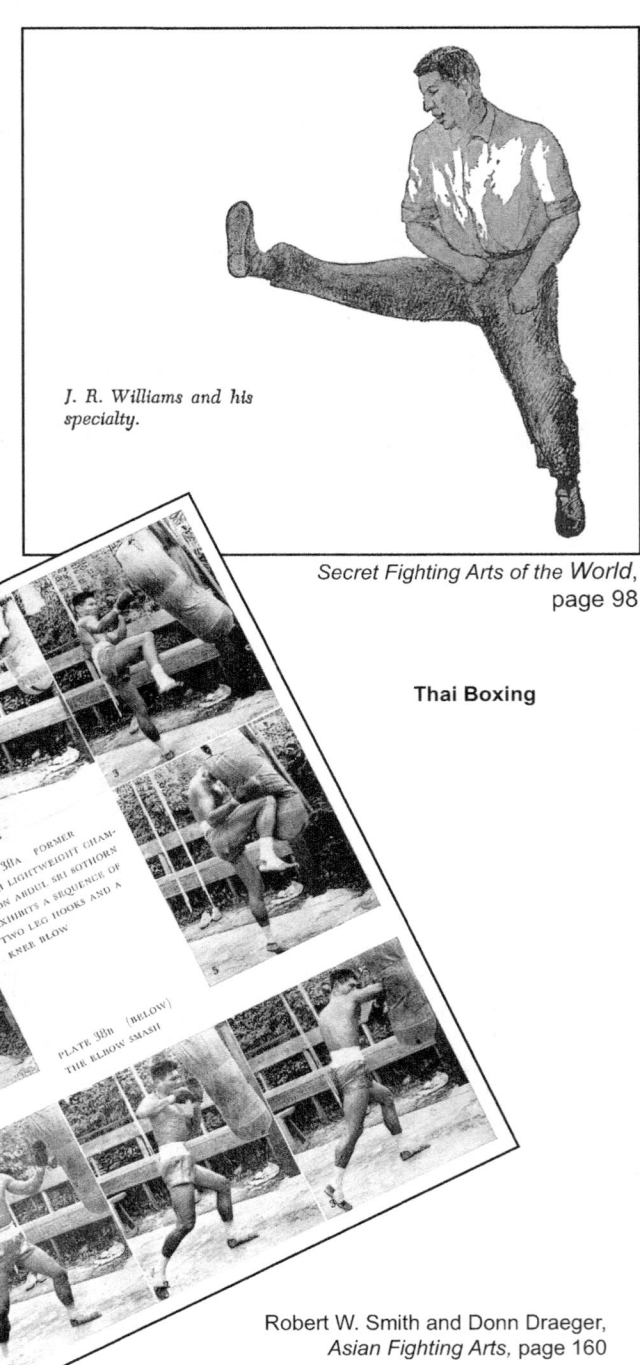

J. R. Williams and his specialty.

Secret Fighting Arts of the World, page 98

Thai Boxing

Robert W. Smith and Donn Draeger, *Asian Fighting Arts,* page 160

Savate

J. DELCOURT, *Black Belt Magazine*, March 1967, pg 22

J. DELCOURT, *Black Belt Magazine*, March 1967, pg 23

J. DELCOURT, *Black Belt Magazine*, March 1967, pg 23

ROBERT BARR; illustrations by HAL HURST, "Fighting with Four Fists" In *McClure's Magazine*, Vol. III, pg 300

ROBERT BARR; illustrations by HAL HURST, "Fighting with Four Fists" In *McClure's Magazine*, Vol. III, pg 295

R. G. ALLANSON-WINN, *Boxing*, pg 58

The lunge (development) remains the safest method at epee of carrying the attack to the opponent. The mechanism of the lunge, which facilitates a speedy recovery out of range of a riposte should the attack fail, has ensured that it should be favoured by most epeeists of class. It is the soundest action of the legs for an offensive movement at a weapon where the slightest loss of balance, or control, may mean that some part of the target has been left unprotected for a fraction of a second. – ROGER CROSNIER, *Fencing with the Epee*, page 31

Like the cobra, the fencer must be able to strike (with the point of his blade) so that his touch is felt before it is seen. – ALDO NADI, *On Fencing*, page 51

Edwin Haislet: The Man Behind the Book

If there was one man whose work was most influential to the contents of the *Tao of Jeet Kune Do*, that man is Edwin Lee Haislet, Ed.D. Haislet's 1940 book, titled *Boxing*, was the source of more material found in the pages of the *Tao of Jeet Kune Do* than any other source. Haislet's book provided the foundation for Bruce Lee's boxing skills.

Edwin Lee Haislet was born on October 2, 1908 in a log cabin on a ranch in Utica, Montana. By the time Haislet reached school age, the family had relocated to Fordville, North Dakota, where the young boy also helped his father in the family printing business. Samuel Haislet would often tell people, with a wry grin, that his son Edwin was a quick study and could "set type before he could walk."

Edwin Haislet and his family moved again to Minneapolis when he was 12. Life was sometimes challenging for Haislet in Minneapolis. He found he was the smallest kid in his neighborhood and a target for bullies. Needing a way to defend himself, Edwin Haislet became interested in boxing as a sport. Soon he was boxing as an amateur. But Haislet didn't just limit himself to boxing; a well-rounded athlete, he also played football at Central High School in Minneapolis.

After high school, Haislet went to the University of Minnesota to study physical education, which had become a passion for him. His commitment to his own physical fitness included a morning routine of 100 pushups, 100 knee bends, 100 sit-ups, and a mile run. Haislet continued his athletic endeavors during his studies, playing basketball and football for the university. By 1925, he was competing as an amateur boxer again, eventually winning the University of Minnesota heavyweight championship title.

Haislet graduated from the University of Minnesota in 1931 with a Bachelor of Science degree in recreation and education. He started a master's degree program at New York University, also in the physical education field, which he completed in 1933. While at New York University, he briefly turned professional boxer, completing six professional fights during that time.

After earning his master's degree, Haislet returned to the University of Minnesota, but this time as a member of the faculty. He became an instructor in physical education at the university as well as an intramural sports assistant and boxing coach.

Seeking to further his career, Haislet left his job at the University of Minnesota in 1935 to return to New York University and complete a doctoral program. While working on his doctorate, he married his wife, Mary McNally, in 1936. Haislet completed his Doctor of Education degree in 1938. His dissertation was on the subject of boxing.

Shortly before completing his doctorate, University of Minnesota Athletic Director Frank McCormick recruited Haislet to return to the university. A newly-minted doctor, he went straight from doctoral school to his second professional stint at the University of Minnesota as an assistant professor in physical education.

Haislet continued to pursue his passion for boxing; he attended frequent boxing matches and became deeply involved in the Golden Gloves organization, a governing body for amateur boxing matches. He would eventually be named the director of the Northwest Golden Gloves district. In 1939, Haislet published his dissertation as a book titled *Boxing in Education* and drafted the official Golden Glove manual of instruction. Haislet also began a stint as a columnist *Minneapolis Star-Journal,* where he wrote a daily boxing column that lasted until 1940.

Edwin Haislet's greatest literary success occurred in 1940, when a reworked version of his first book was published by the A. S. Barnes Company. Simply titled, *Boxing,* the book would become a seminal work on the subject and would go on to influence generations of boxers, including Bruce Lee.

The Two 'H's'

FIGHT EXPERTS SEE 1,200 BOUTS A YEAR

By FRANK DIAMOND

Wanna go to a fight? Sure, everyone likes to see a boxing match, especially of the amateur variety.

But the next time you look around for company at a fight program DON'T ASK Joe Hendrickson or Eddie Haislet to trot along for company.

For one thing, they'll be there be it amateur or professional. And for another thing, they won't be able to sit back and kibitz with you.

JOE HENDRICKSON AND ED HAISLET

Haislet, Dr. Edwin L. Haislet, is director of the Star Journal amateur boxing program and Hendrickson is boxing writer for the Star Journal.

They watch an average of 1,210 fights a year each, travel at least 3,000 miles to see the bouts and yet when spring comes are rarin' to go plotting and planning for the next Golden Glove season.

Haislet for the past 16 years has been connected with amateur boxing. As an amateur fighter he won the University of Minnesota middleweight championship and for the past six years has been in charge of the Star Journal Golden Glove program.

Breaking their program down Haislet and Hendrickson watch 95 novice fights, 125 city tournament bouts, 350 Northwest Golden Glove fights, 400 in the Chicago Golden Glove, 90 professional, 100 district battles and at least 50 Minneapolis amateur bouts.

They both admit they wouldn't miss the excitement, association with the boxers and fans and pleasure of watching the amateurs develop for anything in the world.

As Northwest District Golden Gloves director, Haislet made several progressive changes to the training methodology and programs. His development of that district became a model for other districts across the United States. He was also named the commissioner of Minneapolis boxing. Haislet traveled over 3,000 miles a year to attend boxing matches in other parts of the country. According to a 1941 report in the *Minneapolis Star-Journal,* Haislet's attendance of boxing matches averaged over 1,200 per year.

In June of 1942, during the height of the second World War, Haislet answered his country's call for service by joining the Navy, which was seeking boxing instructors for a new program of combat fitness for its pilots. After a briefing officer training period at Annapolis,

WHO WROTE THE TAO?

* * *

Five Minneapolis p h y s i c a l training experts were assigned to duty as navy officers last week on completion of a special indoctrination course at United States Naval academy, Annapolis, Md. They are **LT. EDWIN L. HAISLET** (former Star Journal and Tribune Golden Gloves director) and **LT. GEORGE H. OTTERNESS, JR.**, assigned to work under Lt. Col. Bernie Bierman at the navy's new pre-flight training school at Iowa City, Iowa; **LT. MICHAEL A. CIELUSAK** and **LT. EDWARD J. FARRELL**, assigned to Wold-Chamberlain naval reserve aviation base, and **ENS. GEORGE FAUST**, assigned to Jacksonville, Fla., naval air station. Faust is on temporary duty at Wold-Chamberlain.

* * *

Lieutenant Edwin Haislet took up his new role as chief Seahawk boxing instructor at the new Pre-Flight Training School in Iowa City, Iowa. The training school was established to provide skills training to Naval pilots in preparation for flight training.

Captain F. T. Ward explained the importance of the boxing program to the Navy's goals:

Sports are used as a training device in the physical training program for Naval Aviation just as mathematics and physics are taught in the academic courses and ordnance and gunnery are employed in the military education of cadets. Physical training was made an integral part of the training plan and is continued progressively throughout the entire training of aviation cadets. Successful coaches were commissioned so that the Navy might have the best instruction available.

Each sport has definite objectives of its own, and, in addition, contributes to the over-all aims and purposes of Naval Aviation training. In such a program it is natural that at times experience may show better means of achieving the desired objectives. Initially, syllabi were prepared by the newly commissioned athletic officers to serve as guides in conducting the various sports and activities. While adhering closely to the original plans, the experience gained in teaching thousands of cadets in varying circumstances has been a valuable supplement to the physical training program.

It is important to understand that in the Naval Aviation program, sports are not used for their own sake or for recreational purposes. The competitive sports embodied in this program were selected for what they contribute to the development of desirable characteristics in the aviation cadet. It is for this reason that the books are unlike other sports publications. The manuals consider sports in the military training sense, in their conditioning values, both mental and physical.

By 1943, Haislet was promoted to assistant athletic director at the base. During this time, he used materials from his previous books to assemble his syllabi and instructional boxing guide for the new Naval officers. The

Preflight Mentor Says Boxing Is Sport Essential to Give Flier What He Needs

IOWA CITY, IA.—(P)—What's tops in an all-around sport to give future fighting pilots just what they need in muscle building, agility and a competitive spirit?

The answer is boxing, says Lieut. Edwin Haislet of the Iowa preflight school.

"We need men who know how to fight and win as well as to fly," Lieut. Haislet, former boxing coach at the University of Iowa explains. "The flier needs confidence and reliance in himself, a sense of timing, and highly developed competitive spirit that can only be satisfied with victory. This is what boxing tries to put into the hearts and heads of future fliers."

When a cadet can't make up his mind about a varsity sport, he's sent to boxing classes. And the popularity of the sport has increased by leaps and bounds.

The assets of boxing to the pilot are varied and many. According to Haislet, head of the boxing program here, boxing "teaches aggressiveness, how to make contact with the opponent, how to find a weakness in the defense, and then to overwhelm it with a furious but directed attack.

"It teaches courage in the face of possible defeat, to face heavy guns without flinching, to gamble of the self to outfight, outgun, outgame and outsmart the opponent even in spite of odds.

"It teaches the ultimate in self confidence and reliance to face the enemy alone and to survive."

instructional guide was adopted as the official instructional guide of the entire Navy and published in 1943 by the United States Naval Institute as *Boxing: The Naval Aviation Physical Training Manual*.

"Boxing is the moral substitute for personal combat," Edwin Haislet would tell one newspaper. "It is the very essence of the fighting man."

"Boxing teaches the lesson of a daring and whirlwind attack, courage in the face of possible defeat, willingness to face heavy odds without flinching, and to gamble on one's chances of out-gunning, out-gaming, and out-smarting the enemy. To the fighting flyer, these lessons mean the difference between defeat and victory, life, or death."

In 1945, with the war's conclusion, Haislet returned to the University of Minnesota as an associate professor in the College of Education and director of recreation training. It was during this time that he developed one of the first four-year degree programs for recreational leadership in the United States.

Haislet also returned to the role of Golden Gloves director, expanding the amateur boxing program to a year-round basis. Children 12-14 years of age were taught the pugilistic art of self-defense at a new outdoor training camp. He served as director of the Northwest district of Golden Gloves for a total of 10 years and was a member of its national rules committee. Haislet was also a member of the national Amateur Athletic Union (AAU) Boxing Committee (as well as the president of the state branch), secretary of the National Collegiate Boxing Coach Association, and served on the National Collegiate Athletic Association (NCAA) Boxing Rules Committee during this time.

Haislet became increasingly concerned about the problem of juvenile delinquency in his community and saw boxing as a means to reach at-risk youth. "I don't know of any

better method for decreasing the outdoor delinquency problem than this outdoor training quarters," he said. In the summer of 1947, Minnesota governor Luther Youngdahl asked Haislet to start the Minnesota Youth Commission – with the goal of tackling the juvenile delinquency problem. He took a leave from the university to work as director of the Youth Conservation Commission's division of prevention and as the executive secretary for the Minnesota governor's youth conference.

During his term on the Minnesota Youth Commission, Haislet advocated for the use of recreation programs as intervention tools with troubled youth. "We spend $1,000 a year on every child committed to a Minnesota correctional institution," he said. "But what do Minnesota communities spend, on the average, for recreation programs? About 76 cents."

After serving on the Minnesota Youth Commission for a year, Edwin Haislet returned to the University of Minnesota. In September of 1948, Haislet was named the director of the University of Minnesota Alumni Relations program. Wanting to fully focus on the Alumni program, Haislet resigned his director role for the Northwest district of Golden Gloves. "He was fiercely loyal to the University of Minnesota," said George Pennock, a former national president of the Alumni association. "He realized what an important role the group could play on campus."

Haislet's contributions to the world of boxing, to his university, and to his community were significant. In 1953, the *Minneapolis Star-Journal* referred to Haislet as a "human dynamo" for the many hats he wore and his copious achievements. During the 1950s, he appeared as a panel member of a local boxing television program. In 1961, he received the Golden Gloves Alumni Achievement Award in recognition of his services to the organization.

The latter part of Haislet's career was largely focused on his role as executive director of the University of Minnesota alumni association and his duties as a university professor. As the director of the alumni association, he started the alumni association's international travel tourism program and the freshman scholarship program.

In addition to his other many accomplishments, Edwin Haislet was also a visionary. In

May of 1970, Haislet foresaw the advent of the modern age of online education, writing about the changing needs of students and what the future would hold:

> "The only answer is working together on behalf of the best possible education for all qualified youth on a predetermined basis – area, state and regional schools sharing facilities, faculty, and libraries, with a free exchange of students from campus to campus. With modern electronic equipment – tape recorders, telephone, radio, television, and computer systems – this kind of sharing becomes increasingly possible, day by day, and in some places is already an actuality.
>
> "Instead of bringing thousands of students to a few hundred professors - professors will be brought to the people – to classrooms all over the city or area, to business and industry, personally or by radio, TV, tape, and computer. The day when you have to go to a campus to take a course is almost antiquated."

Haislet served as executive director of the Minnesota alumni association for 28 years – from 1948 until his retirement in 1976 at the age of 67, when he announced that he was "hanging up his gloves." After receiving notice of Haislet's intention to retire, University President C. Peter Magrath called him "a veteran both in terms of service and in his loyalty and dedication to the University of Minnesota and our state."

In his retirement, Haislet devoted his spare time to a wide variety of professional and civic activities, including acting as athletic chairman of the first Minneapolis Aquatennial, a member of the Minneapolis Planning Commission, the United States Olympic Committee, and the American Athletic Union Board of Governors. He was also active with the American Red Cross, Community Chest, and the Boy Scouts of America.

In his final years he suffered from the effects of Alzheimer's disease. Edwin Lee Haislet died on May 8, 1992 at Colonial Acres Health Care Center in Golden Valley, Minnesota. He was 83. He left behind his wife of 56 years, Mary, his son Charles and daughter Marcia, and a number of grandchildren and great-grandchildren. He also left behind a legion of boxers and martial artists influenced by his boxing theories. And thanks to the *Tao of Jeet Kune Do*, Edwin L. Haislet, Ed.D. is inextricably associated with the name Bruce Lee.

> "It is easy to prepare the body for contest; it is difficult to prepare the mind."

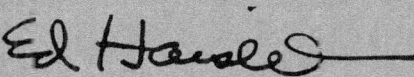

The time-hit is a movement which is quite definitely premeditated. It has a very demoralizing effect on the adversary who has impaled himself on the blade and who, thereafter, will attack less confidently. – ROGER CROSNIER, *Fencing with the Epee*, page 47

Eric Hoffer: Longshoreman Philosopher

Eric Hoffer was one of the most unusual philosophers of the 20th Century, yet he left an indelible mark on the social sciences and human thought.

His early life is shrouded in mystery. Eric Hoffer claimed to be born on July 15, 1902 in New York City, the son of German immigrants, but no records seem to exist to verify these facts. At the age of five, his mother fell down the stairs with him in her arms. Hoffer says the injuries to his mother resulted in her death two years later. For Hoffer, the accident affected his memory and resulted in his loss of sight. As the result of his blindness, he did not go to school. When his vision returned 10 years later, he eagerly began reading again and absorbing knowledge.

After the death of his father, Eric Hoffer used the insurance money to take a bus to Los Angeles where he began a period of drifting down the Pacific coast, working odd jobs and struggling with poverty and depression.

Hoffer eventually began working with migrant field laborers working the crop harvests in California. He continued reading in his spare time and developed a life-long appreciation of the philosophy of Michel de Montaigne.

In 1943 he settled in San Francisco and started working as a longshoreman on the docks. During the same period, he began to write about his observations of the world in his spare time. Written in his tiny one-room apartment in the evenings after a day of back-breaking labor, his first book, *The True Believer: Thoughts on the Nature of Mass Movements*, was published in 1951. In the book, he analyzed the nature of mass movements, revolutions, nationalism, and religious movements. The central thesis of the book is that there is a danger that is inherent in mass movements, and they can easily slip into dogmatism and absolutism. Prophetically, he warned of the coming dangers of religious fanaticism in the Middle East. The book was a revelation to many and immensely successful. President Eisenhower loved it so much that he gave copies to his friends, noted philosopher Bertrand Russell proclaimed that it was intellectually sound and politically timely, and Harvard historian Arthur M. Schlesinger Jr. called it a "brilliant and original inquiry into the nature of mass movements is a genuine contribution to our social thought."

Eric Hoffer was now in the public eye and established as one of the major intellectual thinkers in the United States. Yet, he continued to live his life as a longshoreman, preferring the company of his fellow dock workers. His life as a dock worker and, even after literary success, his unwillingness to leave it, earned him the reputation as the "longshoreman philosopher".

Hoffer's next book was a collection of random thoughts, observations, and aphorisms, titled *The Passionate State of Mind*. This book was a significant influence on Bruce Lee, who copied entire passages from it, many of which were then posthumously credited to Lee in books like *Bruce Lee: Artist of Life* (in a chapter titled, rather obviously, The Passionate State of Mind). Hoffer factors heavily in the *Tao of Jeet Kune Do*; *The Passionate State of Mind* is the true source of 19 passages within its pages.

Eric Hoffer was named an adjunct professor at the University of California at Berkeley in 1964 but continued his other job as a longshoreman until 1967, working three days a week on the docks and one day a week at Berkeley. He continued to write throughout the 1960s, publishing *The Ordeal of Change* (1963), *The Temper of Our Time* (1967), *Nature and the City* (1968), and *Working and Thinking on the Waterfront* (1969). Hoffer announced his retirement in 1970, saying: "I'm going to crawl back into my hole where I started. I don't want to be a public person or anybody's spokesman. Any man can ride a train. Only a wise man knows when to get off."

Retirement did not seem to slow down Eric Hoffer's mind nor his pen. He published six more books during his remaining lifetime, including *First Things, Last Things* (1971), *Reflections on the Human Condition* (1973), *In Our Time* (1976), *Before the Sabbath* (1979), *Between the Devil and the Dragon: The Best Essays and Aphorisms of Eric Hoffer* (1982), and *Truth Imagined* (1983). He also received honorary doctorates from Stonehill College and Michigan Technological University and received the Presidential Medal of Freedom from President Ronald Reagan.

He died at his home in San Francisco on May 21, 1983 at the age of 80. Author and journalist Eric Sevareid offered these thoughts about Hoffer after his passing: "America meant freedom and what is freedom? To Hoffer it is the capacity to feel like oneself. He felt like Eric Hoffer; sometimes like Eric Hoffer, working man. It could be said, I believe, that he was the first important American writer, working class born, who remained working class-in his habits, associations, environment. I cannot think of another. Therefore, he was a national resource. The only one of its kind in the nation's possession."

– HOWARD ALEXANDER, QUINTIN CHAMBERS, and DONN F. DRAEGER, *Pentjak-Silat: The Indonesian Fighting Art*, pages 70-71

| Toe to Back of Neck | Toe to Coccyx | Drop Knee to Groin | Heel to Face |
| Heel on Back | Heel on Ribs | Knee Drop to Head | Drop Knee to Solar Plexus |

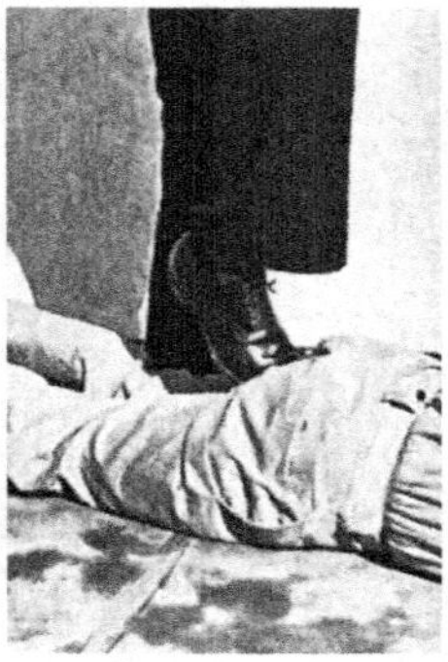

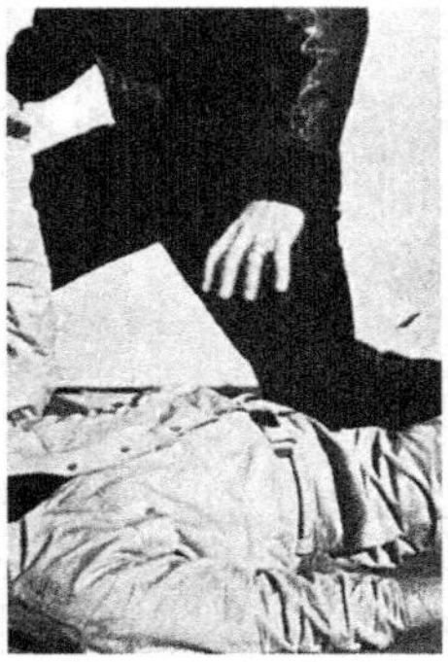

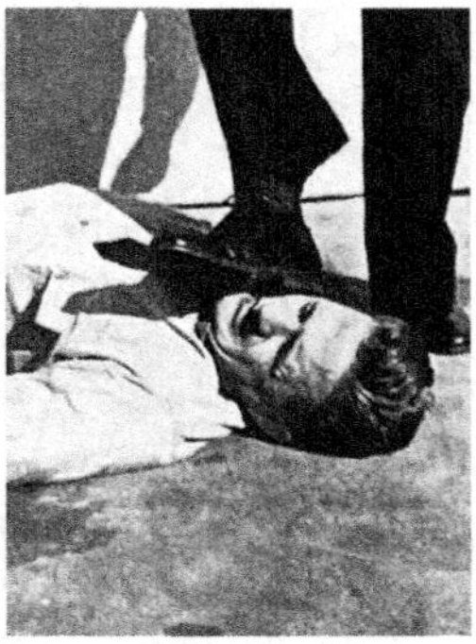

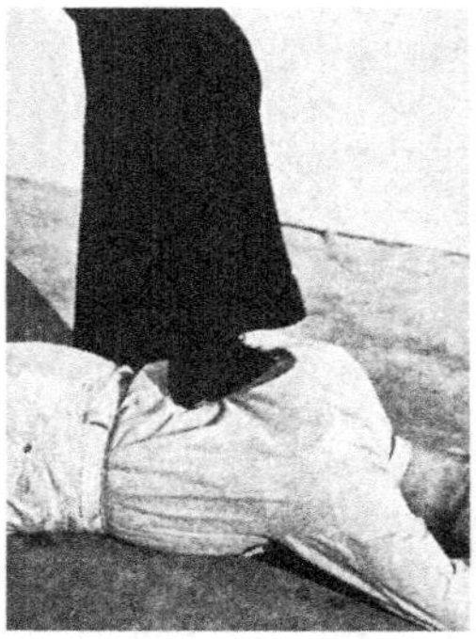

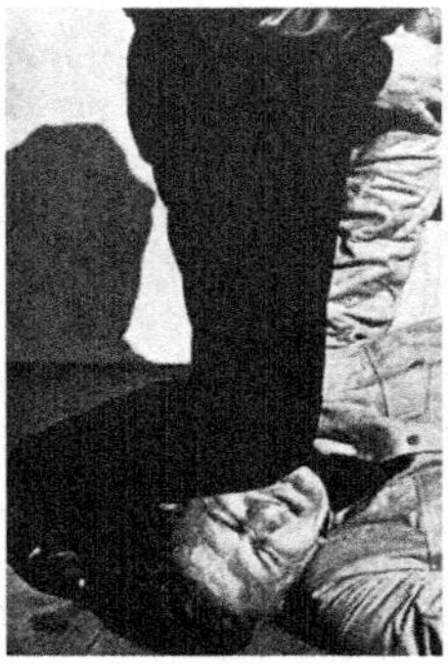

– JOE BEGALA, WESLEY BROWN, JR., and HAROLD LOWE, *Hand to Hand Combat*, pages 38, 37, 34, 42, 41, 41, 33, 34

Striking

Leading Straight Punch

The straight left is generally considered to be the "backbone of boxing," and rightly so. ... Because of its advanced position the left arm is a potent defensive and offensive weapon. It is the reconnoitering squad, the advance skirmisher, the light artillery that foils the opponents best laid plans and paves the way for your right. ... The straight left is the safest blow in boxing, because of the advanced position of the left arm and because, in following through the arm delivery, the body is still farther swung out of range. The follow through also carries your right farther back, from whence it can be snapped forward with added momentum and force. The straight left is the swiftest full-arm blow that can be delivered from the fundamental stance because it has the shortest distance to travel—it is more than half-way there before it starts.
– PHILADELPHIA JACK O'BRIEN, *Boxing*, pages 32, 31

For my money, the obvious superiority of the straight blow over any other type is that it moves directly to its destination, and so is the fastest possible punch. After all, it can hardly be disputed that the shortest distance between two points is a straight line! Another obvious advantage is that the straight blow reduces the chances of missing to a minimum because the opponent has less time for evasive action. – PETER MCINNES, *Tackle Boxing This Way*, page 25

Beware of using just arm power. It is well known that the weight lifter, wrestler, or gymnast, unaccustomed to boxing, relies upon his arm power and a 200 lb. athlete of this kind does not hit as hard as a trained featherweight boxer of about 126 lb. weight. Study upon your sack and punch bag how to get the shoulder into your punches and how correct footwork to suit the punch puts body weight into each blow. ... In most blows it is necessary to time footwork with arm and shoulder extension and at the same time use strong shoulder reverse and body whirl so that, with little apparent effort, every ounce of strength and speed goes into the blow. – THOMAS INCH, *Boxing: The Secret of the Knock-Out*, page 11, 12

Thomas Inch

Thomas Inch was born on December 27, 1881 in Scarborough, a coastal town in North Yorkshire. The son of working-class parents, Inch grew up admiring the strongman Eugene Sandow and became fascinated by strength training during his teens. He started developing his own body using physical labor as his tool.

By the time he reached adulthood, Thomas Inch had earned a reputation as a strongman. At age 19, he was declared the world's strongest youth by a bodybuilding publication.

Inch went on the road exhibiting his feats of strength. He was one of the first strongmen of his era to demonstrate with the use of barbells and dumbells; other bodybuilders of the time often used more theatrical tools like wooden barrels and heavy sacks of grain.

Declared the "Scarborough Hercules", Inch capitalized on his growing notoriety as a strongman by launching a mail order bodybuilding course in 1903 – the first of its kind in the United Kingdom. The course went on to sell over 40,000 copies. He also authored books on strength training, beginning with *Scientific Weightlifting* in 1905 and *Thomas Inch on Strength* in 1907.

In June of 1910, Inch competed in and won the Britain's Strongest Man championship. That title sealed his reputation as the foremost example of physical fitness in the United Kingdom.

A man ahead of his time, Inch was the first person to introduce adjustable plate-loading barbells and dumbbells for increasing strength, the first to promote weight training for the

WHO WROTE THE TAO?

improvement of athletic performance, and the first to promote the use of weight training to correct physical abnormalities and physical rehabilitation.

Perhaps his greatest claim to fame was his invention of the "Thomas Inch" dumbell, which weighed 172 pounds and nine ounces. It's thick handle made it particularly difficult to grip and lift. It is believed that, during his lifetime, no other man but Inch was able to lift it.

Inch worked as a rehabilitation specialist for wounded soldiers at Fulham Military Hospital following World War I. In 1923, he authored a third book, *Inch on Fitness*.

By the 1930s, Inch had become a household name and a leading expert on strength. His physical culture equipment and mail-order business was, at the time, the largest such business in the world, employing over 120 employees. He produced two more books during the 1940s: *Away with Nerves* (1946) and the *Manual of Physical Training* (1947).

Later in life, Inch served as a strength and conditioning coach for boxers, including such luminaries as Bombardier Billy Wells and "Gunner" James Moir. This led to Inch's books on boxing, which included: *Spalding's Book on Boxing and Physical Culture* (1945), *Boxing for Beginners: from Novice to Champion* (1951), and *Boxing: The Secret of the Knock-Out* (1953). All three boxing books provided material for the *Tao of Jeet Kune Do*, with a total of 24 passages and illustrations derived from these sources.

Inch remained active and fit as he aged. In 1939, at the age of 58, he demonstrated his ability to lift the "Thomas Inch" dumbell in a film for the British Pathé news service. Ten years later, at the age of 68, Inch was still deadlifting 540 pounds.

Thomas Inch inspired a generation of bodybuilders and strongmen, including Darth Vader actor David Prowse, who acquired the "Thomas Inch" dumbell for his personal collection and counted it as one of his favorite pieces of memorabilia.

Thomas Inch died on December 12, 1963 in Cobham, Surrey of coronary thrombosis.

Remember that you must take up power from the ground through your legs and back. Sway all your muscles into your punches. Make them drives. Push off from the ground. And, above all, get your timing and your aim right. – JIM DRISCOLL, *The Straight Left and How to Cultivate It*, pages 65-67

To fence well is to be greased lightning with the potential forward speed of a coiled spring. Like the cobra, a fencer must remain coiled in a relaxed position having at the same time the potentiality of leaping from absolute immobility to top speed, power, and precision. The guard position is the only position from which one can attack efficiently. Like the cobra, the fencer must be able to strike (with the point of his blade) so that his touch is felt before it is seen.
— ALDO NADI, *On Fencing*, page 51

Edwin L. Haislet's BOXING presents simply, concisely and graphically the technique of boxing. It is the result of the author's more than twenty years' association with this great sport. BOXING emphasizes the correct sequence in learning the skills necessary for good boxing. It is liberally illustrated with "how-to" drawings.

The Barnes Sports Library

BOXING by Haislet is just one of the volumes in the Barnes Sports Library. Written by experts, these "how-to" books are standard texts on all popular sports. Thoroughly illustrated, they are priced at $1.50 each. Available at all book or sporting goods dealers or send *cash* to A. S. Barnes and Company, Dept. JB, 67 West 44th St., New York 18, N. Y.

ABOVE: 1946 advertisement for Edwin Haislet's book, *Boxing*. This advertisement appeared in the *Official National Collegiate Athletic Association Boxing Guide for 1947*, a booklet owned by Bruce Lee.

Jack Dempsey

Known for his savage boxing style, Jack Dempsey has been called the most vicious heavyweight in boxing history, the Giant Killer, and the Manassa Mauler. *Ring* magazine ranks him the #10 heavyweight of all time and the 7th strongest puncher. The Associated Press called him the greatest fighter of the first half of the 20th Century.

Born William Harrison Dempsey in Manassa, Colorado on June 24, 1895, Dempsey was the son of Mormon missionaries from West Virginia. He spent some of his early childhood in Colorado before his family returned to West Virginia, where he spent the remainder of his childhood.

He left home at age 16 and began traveling, living a vagabond lifestyle. For money, Dempsey would sometimes walk into bars and challenge men to fight.

Jack Dempsey began fighting professionally in the Fall of 1914, at the age of 19. He became heavyweight champion on July 4, 1919 by beating Jess "The Great White Hope" Willard. Dempsey held the heavyweight title for seven years. Boxing writer Rick Espinosa recalled a particular anecdote about Dempsey's time as heavyweight champion:

> "Out of the ring Dempsey was a generous and warm fellow. That showed in his fight with [Billy] Miske in 1920. Miske was a hell of a good light-heavyweight who had fought Dempsey tough two times before. But then he had contracted Bright's Disease and he was dying. He was out of boxing three years when he finally recovered enough to start fighting again. He was trying to cram in as many fights as he could before he died so he could pay off his doctor bills and set up his family.
>
> "He wasn't making any bread, so he came to Dempsey who was a close friend and said he needed a title fight to make some money. Tex Rickard, who promoted Dempsey's bouts, didn't want anything to do with it. Miske was dying and he didn't want the guy to kick off in the ring.
>
> "Dempsey agreed to the fight and had someone else promote it. Miske would get $25,000. But when it came time to fight, Dempsey was in a sort of a quandary. If he knocked the guy out, people would say he beat a sick man. But if he carried the guy 15 rounds, Miske could either get hot right at the end and possibly take Dempsey's title, or the exhaustion might kill the guy. Dempsey finally decided to end it as quick as possible.
>
> "In the third round he used a crushing right hand and knocked Miske out. He said it was the hardest blow he ever hit anyone with. As Miske lay there unconscious, Dempsey knelt over him, trying to revive him. He said he felt nauseous. And when the crowd cheered for him, Dempsey said he felt anger and rage.
>
> "Miske managed to pay off his bills and avoid bankruptcy. He won 24 fights after that, but the day after Christmas in 1924 he died. As he lay on his deathbed, his wife said his last words were 'Tell Jack Dempsey, thanks from Billy Miske.'"

Dempsey's title run ended in September 1926 during his fight with Gene Tunney. He fought Tunney again the following year, but a mistake made by Dempsey after sending Tunney to the canvas gave his opponent extra time to recover, resulting in Dempsey's eventual defeat.

> Jack Dempsey fought in exhibition matches throughout the 1930s before retiring from boxing in 1940. His legacy, nonetheless, was secured; he expanded the appeal of boxing as a sport and was the first fighter to draw a million-dollar gate (for his 1921 title fight with Georges Carpentier). Dempsey was the second-most popular sports figure in America in the 1920s, behind only Babe Ruth.
>
> After retiring from boxing, Dempsey opened a restaurant in New York City and tried his hand at film acting. He also joined the war effort during World War II, serving as a lieutenant commander in the Coast Guard. In 1950, Jack Dempsey authored the book *Championship Fighting: Explosive Punching and Aggressive Defense*. The book was a considerable influence on Bruce Lee, the true source of 23 passages in the *Tao of Jeet Kune Do*. Other books written by Jack Dempsey include *Round by Round* (1940), *Dempsey* (1960), and *Dempsey: The Autobiography of Jack Dempsey* (1977).
>
> Jack Dempsey died as the result of heart failure on May 31, 1983.

The straight left lead to the head ... is the blow that, whether used in attack or defence, leaves its exponent in hitting range for a shorter period than any other; other; and though many " new " moves have been advocated of recent years, we invariably find that great boxers make it their principal stroke. – NORMAN CLARK, *How to Box*, page 52

Necessary Qualities of a straight lead: We have already decided that there are four principles that govern straight hitting, i.e., perfect balance of the body, accuracy of aim, precise timing and coordination, and maximum power of punch. – JIM DRISCOLL, *The Straight Left and How to Cultivate It*, page 41

Some fencers are continually making the alternative movements of engaging and making an absence of blade. This habit can be used to advantage. As the adversary is leaving the blade and moving across to the opposite line, the opportunity of making a straight-thrust can be taken. Others are repeatedly changing from one line to the other. As they are executing this change of line their target is uncovered and, again, a straight-thrust is possible. – ROGER CROSNIER, *Fencing with the Foil*, page 75

It is quite common to meet fencers who lack decision. They extend their arm as if intending to attack and change their minds. They just come back to the on-guard position. The straight-thrust on the return to guard is a paying stroke. – ROGER CROSNIER, *Fencing with the Foil*, page 75

Very often, these defensive errors committed by an opponent are made in conjunction with a step forward and render the chances of bringing off a straight-thrust all the more possible. – ROGER CROSNIER, *Fencing with the Foil*, page 75

Straight blows are the foundation of boxing skill. They developed late in history and therefore are the product of careful thought. Requiring speed and intelligence to use, they travel less distance than round arm blows and will reach the mark first. Straight blows are more accurate than hooks and swings and allow full use of the arm's reach. – EDWIN HAISLET, *Boxing*, page 14

Straight hitting is based upon an understanding of body structure and the value of leverage. It is an attempt to use body weight in every blow, hitting with the body, the arms being merely the vehicle of force. Arm action alone is insufficient to give real power to blows. Real power, quick and accurate, can be obtained only by shifting the weight in such a manner that the hip and shoulder precede the arm to the center line of the body. – EDWIN HAISLET, *Boxing*, pages 7-8

There are only two methods which obtain a complete shift of weight. One method is a pivot or quick turn of the waist allowing the hip and shoulder to precede the arm, the other being a full body pivot, shifting the weight from one leg to the other. The waist pivot is faster and easier to learn and is used as the basis of teaching the art of hitting. – EDWIN HAISLET, *Boxing*, page 8

The waist pivot is faster and easier to learn and is used as the basis of teaching the art of hitting. – EDWIN HAISLET, *Boxing*, page 8

Hitting does not mean *pushing*. True hitting may be likened to a snap of a whip – all the energy is slowly concentrated and then suddenly released with a tremendous outpouring of power. Pushing is exactly the opposite, with the concentrated force at the start of the blow and a subsequent loss of power as the arm leaves the body. In real hitting the feet are always directly under the body. In pushing, the body is often off-balance as the force of the blow does not come from a *pivot* of the body but from a push off the right toe. – EDWIN HAISLET, *Boxing*, page 8

Power in hitting comes from a *quick twist* of the waist, not a swinging, swaying movement, but a *pivot* over the straight left leg. As long as this straight line is maintained, as long as the hips are relaxed and free to swing, as long as the shoulders are turned through to the center line of the body before the arms are extended, power will result and hitting will be an art. – EDWIN HAISLET, *Boxing*, pages 8-9

Once the *straight line* of the left side of the body is broken, power is lost because the straight left side of the body is the anchor, the pivot point, the hinge from which power and force is generated to its greatest height. … So great is the power that may be attained in this manner that a real artist in boxing can deliver a knockout blow without taking a single step forward or displaying any apparent effort. – EDWIN HAISLET, *Boxing*, page 9

The chief fault with beginners – and veterans, too – is a failure to remember the simple process of "leveling" a punch. Punches are not supposed to be thrown with a windup motion. They are made with a well-directed forearm and loose shoulder muscles. The momentum helps carry the arm back to the proper position. – BARNEY ROSS, *Fundamentals of Boxing*, page 31

Barney Ross

Barney Ross was born on December 23, 1909 as Dov-Ber David Rosofsky, the son of Jewish immigrants from Poland. Ross was raised in the Jewish ghetto of Chicago, and his environment introduced him to violence at an early age. His father, a rabbi, hoped that Ross would follow in his rabbinical footsteps, but all that changed when he was murdered during a robbery at the family's small grocery store. The tragedy caused Ross' mother to have a nervous breakdown. Unable to care for her family, his siblings were placed in orphanages and Barney Ross found himself surviving on the street at age 14. He became a street tough, thief, and, for a time, worked for gangster Al Capone.

> His goal in life was to make enough money to bring his family back together. He decided boxing would be that vehicle and began training with another boy from the ghetto, Jack Ruby, who would one day gain his own infamy as the man who shot Kennedy assassin Lee Harvey Oswald.
> The young boxer took on the new name "Barney Ross" in order to protect his late father's reputation and family name. Ross went professional in 1929; from that time and until his retirement from professional boxing in 1938, Barney Ross accumulated a fight record of 74 wins (22 by KO), four losses, and three draws.
> After retiring from boxing, Barney Ross served in the United States Marin Corps during World War II. He was awarded the Silver Star for his performance at the Battle of Guadalcanal and was honored by President Roosevelt in a Rose Garden ceremony.
> Ross spent his remaining years as a celebrity spokesperson for casinos and other businesses. He died of throat cancer on January 18, 1967 at the age of 57.
> Barney Ross wrote a book, *Fundamentals of Boxing*, in 1942. The book is the source of 16 passages in the *Tao of Jeet Kune Do*

Remember that you must *take up power from the ground* through your legs and back. Sway all your muscles into your punches. Make them drives. Push off from the ground. And, above all, get your timing and your aim right. – JIM DRISCOLL, *The Straight Left and How to Cultivate It*, pages 73-74

According to the position of yourself and your man and the time you have to put the punch in, you may occasionally take a short step to the right, just a few inches, with your *right* foot. This will put even more weight into the punch, especially at fairly long range, and take you out of danger of a reply. – THOMAS INCH, *Boxing for Beginners: From Novice to Champion*, page 48

Here is how one should put weight into the left lead or even jab. When you see the opening, step forward with your left foot and then, as you are stepping forward and leaning forward, keeping your chin well within your left shoulder, land the left hand HARD. Your foot must NOT land first, or your body weight will rest upon the floor instead of being behind your left hand. This is most important. – THOMAS INCH, *Boxing for Beginners: From Novice to Champion*, page 111

When it has gone backwards and is about to return, the legs should be bent, then forcibly straightened so that the strong thigh muscles add considerably to the force of the blow. – THOMAS INCH, *Boxing: The Secret of the Knock-Out*, page 104

The step should be long enough to make your reach good and drive your punch slightly through your target. – FRANK GILMER, *Push Yourself: A Book for Amateur Boxers and Boxing Fans*, page 18

The two parts of the motion must be accomplished almost simultaneously, with the extension of the arm only slightly preceding the lunging action of the legs, to form one coordinated movement. – EDITORS OF SPORTS ILLUSTRATED, *Sports Illustrated Book of Fencing*, page 6

You should twist a little at the waist and your head should sway slightly to the right as it moves forward with your step. – FRANK GILMER, *Push Yourself: A Book for Amateur Boxers and Boxing Fans*, page 118

WHO WROTE THE TAO?

> *The follow-through.* There is some confusion in the literature of athletics about the follow-through. In some cases, the term is used to refer to continuation of high rate of movement or even an acceleration from the instant of contact until the ceasing of contact. – JOHN DOBSON LAWTHER, *Psychology of Coaching*, page 304
>
> A punch should increase in speed throughout its run, finishing with 'snap', and this is aided by a quick turn of the wrist, which will make certain of landing the large knuckles of the hand. – THOMAS INCH, *Boxing for Beginners: From Novice to Champion*, page 1

Endeavour never to flinch or close your eyes, but watch your opponent intently all the time. Remember that he is always dangerous, and keep your chin firmly set, and nicely tucked away, otherwise you may get knocked out at a time when you least expect it. – NORMAN CLARK, *How to Box*, page 57

Make up your mind that you will hit as hard as you possibly can, with every ounce of your bodily strength, and above all with every fibre of your mental determination, and also that you will keep on hitting harder and harder as you progress, and you can then rest assured that your hitting powers will develop rapidly. – JIM DRISCOLL, *The Straight Left and How to Cultivate It*, page 73

In boxing, for example, the athlete is taught to "strike through" the opponent: to maintain or increase the rate of movement during the contact so that the "push" carries through farther and changes the opponent's position more sharply. – JOHN DOBSON LAWTHER, *Psychology of Coaching*, page 304

Wrist snaps at the last instant in striking acts are last-moment accelerations that literally do go into the object hit. High speed movies will show that the tennis ball, the golf ball, and the baseball are momentarily flattened by the impact of the blow, and that contact continues for a fraction of time after the first instant of contact. ... Instead of a relaxing follow-through in boxing, the athlete is taught to bring his hands back into defensive position as fast as he thrust them out. – JOHN DOBSON LAWTHER, *Psychology of Coaching*, pages 304, 306

Lead to Body

The left to the body is an effective blow used to bother the opponent and to bring down the opponent's guard. – EDWIN HAISLET, *Boxing*, page 15

TAO FAST FACTS

> One of the principal tools in Bruce Lee's combative arsenal was the straight left punch. Bruce Lee took the mechanics of the straight left from Jim Driscoll's book, *The Straight Left and How to Cultivate It*. Like Lee, Driscoll drew inspiration from fencing to modify his striking and footwork, which he called "sword fencing without a sword". *The Straight Left and How to Cultivate It* is the true source of 14 passages in the *Tao of Jeet Kune Do*.

While not ordinarily a hard blow, it can cause distress if driven to the solar plexus. It is important that the body follow the arm. In other words, a blow to the body is more effective and safer if the body is dropped to the level of the target. – EDWIN HAISLET, Boxing, page 15

Assume the fundamental position. Before a jab to the body can be executed, the body must be on the same level as the mark in order that the blow will be straight. Therefore, drop the body forward from the waist to a position at right angles to the legs. Keep the left leg only slightly bent but the right leg more completely flexed. As the body drops, drive the left arm into forceful extension toward the opponent's solar plexus. The blow is slightly upward, never downward. The right hand is carried high in front of the body ready for the opponent's left hook. Hold the head down so that only the top of the head is visible, which will be protected by the extended left arm. The head should be held tight to the left arm. – EDWIN HAISLET, Boxing, page 22

Training Aids

It is most important for the boxers, after recovering to boxing position from any set maneuver executed on count or 'as you will,' to shuffle about a few seconds on toes and balls of feet for foot work drill and relaxation before repeating the set maneuver. This tactic deftly simulates actual boxing in drill. – CLARENCE E. KENNEDY, Boxing Simplified: Prepared Especially for Teachers, page 3

For the whole secret of the actual force of a terrific punch is the perfect accuracy of its "timing," coordinated, of course, with the accuracy of its aim. – JIM DRISCOLL, The Straight Left and How to Cultivate It, pages 57-58

As a variation, practise shooting out a quick succession of blows, withdrawing the striking arm just sufficient so as to enable full power to be put behind each blow. Do not dab, but hit fiercely and determinedly with each delivery, always aiming in the centre of the face. – JIM DRISCOLL, The Straight Left and How to Cultivate It, page 35

Before learning any stroke, he should be taught to strike correctly from any distance and from a variety of angles. ... Once the master is satisfied with the execution of the hit from the on-guard position, he should then lengthen his distance gradually. – ROGER CROSNIER, Fencing with the Foil, pages 55, 56

With this first attack you have seen that the arm must extend before the right foot moves for the execution of the lunge – a rule that must remain engraved in your mind forever. Hand before foot, always. – ALDO NADI, On Fencing, page 89

TAO OF JEET KUNE DO
by BRUCE LEE
It's all here – Bruce Lee's own in-depth study of combat movement. Bruce's own notes, drawings, philosophies and intricate observations of martial arts dynamics all carefully arranged and honestly presented.
£6.00 (Limited supplies only)
Call in and See the UK's largest selection of Martial Arts Equipment

cimac
Martial Arts Wear Ltd
606 Stratford Rd.
Birmingham B11 4AP
(opposite SPARKHILL Baths) 021 778 2000

Lead Jab

The Left Jab - is a "feeler." It is a light, easy blow, although it stings, jars, and annoys. As in football where the off-tackle play is the basis for a whole sequence of plays, so in boxing the left jab Is the basis of all other blows. It is effective in keeping the opponent off balance and creating openings for other blows. It is a whip rather than a club. – EDWIN HAISLET, *Boxing*, page 14

> You can frequently slip in a sudden and disconcerting jab to the other fellow's face at the very moment when he is about to let go a real punch at you. – JIM DRISCOLL, *The Straight Left and How to Cultivate It*, page 64
>
> Used correctly it is the sign of the scientific boxer, who uses strategy rather than force. It can be used for both defense and offense. It requires skill and finesse as well as speed and deception. Its great advantage is that body balance is not disturbed. – EDWIN HAISLET, *Boxing*, pages 14-15

It is important that upon shooting your left jab you return your left fist to its on guard position ready to jab again or to protect yourself from a counterpunch. – FRANK GILMER, *Push Yourself: A Book for Amateur Boxers and Boxing Fans*, page 20

NEW!
SWORD AND MASQUE
by JULIUS PALFFY-ALPAR,
former Hungarian Olympic Coach

A world-renowned teacher and performing artist here gives his guidance in a masterly text that covers not only the modern fencing technique in all three weapons but also the dramatic and historic aspects of fencing.

To receive your copy just send $6.95 plus $.25 for shipping in check or money order along with this coupon to

MERICAN FENCERS' SUPPLY CO.
2122 FILLMORE STREET ● SAN FRANCISCO, CALIF.

Name _____

Address _____

_____
California residents add 5 % sales tax

ABOVE: 1967 magazine advertisement for Julius Palffy-Alpar's fencing book, *Sword and Masque*. This advertisement appeared in the September 1967 issue of *American Fencing* magazine.

> The jab has been snapped across, not pushed. – JOHN J. WALSH, *Boxing Simplified*, page 26
>
> In all hitting, including the left jab, all force is outward from the body, the arms merely relaxing and sinking back to the body rather than being pulled back. – EDWIN HAISLET, *Boxing*, page 16
>
> This means the left hand is brought back high and kept high to offset a right-hand counter. Just as important as knowing how to deliver a left jab is knowing how to come back into position with the left hand high. – JOHN J. WALSH, *Boxing Simplified*, page 27

Note that, at the time of landing the jab, the chin is tucked down and the shoulder is curved around the chin as a protective covering. – JOHN J. WALSH, *Boxing Simplified*, pages 26-27

In all hitting, including the left jab, all force is outward from the body, the arms merely relaxing and sinking back to the body rather than being pulled back. – EDWIN HAISLET, *Boxing*, page 16

As indicated later, it is often advisable to shoot more than one left jab. Your opponent will many times be able to avoid one left jab, but you will usually be able to hit him by instantly following the first with a second left jab. This second jab also serves to cover up the missed first jab. Of course, you can shoot as many more as you wish. – FRANK GILMER, *Push Yourself: A Book for Amateur Boxers and Boxing Fans*, page 20

The jab should be a light, easy movement. Carry the shoulder and arm relaxed and ready at all times. Continue the jab until it is a natural movement. It requires long diligent practice to make the movement automatic, and to obtain speed and power without apparent effort. Accuracy should be the main objective. – EDWIN HAISLET, *Boxing*, page 16

If you find that your rival is effectively guarding against or blocking every punch you try at his face and is equally good at protecting his body when you switch downstairs, aim at his left biceps until he presents you with another opening to a vulnerable spot. The continuous pounding of his biceps will have the effect of making it difficult for him to lift his arm after a few rounds and then you can score to the face as and when you please. – JIM DRISCOLL, *The Straight Left and How to Cultivate It*, page 67

At the beginning let me impress upon you that the left arm and the fist in the boxing position are not only used to drive a blow at the opponent in attack; they may also be effectively used in fist closed position to stiff-arm opponent away from you in defense. – CLARENCE E. KENNEDY, *Boxing Simplified: Prepared Especially for Teachers*, page 2

Once you have got him on the defensive, keep him there. Never let up in your assault, keep it going methodically, but all the time slightly increasing the pace so that he gets no respite whatsoever. – JIM DRISCOLL, *The Straight Left and How to Cultivate It*, page 67

Leading Finger Jab

To fence well is to be greased lightning with the potential forward speed of a coiled spring. Like the cobra, a fencer must remain coiled in a relaxed position having at the same time the potentiality of leaping from absolute immobility to top speed, power, and precision. The guard position is the only position from which one can attack efficiently. Like the cobra, the fencer must be able to strike (with the point of his blade) so that his touch is felt before it is seen. – ALDO NADI, *On Fencing*, page 51

As indicated later it is often advisable to shoot more than one left jab. Your opponent will many times be able to avoid one left jab, but you will usually be able to hit him by instantly following the first with a second left jab. – FRANK GILMER, *Push Yourself: A Book for Amateur Boxers and Boxing Fans*, page 20

Training Aids

If the athlete tries to continue practicing finely skilled movements after he becomes fatigued, he begins to substitute gross motions for fine ones and generalized efforts for specific ones. – LAURENCE E. MOREHOUSE, PH.D. and PHILIP J. RASCH, *Scientific Basis of Athletic Training*, page 28

GABRIEL LUNA ON THE TAO OF JEET KUNE DO

Gabriel Luna
Actor

"The movement of the exo [in *Terminator: Dark Fate*], and the movement in general, was heavily influenced by Bruce Lee. I read *Tao of Jeet Kune Do*, and he preached efficiency in combat. No extra fluff. He called it organized despair, just flourishes for nothing - fighting for the sake of fighting. That's what Tim wanted too, that we'd have just very streamlined fights. Every move was like a breath in the movie, a breath in the script. So, I was heavily influenced by the great Bruce Lee. He wrote, 'Be like water. Be adaptable. Be able to change and adapt to your circumstances,' and I'm liquid metal as the exo, so it made perfect sense to inhabit those characteristics." SOURCE: *The Austin Chronicle*

Aldo Nadi

Aldo Nadi (1899-1965) is often referred to as the greatest fencer Italy ever produced. The son of a fencing instructor, by age 21 Nadi was an Olympic gold medalist in team foil, team épée, and team sabre.

Aldo Nadi immigrated to New York in 1935 and taught fencing there until he relocated to Los Angeles in 1943. He remained there the rest of his life.

That same year, he published the book, *On Fencing*. The book is often cited as being a principal source of the fencing techniques in the *Tao of Jeet Kune Do*; however, only seven passages in the *Tao of Jeet Kune Do* come from Aldo Nadi's book.

Straight Lead Rear Thrust to Body

The right to the body is a power or force blow. It is used as a counter or after a preliminary feint with the left hand. As in the left jab to the body, the body follows the blow, although added force can be obtained by a body pivot to a position over the left foot. It is effective in pulling down an opponent's guard and can be used with great success against the tall boxer. – EDWIN HAISLET, *Boxing*, page 15

Properly timed and correctly delivered it is a most punishing blow and a comparatively safe one, since you crouch as you drive the punch home, thus avoiding full-arm counters. Opportunities for the use of this blow are rather frequent, since it is one of the best counters to the opponent's left lead, which exposes the left side of his body. – PHILADELPHIA JACK O'BRIEN, *Boxing*, pages 73-74

The left hand is up and open, elbow down, guarding against the opponent's right band. The head is down along the right arm and thus well protected. – EDWIN HAISLET, *Boxing*, page 22

We often ask: "Why hurt your hands on a hard head when there is so much body to punch at?" and then answer: "The point of the chin is only an inch long, whereas there is a foot of body to shoot at." – JOHN J. WALSH, *Boxing Simplified*, page 36

We try to convey to the boys the idea that they have a foot of body to shoot at for each inch of chin. – JOHN J. WALSH, *Boxing Simplified*, page 54

Rear Cross

In your on-guard position your right fist is cocked somewhere under your chin an inch or two out from your chest. Usually, you will hit with your right fist after first having shot a left. When you hit with your left the twist at your waist shifts your right fist, which is at its regular position on guard, back four or five inches to a point from which you can, without telegraphing or drawing back, hit one of the hardest blows in boxing, the right cross. – FRANK GILMER, *Push Yourself: A Book for Amateur Boxers and Boxing Fans*, page 20

WHO WROTE THE TAO?

 The right cross is delivered in much the same manner as the left jab in that it travels in a perfectly straight line. – FRANK GILMER, *Push Yourself: A Book for Amateur Boxers and Boxing Fans*, page 20

The straight right is the opposite of the left jab. It is the heavy artillery. It should be used sparingly and only for apparent openings. It is delivered with a twist of the waist and a forceful extension of the right arm. At the moment of impact, the weight shifts forward to the left leg which gives the power necessary for use as a finishing blow. – EDWIN HAISLET, *Boxing*, page 15

In any power or force blow the bone structure must be aligned so as to form one straight body side or line which enables the bone structure to support the weight of the body, thus freeing the muscles to propel the other side of the body forward and creating terrific force. One side of the body must always form a straight line. – EDWIN HAISLET, *Boxing*, page 18

One side of the body must always form a straight line. This is accomplished by merely shifting body weight over a straight leg, hinging one side of the body, and freeing the other side for a forceful turn or pivot. ... It is the same idea as in slamming a door. – EDWIN HAISLET, *Boxing*, pages 18, 15

As your right fist travels it twists and your right shoulder moves into the blow. You twist at the waist and the weight of your body is shifted forward into the punch and to your left foot. Your right foot moves up a few inches in the direction of the punch. The left fist shifts back to its on-guard position except that your body is twisted to the left. – FRANK GILMER, *Push Yourself: A Book for Amateur Boxers and Boxing Fans*, pages 20-21

The secret of power in the straight right is using the left side of the body as a hinge and allowing the right side of the body to swing free. It is the same idea as in slamming a door. – EDWIN HAISLET, *Boxing*, page 15

For effectiveness and deception, the right cross must be thrown from the regular on-guard position. ... He must not telegraph it by drawing it back or lifting it up. ... The shoulder curves over the chin for protection, and the chin is down. – JOHN J. WALSH, *Boxing Simplified*, pages 29, 28

As the right arm is extended, the left arm is held close to the left side, in the position of guard. This movement must be practiced until it can be easily, quickly, and correctly performed. The arm should drive out with such snapping force as would seem to pull it clear of the socket. Again, the blow must be driven through, not just at, an object. The arm then relaxes back to the on-guard position. – EDWIN HAISLET, *Boxing*, page 19

Also by Thomas Inch
BOXING FOR BEGINNERS

Crown Octavo   9/6 net
With line illustrations throughout by RICHARD CLARKE

From Novice to Champion is the sub-title that Mr. Inch has chosen for this book, and in it the reader can find out the fundamentals of the whole art and science of boxing—and go on to try them out for himself.

Thomas Inch writes as one who knows—as an expert who has trained such boxers as Billy Wells and Gunner Moir, and as an athlete who has held world championships in twice as many sports as most athletes ever think of going in for as a sideline. The personal friend of every boxer and manager who has reached the top since the turn of the century, he knows boxing inside out; and in *Boxing for Beginners* he has put down what fifty years of experience tells him to be most useful to the novice. No young boxer—and no youth club organiser, physical training instructor, or teacher of boxing—can afford to miss what he has to say.

THE WORLD'S WORK (1913) LTD
KINGSWOOD   SURREY

ABOVE: Advertisement for *Boxing for Beginners* by Thomas Inch, which is the source of 12 passages and illustrations in the *Tao of Jeet Kune Do*.

A boxer must not hesitate when throwing the right. If he thinks he has the opening he should let it fly, and not be half-hearted about it. – JOHN J. WALSH, *Boxing Simplified*, page 28

> Because the right cross is a long range blow, to be effective it must be delivered straight as an arrow, fast as a shot and without warning. – FRANK GILMER, *Push Yourself: A Book for Amateur Boxers and Boxing Fans*, page 21
>
> The straighter you keep the cross, the more explosive it will be. – JACK DEMPSEY, *Championship Fighting: Explosive Punching and Aggressive Defense*, page 180

In a Right Stance

Usually, you will hit with your right fist after first having shot a left. – FRANK GILMER, *Push Yourself: A Book for Amateur Boxers and Boxing Fans*, page 20

But the right hand should not be neglected. It is difficult to use, because the fundamental position in boxing has the left side forward and therefore the right hand has farther to travel. Likewise, the use of the right hand will present an opening for your opponent if you miss. – BARNEY ROSS, *Fundamentals of Boxing*, page 36

To deliver the right cross correctly, assume the pose position again – left extended in jab position, right fist near chin, elbow near side and pointing toward floor. Throw the jab out, stepping out with left foot simultaneously. Before it reaches its mark, drive your right fist straight out, (do not pull fist back even a fraction) twist your body to the left, pivoting on the sole of your right foot. As you pivot, get plenty of push and snap from the right side of your body up from the foot through the legs and hips and make sure it is capped off by plenty of snap from your right shoulder. This power is accentuated by the coordination of the body, which is sometimes described in other sports as the "follow through" motion. – ROCKY MARCIANO, *Rocky Marciano's Book of Boxing and Bodybuilding*, pages 82-83

TAO FAST FACTS

> Bruce Lee's *Tao of Jeet Kune Do* is reported to be the best-selling martial arts book of all time. Although exact book sales numbers proved impossible to verify, there is little doubt that the claim is correct. The original edition has gone through at least 45 printings since it debuted in 1975 and has been translated into a minimum of 15 other languages. In addition, in 2011 Bruce Lee Enterprises released a revised and expanded edition which included, among other things, new English translations of the Chinese text and reflections from Bruce's family and notable Jeet Kune Do practitioners.

It is always best to feint the opponent to lead and shoot the right as a counter. ... As a counter your best opening for a righthander is usually just after the opponent leads a left for the head. You step inside of it, allowing his lead to slip over your right shoulder, and shoot the right, meanwhile keeping an eye on his right, which you can block with your left. – PHILADELPHIA JACK O'BRIEN, *Boxing*, pages 68, 69-70

Keep your hands up by your face, your elbows by your side. Bob and weave, shuffle forward, or take short, deliberate steps toward your adversary while moving the head from side to side. Try to gauge your opponent's leads. When he shoots out his punches, make him miss and get inside his swings and close to his stomach. – ROCKY MARCIANO, *Rocky Marciano's Book of Boxing and Bodybuilding*, page 123

Your boxer should be taught that a short, straight right, rather than a hard, telegraphed right will do the trick. The opportunity is usually there only for an instant, hence the short, fast right rather than the looping, hard right. – JOHN J. WALSH, *Boxing Simplified*, pages 52-53

JASON SCOTT LEE ON THE TAO OF JEET KUNE DO

Jason Scott Lee
Actor

Jason Scott Lee is best known for his portrayal of Bruce Lee in *Dragon: The Bruce Lee Story*. For the film, he was trained in Jeet Kune Do by original Bruce Lee student Jerry Poteet. They trained for 10-12 hours a day for four months to prepare for the movie. Intrigued by Jeet Kune Do, Jason continued as Poteet's student until Poteet's death. "The first day I worked with Jerry, he showed me a simple energy exercise Bruce had devised," said Jason. "It was just a quick movement, a pull and hit, but the power was incredible. I was immediately hooked. But not all the training was physical. I would show up in the morning and we would sometimes sit for hours over tea discussing the *Tao of Jeet Kune Do*. When people say they see in my performance the mannerisms and charisma of Bruce Lee, they are really seeing the *Tao of Jeet Kune Do*."

– ROCKY MARCIANO, *Rocky Marciano's Book of Boxing and Bodybuilding*, pages 75, 85, 98, 100, 105

Always try to nail a long-range target (either body or head) with stepping straight punches. However, if your opponent is blocking, evading, or countering those straight blows, you can resort to long-range hooking attempts. You can step in with any type of book, if necessary. – JACK DEMPSEY, *Championship Fighting: Explosive Punching and Aggressive Defense*, page 118

The Hook

A left hook, thrown properly, has a tremendous "kick" to it. It must be a loose, easy, snappy, punch. ... The boxer is on the toe of the front foot, and on the ball of the back foot. Note further that both toes at the finish twist to the right, and the left knee is bent. This is necessary because of the pivot of the body to the right when the left hook is thrown. Much of the "kick" behind the left hook is accomplished by this footwork, thus the shift from the toe of the back foot to the toe of the front foot is vitally important. – JOHN J. WALSH, *Boxing Simplified*, page 39

The left hook must begin from the on-guard position for proper deception. The opponent does not know whether to expect a jab, a cross, a feint, or a hook, as long as they all start from the same position. ... Most boxers will at first pull their left hand back too far before throwing the hook. This should be corrected, and the point stressed that the left shoulder is never pulled back or lowered when the boxer is throwing the hook. – JOHN J. WALSH, *Boxing Simplified*, page 39

The hook is mastered chiefly on the small punching bag, where the most minute fault can be ironed out. The great difficulty is in learning to swing sharply enough without twisting the body out of shape. The hook should be mastered so that it can be thrown from any position, even with both feet parallel, or immediately after finishing a right, which may leave you slightly off balance. – BARNEY ROSS, *Fundamentals of Boxing*, pages 41-42

Lead Hook

The more versatile the boxer, the more alert mentally, and the more agile physically, the more apt he is to shoot the most unorthodox blows from the most impossible angles, with the one idea of taking advantage of an opening. Your position during a bout is not always a matter of your own preference. – PHILADELPHIA JACK O'BRIEN, *Boxing*, page 77

The Left Hook-is used as a counter and finishing blow. It is a short blow, rarely traveling over six inches, and produces tremendous power as the whole body weight is behind it. It should be used *judiciously* and only when an actual opening has been created. It is used best when going in or coming out and is useful against an overreaching left jab or swing, or a straight right or swing. – EDWIN HAISLET, *Boxing*, page 40

It is necessary to know how to hook with either hand if you wish to be a good boxer. Against a clever opponent it is sometimes the only way you can penetrate his defense or force him to vary it so that you can find openings for other types of punches. – BARNEY ROSS, *Fundamentals of Boxing*, page 39

The hook is a short-range blow and is delivered to either head or body. A hook is usually employed as a counter, punch when your opponent is coming to you. It can be used as a lead when your opponent for some reason has lost his ability to move out of the way. – FRANK GILMER, *Push Yourself: A Book for Amateur Boxers and Boxing Fans*, page 21

Horizontal Hook - But there is another great advantage in using this blow. It comes from the side, outside the range of vision as it were. A man sees the straight left coming towards him, he is warned and prepared. He does NOT see the elusive left hook; knows nothing about it until it has landed. It is hard to defend against. If a man goes through a bout with his right-hand guard well up, open glove, he is certainly well defended against straight lefts and left jabs. But NOT against the left hook, because the hook will go round the guard. – THOMAS INCH, *Boxing for Beginners: From Novice to Champion*, page 42

Incidentally, it should be borne in mind that although most boxers automatically try for the head, a large number of contests have been won by a right-hand body-blow. This is actually easier to land because the body is a wider and less mobile target than the head. – PETER MCINNES, *Tackle Boxing This Way*, page 34

The Horizontal Hook

– THOMAS INCH,
*Boxing for Beginners:
From Novice to Champion*,
page 41

It is also a good punch to combine with a sidestep, for you are moving side-wise and it is the natural way to swing at that moment. Similarly, you may land effectively on your opponent with a hook at the instant when he is trying to sidestep; his own momentum will then add power to your blow. – BARNEY ROSS, *Fundamentals of Boxing*, page 39

Remember that if you catch your man coming in the blow will be twice as hard. Remember also to keep your right glove up for fear that you yourself are 'hooked'. – THOMAS INCH, *Boxing: The Secret of the Knock-Out*, page 69

[The Long Lead Hook] - On the other hand, if you're in so close to an opponent that you're almost in a clinch, it would be silly for you to be rearing back and trying to stab your opponent's face with straight punches – when you could be exploding hooks or uppercuts on his chin, or digging them into his body. – JACK DEMPSEY, *Championship Fighting: Explosive Punching and Aggressive Defense*, page 78

The left hook must begin from the on-guard position for proper deception. – JOHN J. WALSH, *Boxing Simplified*, page 39

Most boxers will at first pull their left hand back too far before throwing the hook. This should be corrected, and the point stressed that the left shoulder is never pulled back or lowered when the boxer is throwing the hook. Remember—the hook is a short, snappy punch. Enough power can be put into the punch *without* pulling the arm far back. ... Much of the "kick" behind the left hook is accomplished by this footwork, thus the shift from the toe of the back foot to the toe of the front foot is vitally important. – JOHN J. WALSH, *Boxing Simplified*, pages 41, 39

The Left Hook - The left heel MUST be raised so that the body can pivot and shoulders reverse when the blow lands. – THOMAS INCH, *Boxing: The Secret of the Knock-Out*, page 69

You MUST keep the left shoulder high for full leverage when hooking. – THOMAS INCH, *Boxing: The Secret of the Knock-Out*, page 69

The chief fault with beginners – and veterans, too – is a failure to remember the simple process of "leveling" a punch. Punches are not supposed to be thrown with a windup motion. They are made with a well-directed forearm and loose shoulder muscles. The momentum helps carry the arm back to the proper position. – BARNEY ROSS, *Fundamentals of Boxing*, page 31

Frequently a boxer tries to put too much body behind the punch, thereby making it a push punch. The hook is a loose, arm-propelled punch. The "kick" comes from the looseness of the delivery and the proper pivoting of the feet and body. – JOHN J. WALSH, *Boxing Simplified*, pages 39-40

The weight of the body is shifted with the punch to the side opposite the side you hook from. If you lead a hook, you must step in with the punch to make your reach good. – FRANK GILMER, *Push Yourself: A Book for Amateur Boxers and Boxing Fans*, page 21

It must be a loose, easy, snappy, punch. – JOHN J. WALSH, *Boxing Simplified*, page 39

The whip of the arm is caused by turning the body away from the arm until the range of movement in the shoulder joint is completely used. Then, the arm must turn with the body. Executed quickly, this causes the arm to whip forward as if released from a bow. – EDWIN HAISLET, *Boxing*, page 4

You MUST make the blow *snappy*; always think of speed and more speed. – THOMAS INCH, *Boxing: The Secret of the Knock-Out*, page 69

Always raise your left heel and turn it out as the hook goes in, and always drop a little to your right to get weight into the blow. ... As the left-hand hook goes in always raise your left heel. Thus, you *swivel* on the ball of the foot. Your blow has a better reach; it *goes through* better, it is faster. – THOMAS INCH, *Boxing for Beginners: From Novice to Champion*, pages 42, 48

Remember this: The more you "open" an outside hook, the more it degenerates into a swing. You must keep it tight. ... Moreover, most of those club fighters are easy to nail because: When you open a hook, you open your own defense. – JACK DEMPSEY, *Championship Fighting: Explosive Punching and Aggressive Defense*, pages 109, 110

The great difficulty is in learning to swing sharply without twisting the body out of shape. – BARNEY ROSS, *Fundamentals of Boxing*, page 42

And the more sharply the elbow is bent, the tighter and more explosive is the hook. When you explode a hook against an opponent's jaw, you can feel your good old power line running just as solidly from shoulder through fist as when the line was straight out in a falling-step punch. – JACK DEMPSEY, *Championship Fighting: Explosive Punching and Aggressive Defense*, page 101

Since boxing is a game of hitting it is all-important that a boxer spends most of his time during workouts perfecting his ability to punch properly. There are no wrists in boxing. The forearm and the fist should be used as one solid piece, like a club with a knot on the end of it. The fist should be kept on a straight line with the forearm and there should be no bending of the wrist in any direction. The fists should be kept closed at all times when you are punching. You should hit with the knuckles of your fist and be careful not to hit with your thumb. If you are constantly bruising your thumbs, you are not hitting properly. – FRANK GILMER, *Push Yourself: A Book for Amateur Boxers and Boxing Fans*, page 17

Note that, at the finish of the punch, the left thumb is up, just as it was at the start of the punch. There is no twist of the fist as in delivering the left jab and cross. This is necessary for the proper protection of the hand. Note further that the forearm is rigid from the elbow to the knuckles and does not bend at the wrist. This makes for greater punching power and prevents sprained wrists. The hook is thrown in a half arc to the opponent's chin, and with a complete follow through motion for power. – JOHN J. WALSH, *Boxing Simplified*, page 40

You MUST be ready to follow up with another solid punch *with either hand*. – THOMAS INCH, *Boxing: The Secret of the Knock-Out*, page 69

The natural reaction seems to be to pull away or out from a left hook. This is absolutely the wrong thing to do. If the blocker *moves in*, the hook often ends harmlessly *around* his neck. – JOHN J. WALSH, *Boxing Simplified*, page 341

The hook is mastered chiefly on the small punching bag, where the most minute fault can be ironed out. The great difficulty is in learning to swing sharply enough without twisting the body out of shape. – BARNEY ROSS, *Fundamentals of Boxing*, pages 41-42

Shovel Hook

Generally speaking, there are two types of hooks:

1. SHOVEL HOOKS, which are thrown "inside" with the elbows *in*, pressing tightly against the hips for body blows and pressing tightly against the lower ribs for head blows; and
2. OUTSIDE HOOKS, which are thrown with the elbows "out"– away from the body.

– JACK DEMPSEY,
Championship Fighting: Explosive Punching and Aggressive Defense,
page 101

Pull your elbow "in" and press it firmly against the front edge of your hip bone. Turn your half-opened left hand up slightly so that your palm is partially facing the ceiling. Your palm should slant at an angle of about 45 degrees between floor and ceiling. Meanwhile, keep your right hand in normal guarding position. ... Now without moving your feet, suddenly whirl your body to your right in such fashion that your left hip comes up with a circling, shoveling hunch that sends your exploding left fist solidly into the bag, about solar-plexus high. The slanting angle of the left hand permits you to land solidly with your striking knuckles. ... Try that punch several times. Make certain you have no tension in the elbow, shoulder or legs until the whirl is started from your normal position. *More important:* Make certain that (1) Your hand is at the 45-degree angle, and (2) the hip comes up in a vigorous shoveling bunch. – JACK DEMPSEY, *Championship Fighting: Explosive Punching and Aggressive Defense*, pages 101, 103

Flashback - *Publishers Weekly*, February 28, 1994

"What the trade paperback most in demand at both Ingram and Baker & Taylor this week? Nope, try again. Give up? It's the *Tao of Jeet Kune Do* by the legendary martial artist Bruce Lee. Loosely translated as "the way of the intercepting fist," the book consists of Lee's diaries during year in which he was creating and refining his martial arts style. The book was originally published in 1975 by Ohara Publications, a martial arts publisher in Santa Clarita, California, and reportedly has been selling steadily ever since. In the wake of last May's release of the movie *Dragon: The Bruce Lee Story*, however, and the recent A&E documentary about Lee, sales have suddenly spiked about 7,000 copies a week. While general bookstores are certainly stocking the book, Ohara counts a large number of martial arts specialty stores among its customers. The *Tao of Jeet Kune Do* is in its 37th printing and has been translated into nine languages. After the most recent 70,000-copy printing, there are 422,329 copies in print in the United States."

The *fist angle* and the *hip hunch* are important features of all shovel hooks, whether to body or head. The leg spring used in the hip hunch speeds up your body whirl and, at the same time, deflects the direction of the whirl slightly upward in a surge. Meanwhile, the combination of the angled fist and the bent elbow points your striking knuckles in the same direction as that of the whirl-surge. You have a pure punch. Your fist lands with a solid smash that packs plenty of follow-through. And your pure punch is *angled* to shoot *inside* an opponent's defenses. – JACK DEMPSEY, *Championship Fighting: Explosive Punching and Aggressive Defense*, page 103

Head shovels are delivered from the normal stance at close range. If you have a pear-shaped, inflated punching bag, it will enable you to feel out the head-shovels more satisfactorily than the heavy bag. That is so because your shovels are rising at chin height. ... Stand before either bag. Keep your hands in normal punching position. Fold the left arm in toward the body, keeping your forearm straight up until the thumb knuckle is only a slight distance from your left shoulder. Be sure that your left elbow is well "in" and that it is pressing against your lower left ribs. ... Now, without moving your feet, suddenly give your body the combination shoulder whirl and hip hunch, and let your angled left fist explode the punch against your chin-high target. ... Try four or five of those left shovels making certain each time that your elbow is pressing against the lower ribs, at the start of the whirl, and that your fist, when it lands, is only a short distance from your left shoulder. – JACK DEMPSEY, *Championship Fighting: Explosive Punching and Aggressive Defense*, page 105

You are throwing a full-fledged inside left hook – one of the shortest, yet one of the most explosive, blows in the human arsenal. You're doing that if you're landing with your striking knuckles, and not with the side of your hand. ... Your hands will be in their normal positions before the blows begin. But they will flash instinctively to their shovel posts as your body starts its bunching whirl. Your body will pick them up. – JACK DEMPSEY, *Championship Fighting: Explosive Punching and Aggressive Defense*, pages 105, 108

You can make the range, for example, with any number of attack combinations in which the shovels are used for follow shots. The simplest combination would be a long-left jolt to the head, which failed to knock your opponent backward, followed immediately by a right shovel to head or body. Or you could follow a similar straight left to the head with a left shovel to head or body. Likewise, a long straight right to the head, which failed to accomplish its explosive object, would put you in position for left shovels to either target. ... Also, if a fast opponent steps into you, his speed may be such that you can't catch him with a stepping counterpunch; but that very speed may make him a perfect "clay pigeon" for your short-range artillery. In addition, you'll be in short range for counter-shovels many times when you ward off attacks by means of blocks, parries, slips and the like. – JACK DEMPSEY, *Championship Fighting: Explosive Punching and Aggressive Defense*, page 103

Practice the shovels until you perfect them. They are particularly valuable for the fist-fighter. In importance they rank next to your long, straight punches. They will enable you to knock out or at least "soften up" an opponent who is trying to clinch with you. They will help you, from your normal stance, to keep *inside* the attack of bobber-weavers, most of whom hook from the *outside*. They'll help you to straighten up bobber-weavers, although not as effectively as will uppercuts. They'll eliminate the necessity of your "getting down" in a low crouch to try to beat a bobber-weaver at his own game. Since the shovels are all short, tight blows, you are less likely to get hit while using them than while throwing the more open *outside* hooks. – JACK DEMPSEY, *Championship Fighting: Explosive Punching and Aggressive Defense*, page 109

Corkscrew Hook

The essence of any hook is that the striker raises his elbow at the last possible moment when swinging, for this will bring round his knuckles so that it is they that will make contact when his punch lands. – PETER MCINNES, *Tackle Boxing This Way*, page 30

Try the corkscrew on the bag. Stand in normal position. Do the following movements slowly: Start your shoulder whirl as if you were to shoot a medium-range left jab. No preparatory movement. Instead of jabbing, however, snap your left forearm and fist down and your left elbow up. Your left fist snaps down with a screwing motion that causes your striking knuckles to land properly on the target. When your fist explodes against the target, your forearm is almost parallel to the floor. – JACK DEMPSEY, *Championship Fighting: Explosive Punching and Aggressive Defense*, page 115

But when you step with the corkscrew, you do not move in with the straight-forward falling step. Instead, you move in with "pivot step." You step forward and slightly to your own left, pointing the toe sharply in. Your body pivots on the ball of your left foot as your left arm and fist snap down to the target. At the instant of the fist-landing, your right foot generally is in the air; but it settles immediately behind you. – JACK DEMPSEY, *Championship Fighting: Explosive Punching and Aggressive Defense*, page 121

Moreover, if you have a potent left corkscrew that flashes in without warning, your opponent will be very cautious about menacing you with his right fist. Remember that your left hand, in normal position, is always closer to your opponent's head than his right hand is to your head. As he attempts to start a straight right, you can beat him to the punch with your countering corkscrew. Moreover, if he permits his guarding right hand to creep too far forward as he blocks or parries your left jabs, your corkscrew can snap down behind that guarding right and nail his jaw. – JACK DEMPSEY, *Championship Fighting: Explosive Punching and Aggressive Defense*, page 115

Let me help you at this point by admitting that the corkscrew usually is a medium-range punch, and that it's usually delivered while you are circling to your opponent's right. – JACK DEMPSEY, *Championship Fighting: Explosive Punching and Aggressive Defense*, page 115

As previously stated, the left hook is the most difficult of the punches to master, but I have found that working on the light punching bag is an ideal way to learn this punch. ... Illustrations show the sequence of punches to be used on the bag to obtain the proper form and zip in throwing a left hook. – JOHN J. WALSH, *Boxing Simplified*, page 40

Palm Hook

In the normal punching position, the outside left hook is very useful as a lead that shoots in behind guarding right hand. And it is useful as a counter that "beats to the punch" a straight right started by your opponent. – JACK DEMPSEY, *Championship Fighting: Explosive Punching and Aggressive Defense*, page 114

Uppercut

It is also possible quickly to place the left-hand glove along the left-hand side of your jaw and catch the right hook that way; in that case you have a clear way up to the jaw with your RIGHT upper-cut. Possibilities and combinations are endless at in-fighting, a great science not properly understood by the average boxer. Try to get the inside position always. – THOMAS INCH, *Boxing for Beginners: From Novice to Champion*, page 132

> Sons sometimes become over-exuberant, forget their teaching, and come in swinging wild with head down. A good "object" lesson is readily taught by landing a light uppercut. Be sure and duck that wild right, however. – JOHN J. WALSH, *Boxing Simplified*, page 61
>
> Most obvious way to avoid getting caught with an uppercut is never to get the head and body bent forward in a position to receive this blow, but for those boxers who favour in-fighting this is not possible. – PETER MCINNES, *Tackle Boxing This Way*, page 50

Take my advice and don't waste time with the long-range upper-cut. It can be seen coming and hardly ever succeeds. The upper-cut should be used when close in. ... Turn the hand so that palm is up. When using the right upper-cut BRING THE RIGHT FOOT WELL UP IN LINE WITH THE LEFT. Often at close quarters you will have to lean backwards to get reach into the blow. Put more weight upon the left leg when using the right and more upon the right leg when using the left uppercut. – THOMAS INCH, *Boxing: The Secret of the Knock-Out*, page 72

When upper-cutting with your right, lay the left hand for a moment on your opponent's right shoulder to make sure you don't run into a heavy return. – THOMAS INCH, *Boxing for Beginners: From Novice to Champion*, page 62

The uppercut is delivered by lowering the right on the way across and "scooping" up and to the jaw. ... Note further that the left hand is drawn back and high to protect the chin. – JOHN J. WALSH *Boxing Simplified*, pages 47, 48

The Upward Hook: As its name implies, this is a close relation to the upper-cut. The elbow is turned well out, and you 'screw' the blow in and up so that you can send it to the chin of a man with his face covered by his arm held across it. On the other hand, the horizontal hook and the forward hook will go over that kind of guard. – THOMAS INCH, *Boxing for Beginners: From Novice to Champion*, page 48

– THOMAS INCH, *Boxing for Beginners: From Novice to Champion*, pages 46 and 45

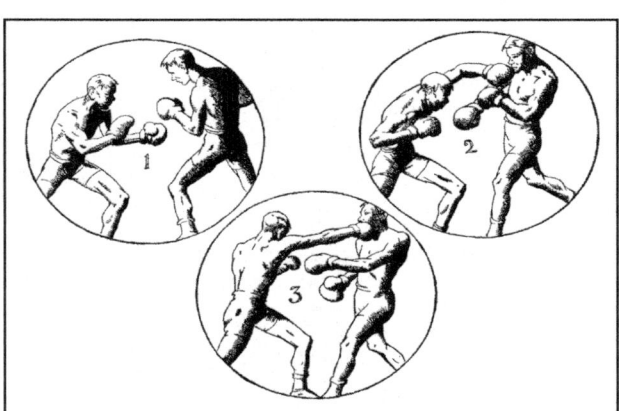

– THOMAS INCH, *Boxing: Secret of the Knock-Out* pages 145 and 111

– THOMAS INCH, *Boxing for Beginners: From Novice to Champion*, page 77

Combination Punching

A good boxer hits from every angle. Each punch sets him in position to deliver the next one. ... Fight from a center and always be in position and balanced to shoot another punch. ... The more good kinds of blows you have, the more guns you have and the more effective and dangerous a boxer you are and the more different kinds of opponents you can beat. – FRANK GILMER, *Push Yourself: A Book for Amateur Boxers and Boxing Fans*, pages 24, 25

The step should be long enough to make your reach good and drive your punch slightly through your target. ... Some observations are applicable to all types of hitting. ... Don't telegraph any punch. If you have to set your fist a certain way for a particular punch, do it in a manner that won't warn your opponent. *Fight from a center* and *always be in position and balanced to shoot another punch.* ... If your opponent is doing the leading, always hit back. Never let him escape your counterpunches. After hitting get back on guard. *End a series of punches with a left.* – FRANK GILMER, *Push Yourself: A Book for Amateur Boxers and Boxing Fans*, pages 18, 25

For long range fighting, jab with your left and cross with your right. For short range fighting use hooks, uppercuts and right-hand body blows. – FRANK GILMER, *Push Yourself: A Book for Amateur Boxers and Boxing Fans*, page 25

Sway a little as you hit and remember a hard punch must be delivered from a solid base; light punches are delivered by a boxer on his toes. – FRANK GILMER, *Push Yourself: A Book for Amateur Boxers and Boxing Fans*, page 25

Learn to hold your fire until you can hit something; don't waste your energy missing. ... If your opponent is doing the leading, always hit back. Never let him escape your counterpunches. – FRANK GILMER, *Push Yourself: A Book for Amateur Boxers and Boxing Fans* page 25

Keep loose and relaxed except when actually fighting. Develop speed and your timing and judgment of distance by many good workouts with all types of sparring partners. With this practice your authority, hit confidently and hard. – FRANK GILMER, *Push Yourself: A Book for Amateur Boxers and Boxing Fans*, page 25

JOHN LITTLE ON THE TAO OF JEET KUNE DO

John Little
Author, director, editor of the *Bruce Lee Library Series*

What amazed me was that a man of 32 years of age could be so prolific, especially one who he had a full time teaching schedule of private lessons, one who made movies full time, television series, and also managed to be a father and a husband and all of those sort of things. I was particularly impressed with Bruce Lee's day-timer diaries which no one for some reason, when they did the *Tao of Jeet Kune Do,* no one touched on these, no one put that into the training component. When you look at the *Tao of Jeet Kune Do* – which is only 208 pages long – and you consider what I just said that there is at least 6,000 pages of material, obviously an enormous amount of material was not put into it. That to me does not do justice to Bruce Lee. It's giving you a segment of his totality and what you need is everything that he wrote.

Bruce's whole thing was to absorb what is useful and discard the rest – *for you.* In order for the reader to be able to do that, then you would have to be able to open the book and see something of value or something meaningful to you in your quest for self-improvement. Maybe you'd find something of use or maybe you wouldn't, but maybe the next time you go to the book and crack it open you're going to get something meaningful from it. *(Excerpted from the book,* Disciples of the Dragon, *by Paul Bax)*

WHO WROTE THE TAO?

Takedown Methods

1. Circle step single leg tackle
2. Drop step leg tackle
3. Draw step leg tackle

– ROBERT L. BROWN and THOMAS E. ROBERTSON, *Illustrated Guide to Takedown in Wrestling* (List of techniques described on pages 23-28; "shuffle step" omitted)

– ROBERT L. BROWN and THOMAS E. ROBERTSON, *Illustrated Guide to Takedown in Wrestling,* pages 24, 27, 28, 29

Do's of Take-Down Wrestling:

1. Always keep moving.
2. Be prepared for countermoves.
3. Develop catlike movement.
4. Make opponent wrestle your way.
5. Be aggressive – Make your opponent think defense.

Don'ts of Take-Down Wrestling:

1. Don't cross your legs.
2. Don't commit your arms too deeply.
3. Don't chase your opponent.
4. Don't rely on one takedown. Be ready for other openings.
5. Don't let your opponent circle you.

– ROBERT L. BROWN and THOMAS E. ROBERTSON, *Illustrated Guide to Takedown in Wrestling, page* 30

TAO FAST FACTS

Compare the images from the *Illustrated Guide to the Takedown in Wrestling* presented here to the images found on pages 116 and 117 of *The Tao of Jeet Kune Do.* You will note some subtle and not-so-subtle differences between them.

That is because, much like he often did with his fencing and boxing drawings, Bruce Lee altered the images when he redrew them – modifying the stances for his use in Jeet Kune Do. His modifications included adding non-wrestling techniques like attacks to the eyes and groin strikes.

Double Leg Attacks

Photographs on this page – ROBERT L. BROWN and THOMAS E. ROBERTSON, *Illustrated Guide to Takedown in Wrestling*, pages 37, 38, 39, 47, 48, 51, 54

Drawing (below) - MOSHE FELDENKRAIS, *Higher Judo: Groundwork*, page 93

Drawing (bottom right) - MIKINOSUKE KAWAISHI, *My Method of Self-Defense*, page 44

Single Leg Attacks
Back Trip to Groin Strike

 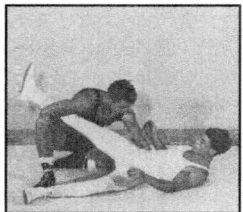

Forward Trip to Side Strangulation

The Smash and Groin Strike

Snap & Heel to Leg Lock

Double Leg Locks

Single Leg Locks

- MOSHE FELDENKRAIS,
Higher Judo: Groundwork,
page 91

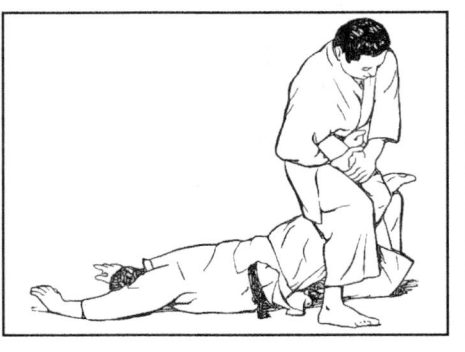

Toe Holds *(with single leg locks)*

- FRANK GOTCH,
Wrestling and How to Train,
page 78

Arm Blast

– ROBERT L. BROWN and THOMAS E. ROBERTSON, *Illustrated Guide to Takedown in Wrestling,* page 61

Wrist Post

— ROBERT L. BROWN and THOMAS E. ROBERTSON, *Illustrated Guide to Takedown in Wrestling*, page 62

Touch (Jab) and Go

— ROBERT L. BROWN and THOMAS E. ROBERTSON, *Illustrated Guide to Takedown in Wrestling*, page 66

Elbow Throw-Bys

— ROBERT L. BROWN and THOMAS E. ROBERTSON, *Illustrated Guide to Takedown in Wrestling*, page 88

Arm Drag

— ROBERT L. BROWN and THOMAS E. ROBERTSON, *Illustrated Guide to Takedown in Wrestling*, page 93

Head and Neck Manipulations

- MOSHE FELDENKRAIS, *Higher Judo: Groundwork*, page 216

- MOSHE FELDENKRAIS, *Higher Judo: Groundwork*, page 216

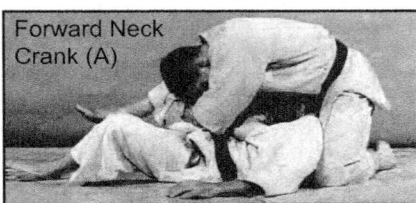

- MOSHE FELDENKRAIS, *Higher Judo: Groundwork*, page 204

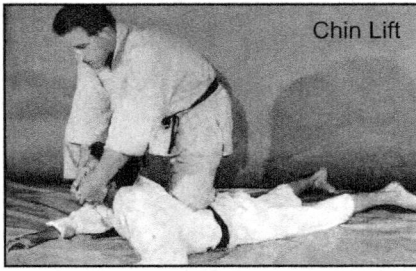

Forward Neck Crank (A) • Forward Neck Crank (B)

- GENE LEBELL and L. C. COUGHRAN, *The Handbook of Judo*, pages 168, 169

Chin Lift • Spine Stretch

- GENE LEBELL and L. C. COUGHRAN, *The Handbook of Judo*, pages 172, 173

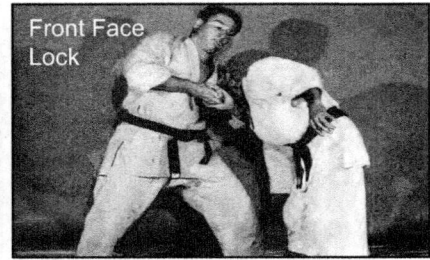

Reverse Figure 4 Neck Lock • Front Face Lock

- GENE LEBELL and L. C. COUGHRAN, *The Handbook of Judo*, pages 169, 171

Head and Neck Manipulations

Side Strangle Hold

Front Strangle Hold

Above - HUGH F. LEONARD, *A Handbook of Wrestling*, page 240

Right - MIKINOSUKE KAWAISHI, *My Method of Self-Defense*, page 44

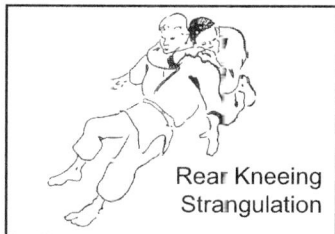

Rear Kneeing Strangulation

Head and Arm Manipulations

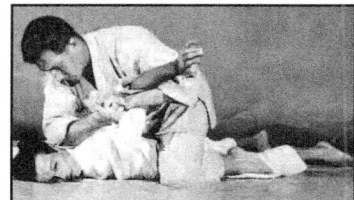

Neck and Arm Lever

Half-Nelson and Arm Bar

- GENE LEBELL and L. C. COUGHRAN, *The Handbook of Judo*, page 129

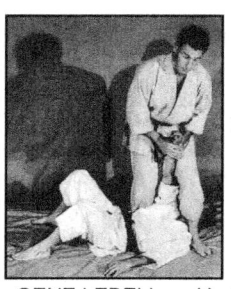

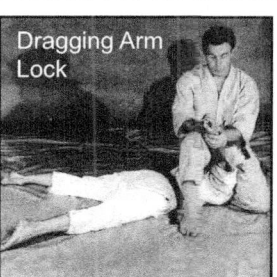

Dragging Arm Lock

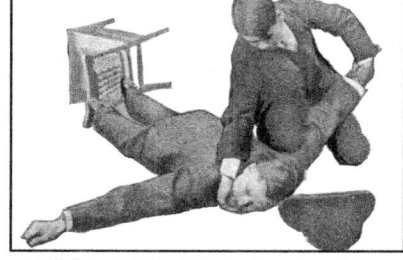

- GENE LEBELL and L. C. COUGHRAN, *The Handbook of Judo*, page 150

- HARRY H. SKINNER, *Jiu-Jitsu: A Comprehensive and Copiously Illustrated Treatise*, page 150

Half Nelson and Hammerlock

Half-Nelson and Top Scissors

- EARLE LIEDERMAN, *The Science of Wrestling and the Art of Jiu Jitsu*, pages 131, 158

Studies on Judo and Ju-Jitsu

 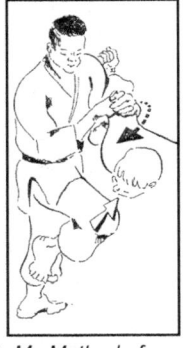

- MIKINOSUKE KAWAISHI, *My Method of Self-Defense*, pages 15, 27

- E. G. BARTLETT, *Judo and Self-Defense: One Hundred Lessons*, pages 151, 150

- MIKINOSUKE KAWAISHI, *My Method of Self-Defense*, page 29

 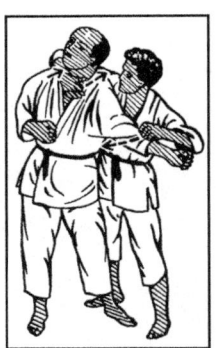

- E. G. BARTLETT, *Judo and Self-Defense: One Hundred Lessons*, pages 124, 122

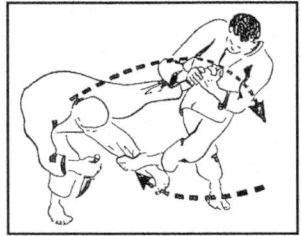 

- MIKINOSUKE KAWAISHI, *My Method of Self-Defense*, page 58

- E. G. BARTLETT, *Judo and Self-Defense: One Hundred Lessons*, page 72

- E. G. BARTLETT, *Judo and Self-Defense: One Hundred Lessons*, pages 52, 58, 63

- GENE LEBELL and L. C. COUGHRAN, *Your Personal Handbook of Self-Defense*, page 91

  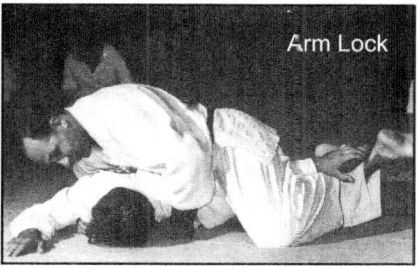

- GENE KENNETH, "Mat Work - Judo's Neglected Art"; *Black Belt September 1970*, page 24

  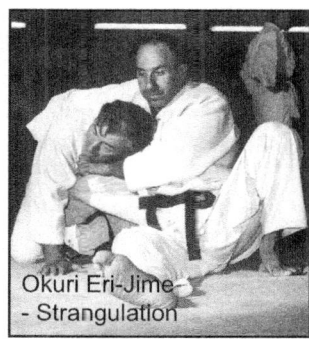

- GENE KENNETH, "Mat Work - Judo's Neglected Art"; *Black Belt September 1970*, page 24

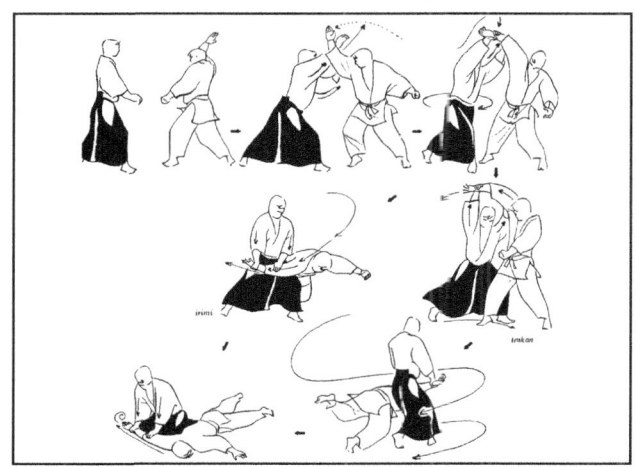 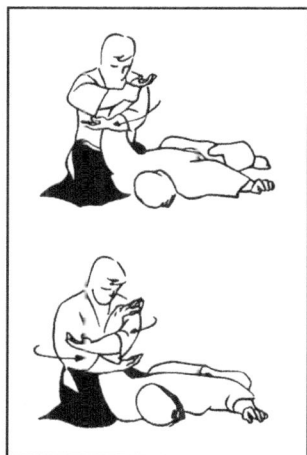

- A. WESTBROOK and O. RATTI, *Aikido and the Dynamic Sphere*, pages 172, 179

PREPARATIONS

INTELLIGENCE is sometimes defined as the capacity of the individual to adjust himself successfully to his environment, or to adjust the environment to his needs.

— JESSE FEIRING WILLIAMS, M.D.
and EUGENE WHITE NIXON, M.A.,
The Athlete in the Making,
page 60

Feints

There is a lead, or counter, to the body which can be performed with the left hand in exactly the same style as to the head, and this should be preceded by a feint to the head with either the left or the right hand. – THOMAS INCH, *Boxing for Beginners: From Novice to Champion*, page 28

A slight wave of the opponent's hand, a stamp of the foot, or a sudden shout from a spectator can produce *sensory irradiations* sufficient to reduce coordination. This mechanism is at the reflex level of human behavior, and even many seasons of athletic experience cannot erase the distracting effects of extraneous stimuli. – LAURENCE ENGLEMOHR MOREHOUSE and PHILIP J. RASH, *Sports Medicine for Trainers*, page 36

No feint at any weapon can be counted effective unless it *forces the opponent to move* to parry it. To be successful it must appear to be a simple movement of attack. – CHARLES LOUIS DE BEAUMONT, *Fencing: Ancient Art and Modern Sport*, page 162

Good feints are *decisive, expressive*, and *threatening*, and executed from a distance which the opponent considers really dangerous. – JOHN KARDOSS, *Sabre Fencing: History, Theory, Practice*, page 51

The feint is a deceiving or false thrust which invites and lures the opponent to make the appropriate parry. As the opponent takes the parry, the fencer's blade passes the opponent's parrying blade and the thrust is completed in the opened line. The feint is composed of a *false thrust* and a *real, evasive thrust*. – JULIUS PALFFY-ALPAR, *Sword and Masque*, page 101

The false thrust from the middle distance is made in two movements: the first is an extension of the arm with a slight forward movement of the upper body; the second is the evasive thrust with a lunge. ... The false thrust must appear to be the real thrust in order to convince the opponent to take the parry (trompement). – JULIUS PALFFY-ALPAR, *Sword and Masque*, pages 101-102; 101

Feints should be made with the arm extended if they precede a lunge, with the arm bent, if made after a parry and the adversary can be reached without a lunge. The correct feint should be made with the arm and fingers only, keeping the body motionless. – JULIO MARTINEZ CASTELLÓ, *The Theory and Practice of Fencing*, page 32

The advantage of a feint, or feints, must be that the attacker can start lunging with his feint and thus be *gaining distance* from the outset. He will have shortened the distance his point had to travel by a good half with his feint and leave to his second movement only the second half of the distance. Thus, he is at the same time gaining distance by starting his lunge with his feint, and simultaneously *gaining time* by deceiving the parry while doing so. – ROGER CROSNIER, *Fencing with the Foil*, page 130

WHO WROTE THE TAO?

A boxer can make openings or keep his rival in a state of suspense by such tactics, for feinting is an essential part of attack by manoeuvre. Such moves must be realistic, and they can only be that if they are made vigorously. The more an opponent can be caught off-guard or, more important still, off-balance by means of feints, the better. – PETER MCINNES, *Tackle Boxing This Way*, page 39

That is to say, excessive speed can be a severe handicap, if it is not regulated to that of the opposing fencer. – ROGER CROSNIER, *Fencing with the Sabre*, page 186

In a manner similar to simple attacks, feints can be executed with either a perpendicular or a lateral character. The choice of either will depend, partly, on the defence used or the opponent's preference for the combination of parries belonging to one triangle or to the other. – ROGER CROSNIER, *Fencing with the Sabre*, page 108

The first movement, i.e. the feint, must be long and deep, or *penetrating*, to draw the parry. The second movement must be fast and decisive in its deception of the parry, allowing the defender no possibility of recovery. It can be said, therefore, that for compound attacks of one feint the rhythm is, *long-short*. – ROGER CROSNIER, *Fencing with the Sabre*, page 107

Even in the delivery of compound attacks with two feints, *the depth of the first feint must force the opponent to move to the defense*. But, as at this stage the measure has been considerably shortened, the second feint cannot also be long. There is no room and no time to do so. Thus, the rhythm, or cadence, of a two-feint compound attack will be: *long-short-short*. – ROGER CROSNIER, *Fencing with the Sabre*, page 107

A more advanced form of feinting with a *change of cadence* could be described as: *short-long-short*. The object of this variation would be to mislead the adversary, making him believe that the second feint (*long*) was the final action of a compound attack, thus drawing the parry. – ROGER CROSNIER, *Fencing with the Sabre*, pages 107-108

BENEDICT WONG ON THE TAO OF JEET KUNE DO

Benedict Wong
Actor

"I happened on his book, *Tao of Jeet Kune Do*, which has played an intrinsic part in guiding me through my career. When I embarked as an actor 30 years ago, other than some encouraging advice from the legendary Burt Kwouk ("You can do it, Kid!"), whom I was lucky enough to work on radio plays with early on in my career, there were no East Asian actors to guide me through this relatively uncharted path. *Tao of Jeet Kune Do* is more than just a book, it's a philosophical guide that I would highly recommend to all young actors starting out." SOURCE: *The Hollywood Reporter* (photo by Gage Skidmore)

The terms 'long' and 'short' have been used in preference to 'slow' and 'quick', to avoid the danger that the sabreur should think that the first feint is a long, slow, movement. While penetrating deeply towards the opponent, the feint must be fast. The combination of speed and penetration are the factors which draw the desired reaction from the defence. – ROGER CROSNIER, *Fencing with the Sabre*, page 108

If one is fencing with an opponent who doesn't react to feints, for example, an attack with straight or simple movements is advisable. – JULIO MARTINEZ CASTELLÓ, *The Theory and Practice of Fencing*, page 58

By making several simple attacks first, the feints will be more effective as the opponent will not know whether a simple attack or a feint followed by a deceive is being executed. – JULIO MARTINEZ CASTELLÓ, *The Theory and Practice of Fencing*, page 32

This is not a real attack, but is a calculated feint made in order to *parry the opponent's counter-attack* or return and make a fast return or counter return. – JULIO MARTINEZ CASTELLÓ, *The Theory and Practice of Fencing*, page 39

Feints are any motion of the weapon which would lead the opponent to believe he is about to be attacked. The object of the feint is either to open the line in which one intends to attack or to deceive the parry which the feint provokes. – JULIO MARTINEZ CASTELLÓ, *The Theory and Practice of Fencing*, page 32

The introduction of the feint can be:

- direct thrust
- disengagement
- evasive thrust
- cut-over
- engagement
- pressure
- violent pressure
- beat

– JULIUS PALFFY-ALPAR, *Sword and Masque*, page 102

The quality of the taken parry can be:

- simple
- circular (counter or changing parries)

– JULIUS PALFFY-ALPAR, *Sword and Masque*, page 102

The number of evading parries can be:

- single
- dual
- plural

– JULIUS PALFFY-ALPAR, *Sword and Masque*, page 102

Execution

Assume the fundamental position. Advance slowly. While advancing, give a quick bend of the left knee. This gives the impression that the arms are moving as well as the legs. In reality, the arms are held relaxed and ready. – EDWIN HAISLET, *Boxing*, page 67

Make a slight forward movement of the upper body, bending the left knee and moving the left band slightly forward. While advancing, take a longer step forward with the left foot, as in the quick advance, and jab the left arm into extension without hitting the opponent. From his close position, fold the left arm back to the body and jab to the chin. – EDWIN HAISLET, *Boxing*, pages 67-68

Another effective feint is a short bend of the body to the right while moving forward. – EDWIN HAISLET, *Boxing*, page 68

The step in, step out, feint means stepping forward one step as if to jab with the left hand but, instead, step out of range by pushing off with the left leg, pivoting to the left. Now step in as if to feint but drive a left jab to the chin. Step out immediately. Continue, one time feinting, the next time actually jabbing with the left hand. If possible, follow the left jab with a straight right to the chin. – EDWIN HAISLET, *Boxing*, page 68

Other feints that may be used are: Feint a left jab to the face and jab to the stomach; feint a left jab to the stomach and jab for the face; feint a left jab to the face, feint a right to the face and then jab the left to the chin; feint a straight right to the jaw and hook the left to the body; feint a jab to the chin and deliver a right uppercut to the body. – EDWIN HAISLET, *Boxing*, page 68

Tao of Jeet Kune Do - Personal Impacts

[Sean Madigan, who passed away in December 2020 at the age of 55, was a Jeet Kune Do instructor under original Bruce Lee student Steve Golden. Sean provided these comments for a previous project of mine, and I have included his comments here to honor his memory.]

The *Tao of Jeet Kune Do* is a unique blend of both the physical and mental aspects of the martial arts. It is more than just a book on Jeet Kune Do, rather it is a book on what Bruce Lee found to be the many truths inherent in combat, regardless of what faction of the martial arts you studied. Bruce Lee, in his quest for self-perfection, took notes on everything. He later examined them and built his art, Jeet Kune Do, from the information found in them. The *Tao of Jeet Kune Do* is an example of these notes. Simply put, the information that is found in The *Tao of Jeet Kune Do* will, over time, help you to become a better martial artist.

Sean Madigan
Brooklyn, New York

Julius Palffy-Alpar: Renaissance Man

Julius Palffy-Alpar was born on May 19, 1908 in Hunyard-Kristyor, Transylvania, which would later become a part of Hungary. His ancestry was a mix of German settlers and Hungarian nobility.

He graduated from high school in 1927 and spent the following three years in the army at Békés-Csaba. He was a gifted athlete and came in first in his class at the Toldi Miklos Royal Hungarian Sports Institute. He earned his master's degree and the diploma Maître d'Armes of fencing. The Hungarian government sent him to Austria to develop proficiencies in alpine skiing and glacier climbing, and he won the army individual ski championship three times. He also was a member of the army's Ski Biathlon Team and the Modern Pentathlon Squad (fencing, shooting, swimming, running, and horseback riding).

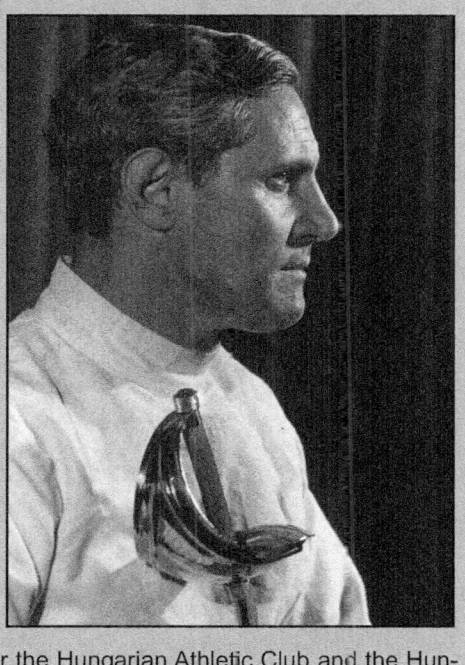

After graduating from the Royal Hungarian Sports Institute he took on a role as captain at the Hungarian Military Academy, where he taught fencing. He also coached for the Hungarian Athletic Club and the Hungarian Officers' Club.

Julius Palffy-Alpar coached the Hungarian Olympic fencing team that won the sabre competition at the 1936 Berlin Olympics. His student Adam Paul Kovacs took the gold.

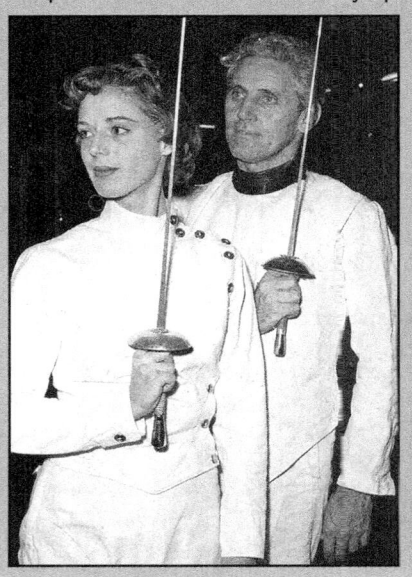

Palffy-Alpar fled Hungary in 1945 with his wife Eva after the post-World War II Soviet occupation began. He moved around a bit, working as as a sports director for the U.S. Army in Europe at Garmisch-Partenkirchen, Bavaria, where he was in charge of arranging a wide range of sports activities for troops and officers. Upon leaving the recreation center, he spent a year in Coblenz with the Tenth French Division, where he worked with the master épée champion, Maître d'Armes Devimeux. He also taught fencing at the Racing Club de France, and it was there that he had opportunities to compare the French style of foil fencing with the Italian style that he had learned in Hungary. He took pride in the certificate of appreciation that he received from the Fédération Francaise D'Escrime.

Among his students was French actor Marcel Marceau, who said of Palffy-Alpar: "I thank Julius Alpar for bringing the love of fencing to my soul."

In 1949 the Palffy-Alpars relocated to Canada, where he became maître d'armes at the University of Toronto and also taught at the Royal Conservatory of Music and with other groups in that city. In 1960 he was invited to become chief instructor at the San Francisco Sports Academy. Two years later he became a member of the faculty of the Department of Physical Education at the University of California, Berkeley, where he served with distinction until his retirement in 1975. An exacting yet kind and considerate teacher, he was greatly admired by both students and colleagues. His counsel was often sought by young men and women who were struggling with the social upheavals and military involvements of the 1960s and 1970s. While he staunchly refused to advise another person on how and what to think, his wide experiences with several cultures, the turmoil of a Europe devastated by World War II, and the occupation of his native country by a foreign power offered enlightening perspectives to which the vast majority of individuals in the United States had not been exposed. Hundreds of Berkeley undergraduates and graduates were eager to enroll in one of the foil, sabre, and épée classes that he taught each semester, and many who had started as "beginners" went on to attain considerable proficiency in his more advanced classes. He brought the UC Fencing Team to a level of distinction, with several of his students qualifying for participation in the Western and U.S. National Championships of the Amateur Fencers League of America as well as (for undergraduates) National Collegiate Athletic Association competitions.

Julius Palffy-Alpar had begun working with faculty of the Department of Dramatic Art in 1963, when he choreographed the combat scenes for Moliére's *Don Juan*. His course titled, "Theory and Practice of Staged Combat," was highly valued by Dramatic Art faculty and students; by the time he retired he had been involved in many other productions (e. g., *Coriolanus, Hamlet, King Lear, Cyrano de Bergerac*). For this work he frequently received accolades from colleagues and in the press. His excellence as a teacher was recognized by the campus when he received Berkeley's Distinguished Teaching Award in 1976. He also choreographed combat scenes for productions of the Marin Shakespeare Festival and the A.C.T. During his career he gave fencing lessons to such noted individuals as actor Robert Goulet; Marcel Marceau occasionally took instruction from Maestro Palffy-Alpar in Hearst Gymnasium, where students and staff could have the pleasure of observing the famous French mime "in action."

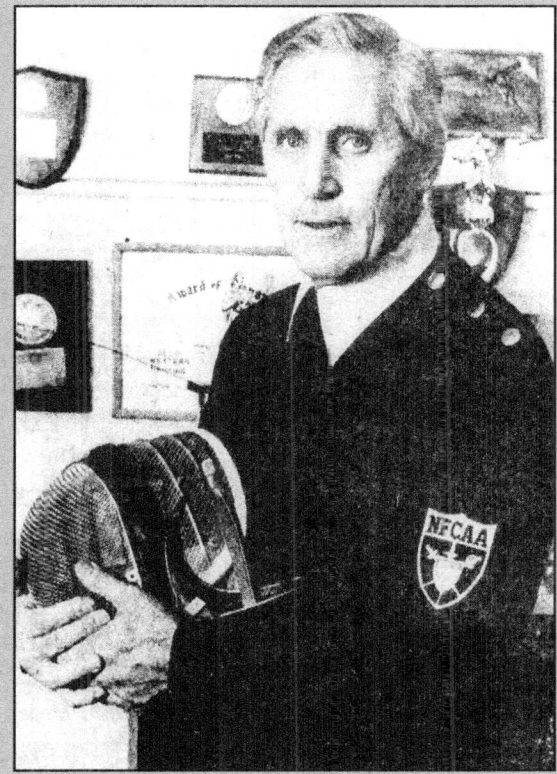

In 1967 Julius Palffy-Alpar authored the book *Sword and Masque*, his personal treatise on fencing and its applications to sport and theater. His book was widely recognized as the standard work in its field. *Sword and Masque* was a significant influence on Bruce Lee, accounting for 37 passages and illustrations in the *Tao of Jeet Kune Do*.

Palffy-Alpar was a real-life renaissance man. A professor, author, pentathlon athlete, champion fencer and skier, and even an inventor. While a member of the Berkeley faculty, Julius Palffy-Alpar had introduced fencing to a small group of youngsters at the California State Orientation Center for the Blind in Albany. In order to facilitate the teaching, he patented a device to teach the students to fence based on sound.

During his long retirement years, he remained active with various community groups as well as physically active, as one might expect of a man with his professional and personal history. Palffy-Alpar later invented a teaching tool that involved a series of straight and semi-circular templates that could be put together in different configurations and utilized for teaching children how to form all the letters of the alphabet.

Three weeks before he passed away at the age of 93, Julius Palffy-Alpar was photographed demonstrating (with outstretched arm and hand) to a local police officer how a fencer parries an opponent's blade, sharing his love of fencing until the very end. He died on February 14, 2001 in Oakland, California after a brief illness. "He was an absolutely marvelous figure," remembered his UC Berkeley colleague Dr. Roberta J. Parks, "a demanding teacher and a compassionate man."

Additional material for this biography courtesy of the California Digital Library

Parrying is a sudden movement of the hand from the inside or outside, onto an oncoming blow, to deflect the blow from its original path. It is a *light, easy* movement depending on *timing* rather than force. A blow is never parried until the last moment and always when close to the body. – EDWIN HAISLET, *Boxing*, page 48

Simple defence is divided into three categories:

1. Simple, direct, (or instinctive) parries.
2. Semi-circular, (or indirect) parries.
3. Circular, counter, (or acquired) parries

. – ROGER CROSNIER, *Fencing with the Foil*, page 94

In the first instance, if the attacker's movements are large and badly directed, it is often difficult to gather the blade with a circular parry; a *simple parry* is then the obvious answer. ... Being based on an instinctive movement the simple parries are the easiest to acquire, but, because of their instinctive nature, are very apt to be used without discrimination. As the fencer is inclined to use them unconsciously, great care must be taken that they are, even then, well controlled. Constant practice must be the means of ensuring that the parry is halted neatly when the line is closed, and that the weight of the hand is not being allowed to carry the sword any further than is necessary. The uncontrolled use of the simple parry is conducive to large arm movements and slashing actions of the blade. – ROGER CROSNIER, *Fencing with the Foil*, pages 107, 96

The object in the parry is to use just enough deflecting motion to protect the threatened area. If you overprotect, moving the foil hand too far to one side , you are immediately vulnerable to a disengage or cutover and have only postponed your fate. – EDITORS OF SPORTS ILLUSTRATED, *Sports Illustrated Book of Fencing*, page 23

To reach out to parry a blow not only makes openings for counter blows but enables the opponent to change the direction of his blow. Parry late rather than early. – EDWIN HAISLET, *Boxing*, page 49

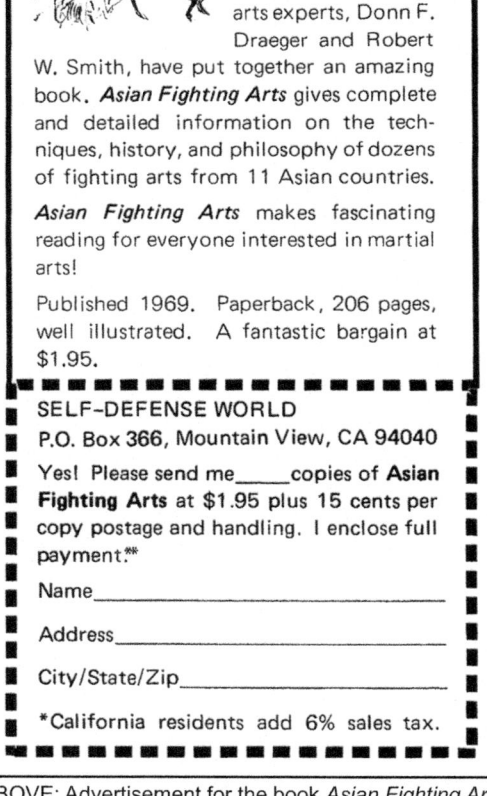

ABOVE: Advertisement for the book *Asian Fighting Arts* – source of two illustrations in the *Tao of Jeet Kune Do*.

Parrying is an extremely useful form of defense. It is easily learned, and easily performed, and should be used whenever possible. *Advantageous openings are created which are essential to counter-fighting.* – EDWIN HAISLET, *Boxing*, page 49

Blocking is the first line of defense. It means taking a blow on some part of the body which is less susceptible to injury. However, considerable resistance is necessary to block a bard blow which causes contusion of the tissue, nerves, and bone. Blocking, therefore, tends to weaken rather than conserve bodily forces. A well delivered blow, even if blocked, will disturb balance, prevent countering, and create openings for other blows. Blocking may be used against all types of blows, either to face or body. It should be learned first and learned well. Later it should be used only when necessary. – EDWIN HAISLET, *Boxing*, page 48

Successful defensive movements are brought about by placing the defensive blade across the path of the cut, so that should there be any force in the blow of the attacking blade it would cause it to slip into the defensive sabre's guard. Such defensive actions are called parries. – ROGER CROSNIER, *Fencing with the Sabre*, page 69

The parry by opposition is obviously the safer of the two and is therefore particularly used with the electric foil and at epee because it prevents a renewed attack being made in the same line. Further, by maintaining contact with the blade the defender retains possession of it and can feel his opponent's reaction on the blade. – CHARLES LOUIS DE BEAUMONT, *Teach Yourself Fencing*, pages 43-44

The fencer should remember to only use a parry against a real attack. The opponent's false attacks can be followed with half positions. – JULIUS PALFFY-ALPAR, *Sword and Masque*, page 43

The master directs cuts or thrusts to different parts of the target. The student follows these movements but stops when the master stops, parrying only the real attacks. Next, the master makes the same threats, but the student does not follow with his blade. Again, the parry is taken only when the real cut or thrust comes. This procedure teaches the student to parry only at the last moment. – JULIUS PALFFY-ALPAR, *Sword and Masque*, page 44

In making the opposition parry and the *beat* parry, the point of the blade should not swing too far to the right or to the left, but merely close the line or deflect the opponent's blade just enough to prevent his point arriving on the target. – JULIO MARTINEZ CASTELLÓ, *Theory and Practice of Fencing*, page 85

The beat parry is usually followed by a fast return. – JULIO MARTINEZ CASTELLÓ, *Theory and Practice of Fencing*, page 45

TAO FAST FACTS

When Bruce Lee injured his back in 1970 after neglecting to properly warm up before a training session, he was left debilitated for several months. During this period of recovery, Lee began going through his library of books and transcribing the passages he had previously underlined as well as the notes he made about them. He organized the material into several volumes from which he intended to draft the *Tao of Jeet Kune Do*.

Semi-circular parries are those which are taken from a high line engagement to deflect an attack directed in the low line, or from a low line engagement to a high line. They describe a half circle and, when taken from high to low lines, form the parries of septime or octave. – ROGER CROSNIER, *Fencing with the Foil*, page 101

The parries of octave and septime are those used for defence against attacks directed in the low line, but it is extraordinary how few fencers realize that they can be an alternative to the parries of quarte and sixte. – ROGER CROSNIER, *Fencing with the Foil*, page 101-102

Against a very fast fencer or one with a marked superiority of height or reach, it is often necessary to step backwards when making a parry. ... When parrying with a step backwards, the parry should be taken as the rear foot moves backwards in the course of breaking ground; in other words, the parry should be formed with the step back and not after it has been completed. – CHARLES LOUIS DE BEAUMONT, *Fencing: Ancient Art and Modern Sport*, page 76

The step back as a defensive movement should always be adjusted to the length of the opponent's attacking movements, to ensure that the required measure is maintained for a successful parry and riposte. – CHARLES LOUIS DE BEAUMONT, *Fencing: Ancient Art and Modern Sport*, page 76

Circular parries, also called counter-parries, are made by a circular movement of the defender's blade which envelops the attacker's blade and brings it back to the original line of engagement, while deflecting it off the target. – CHARLES LOUIS DE BEAUMONT, *Fencing: Ancient Art and Modern Sport*, page 75

When making a counter-parry it is obviously necessary to sweep the opponent's blade away from the target by the shortest route. Thus counter of sixte is taken by moving the blade clockwise, while counter of quarte will require an anti-clockwise rotation of the blade. – CHARLES LOUIS DE BEAUMONT, *Fencing: Ancient Art and Modern Sport*, page 76

When used in the high line, the circle is started under the adversary's blade; when used in the low line, it is started over the opponent's blade. ... The advantage of counter parries over opposition or beat parries is that they protect a larger amount of the target and are more difficult to deceive. However, they are not as rapid as the simple parries. – JULIO MARTINEZ CASTELLÓ, *Theory and Practice of Fencing*, pages 45-46, 48

In using the counter parries be sure that the point describes a perfect circle so that the blade finishes in its original position. Do not start or finish the parry too soon, for your blade must follow the opponent's, and should meet it just before his point is about to arrive on the target. – JULIO MARTINEZ CASTELLÓ, *Theory and Practice of Fencing*, page 88

Compound Parries. These parries consist of either two or more simple or counter parries or a combination of these parries together. – JULIO MARTINEZ CASTELLÓ, *Theory and Practice of Fencing*, page 48

In making these parries, each single parry must be finished, bringing the hand to the right position before making the succeeding parry; otherwise, the result will be a contraction parry. – JULIO MARTINEZ CASTELLÓ, *Theory and Practice of Fencing*, pages 47-48

It can be readily understood that it would be a weakness to repeat the same parry in succession. The adversary, if he has the slightest sense of observation, will quickly detect this and will have little difficulty in deceiving the parries. It is advisable, therefore, to mix one's parries as much as possible, and by so doing, leave the opponent in doubt as to the order in which they will be made. … When one is faced with an opponent of some fencing experience who has learnt to observe his opponent's tactics and apply the correct corresponding movements, the continual use of any one type of parry, no matter how well it may be performed, can be a weakness. The defender must, therefore, vary his parries as much as possible. In this way he will keep his opponent guessing as to the form of defence that he is about to take It will cause a certain amount of hesitation on the part of the attacker, whose offensive actions will suffer in their confidence and penetration. – ROGER CROSNIER, *Fencing with the Foil*, pages 140, 107-108

Julio Martinez Castelló

Julio Martinez Castelló, born in the Basque region of Spain in 1882. He studied fencing at the Royal Academy in Madrid, graduating in 1905. He then served as an officer the in the Spanish Army.

As Castelló's fencing reputation grew, he became much sought after as a fencing instructor. He was the fencing instructor for King Alfonso XIII of Spain.

Castelló immigrated to the United States in 1914 and began teaching at the New York Athletic Club. At the same time, he opened a fencing equipment company that he, and later his sons, managed. During that time, Julio Martinez Castelló became the fencing teacher of famous movie star Rudolph Valentino, and Castelló appeared in a number of Valentino's films.

In 1924, Julio Martinez Castelló served as the coach of the United States Olympic fencing team. The next year he was hired as the coach for New York University's new fencing program. He taught there from 1927 until his retirement in 1947, building New York University into a national fencing power. His teams won 19 International Fencing Association titles and nine National Collegiate Athletic Association titles.

Julio Martinez Castelló wrote the book *Theory and Practice of Fencing* in 1933. The book is responsible for 34 passages in the *Tao of Jeet Kune Do*.

When he retired from New York University, Castelló was replaced by his son Hugo. Hugo's brother James served under his brother as assistant coach. Hugo and James Castelló's 1962 book, *Fencing*, is responsible for seven passages in the *Tao of Jeet Kune Do*.

Castelló died at his home in Tampa, Florida on January 15, 1973 at the age of 91.

A crisp movement of the blade made against the opponent's with the object of knocking it aside or obtaining a reaction, is called a *beat*. ... In most cases it also provokes in the opponent the reaction of beating back. ... In making the fencer beat back we have obtained a movement which we can deceive and gain time upon." – ROGER CROSNIER, *Fencing with the Foil*, pages 170, 171

Once more, because of the distance between the fencers, the beat cannot be made at will. The correct opportunity must be waited for and seized. ... The continual change of hand position often takes the form of half feints and false attacks, which bring the blade well within reach of a beat. – ROGER CROSNIER, *Fencing with the Sabre*, page 141

The beat is made by hitting either the middle or the weak part of the opponent's blade with the middle part of yours, this being done in the same line in which the blades are engaged. This should be done with the hand in the normal guard position. If the change is made with the beat, the action is called the *change beat*. – JULIO MARTINEZ CASTELLÓ, *Theory and Practice of Fencing*, pages 35-36

The Most Unusual Martial Arts Book Ever Written!

FIGHTING ARTS OF THE WORLD

Here is a book crammed full of secret fighting techniques never before divulged in print, secrets such as: the Oriental delayed death touch, the shout of doom, a halitosis attack capable of inflicting unconsciousness . . .

These and twenty other of "the world's most closely-guarded fighting techniques" are vividly described in this one volume.

We must note that a lot of skepticism surrounds this book. However, if even one third of it is true, it belongs on your bookshelf for its startling revelations. And if the other two thirds is fiction, you should read it to appreciate the author's incredible imagination!

If you've got an open mind, send $6.50 per copy plus 15 cents postage and handling for *Secret Fighting Arts of the World*.

Self-Defense World, Box 366, Mountain View, CA 94040.

ABOVE: Advertisement for the book *Secret Fighting Arts of the World* by John Gilby, pseudonym for Robert W. Smith. Smith wrote the book as a farce (the halitosis attack mentioned above should be a hint), but Bruce Lee took it seriously.

Care should be taken to make beats as sharp and as close to the blade as possible, using only the fingers and hand; otherwise, they will be easily avoided by the adversary. There are three purposes of making beats on the blade:

1. Opening the line.
2. As a feint before an attack.
3. As an invitation to the opponent's attack.

– JULIO MARTINEZ CASTELLÓ, *Theory and Practice of Fencing*, page 36

In the first case, the beat on the blade should be made sharply and quickly; in the second, lightly and fast, so as to pass the point quickly and execute the attack; in the third case it should be made lightly and not too quickly, at the same time being ready to parry the attack of the adversary. – JULIO MARTINEZ CASTELLÓ, *Theory and Practice of Fencing*, page 36

The Bind

With the blades engaged, the action of carrying the opponent's blade diagonally across from a high to a low line, or vice versa, is called a bind. – ROGER CROSNIER, *Fencing with the Foil*, page 180

The Croisé

The croise carries the opponent's blade from high to low line on the same side as the engagement and does not, as in the bind, carry it diagonally across. It is not executed from low to high line. – ROGER CROSNIER, *Fencing with the Foil*, pages 182-183

The Envelopment

The envelopment is the action of taking the foible of the opposing blade in the forte of one's own and, by describing a circle with both blades in contact, returning to the line of engagement. – ROGER CROSNIER, *Fencing with the Foil*, pages 177-178

The Pressure

The pressure is the action of pressing upon the opponent's blade in order to deflect it or to obtain a reaction from it. – ROGER CROSNIER, *Fencing with the Foil*, page 173

A crisp movement of the blade made against the opponent's with the object of knocking it aside or obtaining a reaction, is called a beat. – ROGER CROSNIER, *Fencing with the Foil*, page 170

Laurence Morehouse

Laurence Englemohr Morehouse was born July 13, 1913 in Danbury, Connecticut. He received both an undergraduate and a master's degree in physical education from Springfield College in Massachusetts and a doctoral degree in physical education and physiology from State University of Iowa.

Dr. Morehouse began his professorship at UCLA in 1954. He retired as Professor of Kinesiology in 1984. His professional and academic career was focused on the physiology of exercise and fitness.

Morehouse was recognized professionally, both nationally and internationally, for his textbook, *Physiology of Exercise*, which was published in seven editions and translated into five languages. But Dr. Morehouse was best recognized by the general public for his book, *Total Fitness in 30 Minutes a Week*, which was on the top 10 national bestseller list for 35 weeks. This book was translated into 11 languages, and more than 1.5 million copies were sold. The concepts in this book were quite controversial among his contemporaries, but many of his ideas remain viable today.

Laurence Morehouse passed away on April 2, 1995.

(Biography written by V. Reggie Edgerton - courtesy of the Online Archive of California; photograph by Dean Gordon - courtesy of the Los Angeles Public Library)

MOBILITY

I am moving all day and not moving at all. I am like the moon underneath the waves that ever go on rolling and rocking.

– D. T. SUZUKI,
Zen and Japanese Culture,
page 165

Distance

In the ordinary bout, distance is a continually shifting relationship, depending on the speed, agility, and control of both fencers. – HUGO CASTELLÓ and JAMES CASTELLÓ, *Fencing*, page 73

It is a constant rapid shifting of ground, seeking the slight closing of distance, which will greatly increase the chances of hitting the opponent. – EDITORS OF SPORTS ILLUSTRATED, *Sports Illustrated Book of Fencing*, page 7

The maintenance of the proper fencing distance has a decisive effect on the outcome of fencing. – JULIUS PALFFY-ALPAR, *Sword and Masque*, page 42

There must be close synchronization between closing and opening distances and the various actions of the hand. – JULIUS PALFFY-ALPAR, *Sword and Masque*, page 42

To fence for any length of time within distance is safe only if you overwhelmingly outclass your opponent in speed and agility. – HUGO CASTELLÓ and JAMES CASTELLÓ, *Fencing*, pages 73-74

When taking the guard, it is preferable to fall back a little too far than to come too close to your opponent. – LUIGI BARBASETTI, *The Art of the Sabre and the Épée*, page 16

No matter how fast you are able to parry, if a man is close enough to you, he will arrive with his point, for the nature of an attack is such as to give the advantage of the initiative to the attacker. Likewise, in attacking, however accurate, fast, and timely your attack may be, it will fall short unless you have calculated your distance well. – JULIO MARTINEZ CASTELLÓ, *Theory and Practice of Fencing*, page 55

The fencing measure is the distance which a fencer keeps in relationship to his opponent. It is such that he cannot be hit unless his opponent lunges fully at him. – ROGER CROSNIER, *Fencing with the Foil*, page 39

Therefore, it is essential that each man learn his own attacking and defensive distances. This means that in the fencing bout you must allow for the relative agility and speed of yourself and your opponent. That is, you should *consistently stay out of distance* in the sense that your opponent cannot reach you with a simple lunge, but not so far that with a short advance you cannot regain the distance and be able to reach him with your attack. – JULIO MARTINEZ CASTELLÓ, *Theory and Practice of Fencing*, page 55

If fencers are constantly on the move when fighting, it is because they are trying to make their opponent misjudge his distance while being quite well aware of their own. – ROGER CROSNIER, *Fencing with the Foil*, page 39

Hence, of necessity, the fencers are continually gaining and breaking ground in their effort to obtain the distance which suits them best. It will be more easily understood, therefore, why the practice of gaining and breaking ground must be worked at assiduously from the beginning in order to develop the reflex of maintaining a correct measure. – ROGER CROSNIER, *Fencing with the Foil*, page 39

Thus, it is that in an actual bout the skilled fencer always keeps himself just out of distance of the opponent's attack and waits for his opportunity to close the distance himself or to *steal a march* on the opponent's move to close in.

- *Attack on the opponent's advance* or change of distance forward. You may retreat to draw an advance.
- Back the opponent to the end of the strip to cut off his retreat.

– HUGO CASTELLÓ and JAMES CASTELLÓ, *Fencing*, page 75

The majority of *fencers*, when they are preparing an attack or trying to avoid one, advance and retreat very much as boxers do who are sparring for an opening. This procedure is not advisable because the advance and retreat during the assault must be made rapidly, by bounds and at irregular intervals in such a fashion that the adversary may not notice the action until it is too late. The attack should then be launched as suddenly as possible accommodating itself to the automatic movements of the opponent. – LUIGI BARBASETTI, *The Art of the Sabre and the Épée*, page 156

An attack should be aimed at the distance where the opponent will be when he realizes he will be attacked and not at the distance prior to the attack. – JULIUS PALFFY-ALPAR, *Sword and Masque*, page 42

It is of the utmost importance that you acquire the correct "eye" or even an instinctive feeling for distance. By failing to master this fundamental principle of the fencer's art, you will find it impossible to estimate correctly the relation between the length of your adversary's lunge and the speed with which he prepares his defense. The slightest error in calculation can render the attack harmless. – LUIGI BARBASETTI, *The Art of the Foil: With a Short History of Fencing*, page 16

An attack can rarely succeed unless one can 'lodge' oneself at the correct distance *at the moment it is launched*. A parry is most likely to succeed if it can be made just as the opponent is at the end of his lunge. Many a chance to riposte is missed by the defender stepping

back out of distance when he parries. To these examples must be added the obvious importance of choosing the correct measure when making a counter-attack by stop hit or time hit.
– CHARLES LOUIS DE BEAUMONT, *Fencing: Ancient Art and Modern Sport*, page 200

And further: The question whether it is necessary to know in advance the tempo or the distance is a matter rather for the philosopher rather than the swordsman to decide. Just the same it is certain that the combatant has to observe simultaneously both the tempo and the distance. And he has to comply with both simultaneously, with the action, if he wishes to reach his object. – LUIGI BARBASETTI, *The Art of the Foil: With a Short History of Fencing*, page 251

Whatever may be the weapon, the fencing measure is governed by the amount of target to be protected and the parts of the body which are most easily within the adversary's reach. ... We know that at epee the hand is most vulnerable and that it is constantly threatened. Thus, if the foilist is accustomed to measure his distance from chest to chest, the epeeist has to take his measure from hand to hand. – ROGER CROSNIER, *Fencing with the Epee*, page 29

However, he must close the distance so that he is also ready for a parry riposte. When the correct distance is attained, the attack should be carried through with an instantaneous burst of energy and speed. An attack should be aimed at the distance where the opponent will be when he realizes he will be attacked and not at the distance prior to the attack. – JULIUS PALFFY-ALPAR, *Sword and Masque*, page 42

Distance in Attack

This is the true conception of tempo – choosing the exact psychological and physical moment of weakness in an opponent. – JOHN KARDOSS, *Sabre Fencing: History, Theory, Practice*, page 59

Finally, courage and decision are essential factors to success in competitive sabre fencing. – CHARLES LOUIS DE BEAUMONT, *Fencing: Ancient Art and Modern Sport*, page 196

DELUXE EDITION

Tao of Jeet Kune Do

by *Bruce Lee*

If you're really a Bruce Lee fan you will want the distinguished, hardbound edition of his *Tao of Jeet Kune Do*. The final legacy of Bruce Lee, his notes, his descriptions of "alive" combat motion—all bound in rich leatherette with a gold stamped signature. A collector's dream!

No. 401-H $9.95

Also available in a Soft-cover edition.

No. 401-S $6.95

ABOVE: 1976 Advertisement for the *Tao of Jeet Kune Do* deluxe edition.

Footwork

This judgment of distance must become instinctive and can only be acquired through assiduous training to that end. But the fencer can only develop this instinctive sense of distance if he is able to move about smoothly and speedily. – ROGER CROSNIER, *Fencing with the Electric Foil*, page 32

You cannot use your hands effectively until your feet have put you into a position in which you can do so. Your feet are your foundation, and on the way you use them depends the all-important question of balance, which in my opinion is the single greatest factor in the business of learning how to box. – BOBBY NEILL, *Instruction to Young Boxers*, page 13

He will soon develop a springiness of footwork which will enable him to move in any desired direction readily and speedily. He will find an alertness of foot which will be transmuted into an alertness of mind. His reactions will be all the more spontaneous. – ROGER CROSNIER, *Fencing with the Electric Foil*, pages 33-34

ABOVE: Ring's Athletic Library series advertisement. Most were owned by Bruce Lee, and at least two influenced the *Tao of Jeet Kune Do* (Gotch's *Wrestling* and Driscoll's *The Straight Left*).

If fencers are constantly on the move when fighting, it is because they are trying to make their opponent misjudge his distance, while being quite well aware of their own. … The length of the step forward, or backward, should be, approximately, regulated to that of the opponent, but must never be permitted to develop into a large and ungainly stride. – ROGER CROSNIER, *Fencing with the Foil*, pages 39, 37

Clever, well-timed footwork enables you to avoid blows. The more adept a boxer is at footwork the less does he make use of his arms in avoiding blows. By means of skillful and timely side-stepping and slipping he can get clear of almost any punch, thus preserving both of his guns for counters. – PHILADELPHIA JACK O'BRIEN, *Boxing*, page 59

Points to remember:

1. Keep your balance at all times.
2. Coordinate foot-and-hand actions.
3. Start all attacks from the weapon hand.
4. Keep your feet close to the floor when in motion.
5. Keep your steps short.
6. Remember that when you advance you are highly vulnerable to attack.
7. Vary the length and speed of your steps to confuse the opponent.

– HUGO CASTELLÓ and JAMES CASTELLÓ, *Fencing*, page 19

A veteran fencer knows that to reach the top ranks of competition, it is not necessary to possess a large bag of tricks. These simple attacks executed with an absolute minimum of movement and with flawless timing can go very far. – EDITORS OF SPORTS ILLUSTRATED, *Sports Illustrated Book of Fencing*, page 17

Footwork does not mean leg work, nor does it mean jumping around. It means moving just enough to accomplish a purpose, in order to make an opponent miss or to deliver a counter blow effectively. – EDWIN HAISLET, *Boxing*, page 30

The feet should be kept an easy and comfortable distance apart and brought together in proportion as a man is prepared to keep up a battery of two-handed hitting. – VISCOUNT KNEBWORTH, *Boxing: A Guide to Modern Methods*, page 174

The boxer must provide himself with a firm but highly mobile base, capable of being shifted in any direction at a split second's notice. – BOBBY NEILL, *Instruction to Young Boxers*, page 13

In England, footwork was used very little before the time of John Jackson (1768) and it was not until the beginning of the Nineteenth Century and the school of Belcher, Bendigo and Sayer that moving in the ring was used as a means of defense as well as a means of conserving energy. ... Footwork developed with the use of the glove because it called for speed and skill. Today, the essence of boxing is the art of moving, moving in to attack or defend, moving out to defend or "pull off" balance. – EDWIN HAISLET, *Boxing*, page 30

Clever footwork enables you to avoid his blows and yet remain within firing range. Many a husky slugger raining potential destruction exhausts himself trying to corner and sting a dancing-master. The few moments of rest bring new pep into the arms. – PHILADELPHIA JACK O'BRIEN, *Boxing*, pages 61, 59, 62

The greatest phase of footwork is the coordination of the hands and feet. When the feet and hands work together automatically, the art of moving is perfection itself. – EDWIN HAISLET, *Boxing*, page 31

Without footwork, he is like artillery that cannot be moved or a policeman always where not wanted. – NORMAN CLARK, *How to Box*, page 46

WHO WROTE THE TAO?

> The value of a couple of good hands depends almost entirely on their being upon a well-balanced and quickly movable base, and footwork must be regarded as the essential foundation upon which all other things are to be built. – NORMAN CLARK, *How to Box*, page 46
>
> Retain the fundamental stance. It is essential to preserve the balance and poise of the fighting-turret carrying your artillery. No matter in what direction or at what speed you move, your aim is to retain the stance which has been found the most effective for boxing. Let the movable pedestal be as nimble as possible. – PHILADELPHIA JACK O'BRIEN, *Boxing*, page 61

There is really only one-correct style of boxing-that which in its absolute naturalness combines velocity and power of hitting with the soundest defence. – NORMAN CLARK, *How to Box*, page 36

Good footwork means good balance in action, and from this springs hitting-power and the ability to avoid punishment. Every ring movement involves the co-ordination of hands, feet and brain. – PETER MCINNES, *Tackle Boxing This Way*, page 78

A boxer should *feel* the floor with the balls of his feet, the right heel being slightly raised. – PETER MCINNES, *Tackle Boxing This Way*, page 22

Points to remember:

1. Make your own attacks with an advance.
2. Attack on the opponent's advance or change of distance forward. You may retreat to draw an advance.
3. Back the opponent to the end of the strip to cut off his retreat.
4. Use your own footwork and the opponent's for your advantage. Note his pattern, if any, of advancing and retreating. Vary the length and/or speed of your own steps.

– HUGO CASTELLÓ and JAMES CASTELLÓ, *Fencing*, page 75

The length of the step forward or backward should be, approximately, regulated to that of the opponent, but must never be permitted to develop into a large and ungainly stride. – ROGER CROSNIER, *Fencing with the Foil*, page 37

Variations of measure will make it more difficult for the opponent to time his attacks or preparations. A fencer with a good sense of distance, or one who is difficult to reach to launch an attack, may often be brought to the desired measure by progressive shortening of a series of steps backward or by the movement known as gaining on the lunge. – CHARLES LOUIS DE BEAUMONT, *Fencing: Ancient Art and Modern Sport*, page 200

The simplest and most fundamental tactic to use on an opponent is to gain just enough distance to facilitate a hit. You may do this by pressing the opponent, forcing him to retreat. But at the same time, the attacker must be extremely alert to the possibility of the opponent's suddenly taking over the initiative with a counterattack. The idea is to press on (advance) a step or so and then fall back (retreat), inviting the opponent to follow. Allow your opponent to advance a step or two and then, at the precise moment he lifts his foot for still another step, you must suddenly lunge forward into this step. – EDITORS OF SPORTS ILLUSTRATED, *Sports Illustrated Book of Fencing*, page 32

A fencer with a good sense of distance, or one who is difficult to reach to launch an attack, may often be brought to the desired measure by progressive shortering of a series of steps backward or by the movement known as gaining on the lunge. – CHARLES LOUIS DE BEAUMONT, *Fencing: Ancient Art and Modern Sport*, page 200

Small and rapid steps are recommended as the only way to keep perfect balance, exact distance and the ability to develop sudden attacks or counterattacks. – EDITORS OF SPORTS ILLUSTRATED, *Sports Illustrated Book of Fencing*, page 43

This indicates the necessity of sure foot work and balance in order to be able to advance and retreat in and out of distance with respect to both your own and your opponent's reach. Many are the wiles and resources relied upon by the seasoned veteran in stealing, creating, and changing that vital spatial relation to the confusion of his opponent. These are purely personal developments of thought and intention; so that the determination of when to advance and to retreat is the same as saying when to attack and when to protect. – JULIO MARTINEZ CASTELLÓ, *Theory and Practice of Fencing*, page 55

Many are the wiles and resources relied upon by the seasoned veteran in stealing, creating, and changing that vital spatial relation to the confusion of his opponent. – JULIO MARTINEZ CASTELLÓ, *Theory and Practice of Fencing*, page 56

The pupil should practise his footwork with a view to keeping a very correct and precise distance in relationship to his opponent. – ROGER CROSNIER, *Fencing with the Foil*, page 38

The ability to move at the right time is the foundation of great skill in boxing. Footwork means moving the body so as to be in the best position for attack or defense. It means balance--*but movement and balance together.* – EDWIN HAISLET, *Boxing*, page 30

Having your feet in the correct position serves as a pivot for your entire attack. It balances you properly and lends unseen power to your blows, just as it does in sports like baseball and golf where drive and power seem to come up from the legs. – BARNEY ROSS, *Fundamentals of Boxing*, page 51

To maintain balance while constantly shifting body weight is an art few ever acquire. – EDWIN HAISLET, *Boxing*, page 30

The position of the legs and feet in the on-guard position is known as the stance and is of great importance to ensure balance and mobility. Each fencer must find by trial and error the distance between the heels which best suits his height and weight. If this distance is too short, there will be a lack of balance and if too wide the lunge will be correspondingly reduced and there will be lack of mobility. – CHARLES LOUIS DE BEAUMONT, *Fencing: Ancient Art and Modern Sport*, page 31

With the feet too close together you cannot get full force into a blow and you are easily carried off your feet by a sudden attack; with the feet too far apart the inside leg muscles are strained and you will find yourself unable to move quickly in any direction to take advantage of an opening or to evade a rush. – FRANK F. O'NEILL, *Boxing: A Guide to the Manly Art of Self Defense*, page 4

The ideal position of the feet is one that enables you to move quickly in any direction and to be so balanced as to resist blows from all angles. – NORMAN CLARK, *How to Box*, page 46

– EDWIN HAISLET, *Boxing*, page 91

The left leg is not just a prop. It is the spark plug, or better still the piston of the whole fencing machine. This leg provides a great deal of the power and speed that are needed for a correct, fast lunge. – ALDO NADI, *On Fencing*, page 51

If balance is to be maintained at all times, it is absolutely necessary that the feet be always directly under the body. Any movement of the feet which tends to unbalance the body must be *eliminated*. The fundamental position is one of perfect body balance, and should always be maintained, especially as regards the feet. *Wide steps or leg movements which require a constant shift of weight from one leg to the other cannot be used.* During this shift of weight there is a moment when balance is precarious, and so renders attack or defense ineffective. – EDWIN HAISLET, *Boxing*, pages 30-31

TAO FAST FACTS

Photographs and illustrations used in boxing and wrestling books in the early 20th Century were sometimes re-used by publishers. Some of the illustrations originating in Edwin Haislet's book *Boxing* (1940) can also be found in *A Handy Illustrated Guide to Boxing* (1949), edited by Sam Nisenson.

Advancing and retiring, called in fencing parlance gaining and breaking ground, is done by taking short steps on the piste in order to achieve or maintain the desired distance from the opponent. The way this is carried out ensures that the balance of the body is always maintained, so that any offensive or defensive movement required is not limited or impaired as the fencer moves up or down the piste. ... It is better to take two medium steps rather than one long one to cover the same distance. – CHARLES LOUIS DE BEAUMONT, Fencing: Ancient Art and Modern Sport, page 34

Variations of measure will make it more difficult for the opponent to time his attacks or preparations. – CHARLES LOUIS DE BEAUMONT, Fencing: Ancient Art and Modern Sport, page 200

Unless there is a tactical reason for acting otherwise, gaining and breaking of ground is executed by means of *small* and *rapid steps*. A correct distribution of weight on both legs will make for perfect balance, enabling the fencer to get off the mark quickly and easily, whenever the measure is right for attacks which are intended to land on the body or on the arm (advanced target). – ROGER CROSNIER, Fencing with the Epee, page 30

The best way to learn proper footwork is to shadow box many rounds giving particular attention to becoming light on your feet and moving around according to instructions. Gradually this way of stepping around will become natural to you and you will do it easily and mechanically without giving it a thought. – FRANK GILMER, Push Yourself: A Book for Amateur Boxers and Boxing Fans, page 16

You should operate in the same manner as a good ballroom dancer who uses the feet, ankles and calves. He slithers round the floor, being poised to rise on his toes as the occasion demands. – PETER MCINNES, Tackle Boxing This Way, page 74

The basic handbook!

FENCING WITH THE EPEE

by Roger Crosnier

Former Olympic Fencing Coach for Great Britain, Professor Crosnier completes his series of handbooks on modern fencing weapons and techniques with this meticulously illustrated text or *Fencing with the Epee*. His first two books, *Fencing with the Sabre* and *Fencing with the Foil* contained definitions, terminology, classical execution of strokes, and tactics. To avoid repetition of points the three weapons have in common, *Fencing with the Epee* concentrates on individual fencing strokes and positions of the Epee.

Sample lessons for both individual and class instruction make this book invaluable for both students and coaches.

Each volume, illustrated $4.50

A. S. BARNES & CO.
New York 16, N. Y.

We have mentioned the athletic character of present-day foil fencing, and the accent which has been put on speedy footwork. We have also spoken of the tendency towards attacks with a step forward, often combined with an attack on the *blade* or a *prise de fer*. – ROGER CROSNIER, Fencing with the Electric Foil, page 64

There are only four moves possible in footwork – advancing, retreating, circling left, and circling right. However, there are important variations of advancing and retreating as well as the necessity of coordinating each fundamental movement with the arms – EDWIN HAISLET, Boxing, page 31

The Forward Shuffle: This is a forward advance of the body without disturbing body balance which can only be performed through a series of short steps forward. These steps must be so small that the feet are not lifted at all but slide along the floor. ... The Forward Shuffle is a slow movement forward in such a manner that both feet are on the floor at all times, with the body poised for either a sudden attack or a defensive maneuver. Its primary purpose is to create openings and to draw leads. – EDWIN HAISLET, *Boxing*, pages 32, 31

The Backward Shuffle: The principle of the backward shuffle is the same as that of the forward shuffle, that is, a slow backward movement without disturbance of the fundamental position. ... The Backward Shuffle is a slow movement backward in such a manner that both feet are on the floor *at all times* permitting balance to be maintained for attack or defense. It is used to draw leads or to draw the opponent off balance, thus creating openings. – EDWIN HAISLET, *Boxing*, pages 32, 31

The Quick Advance: The body *flattens toward the floor* rather than leaping into the air. It is not a hop. In all respects it is the same as a wide step forward-a long step with the left foot, bringing the right foot immediately into position. – EDWIN HAISLET, *Boxing*, page 34

The Step Forward and the Step Back: Gaining and breaking ground may be used as a preparation of attack. The step forward is obviously used to obtain the correct distance for attacking and the step back can be used to draw the opponent within distance. – CHARLES LOUIS DE BEAUMONT, *Fencing: Ancient Art and Modern Sport*, page 101

Its object is to lure your opponent within reach at a crucial moment, while staying out of reach yourself. – EDITORS OF SPORTS ILLUSTRATED, *Sports Illustrated Book of Fencing*, page 7

The step forward may precede an attack or may be combined with a feint or a preparation for the attack. To combine it with a blade movement such as a preparation or a feint will add speed to the attack, but the attacker is vulnerable to a stop hit which deceives the blade movement. ... If the step forward is made with the line of engagement covered, the attacker will be in the best position to deal with a stop hit launched during this movement. – CHARLES LOUIS DE BEAUMONT, *Fencing: Ancient Art and Modern Sport*, page 101

The step back can be used tactically against an opponent who has formed the habit of retiring whenever any feint or other offensive movement is made, and is therefore very difficult to reach, especially if he is superior in height or length. – CHARLES LOUIS DE BEAUMONT, *Fencing: Ancient Art and Modern Sport*, page 101

Constant steps forward and back, with a carefully regulated length of step, can *conceal a fencer's intentions*, and enable him to lodge himself at the ideal distance for an attack, often as the opponent is momentarily off balance. – CHARLES LOUIS DE BEAUMONT, *Fencing: Ancient Art and Modern Sport*, page 101

Circling to the Left: In this movement the left leg becomes a movable pivot. Assume the fundamental position. Step six to eight inches to the left with the left foot. Then, using the left leg as a pivot-point, wheel the whole body to the left until the correct position is resumed. The first step with the left foot may be as short or as long as necessary, the longer the step, the greater the pivot. The fundamental position must be maintained at all times. The left hand should be carried a little higher than ordinarily in readiness for the opponent's right counter. ... Circling left may be used to nullify an opponent's left hook. It may be used to get into position for terrific right-handed counters, and it can be used to throw an opponent off balance. The important things to remember are not to cross the feet while circling, to move deliberately rather than wildly, and with very little motion. – EDWIN HAISLET, *Boxing*, pages 35, 32

Circling to the Right: This is a more precise movement requiring shorter steps. Assume the fundamental position. Step from four to six inches to the right with the left foot and immediately follow with the right foot to the fundamental stance position. The step with the left foot must be short. Carry the right hand high, ready for the opponent's left hook. ... Circling to the Right is used to keep out of the range of right-hand blows and to obtain a good position for the delivery of a left hook and a left jab. It is safer but more difficult than circling to the left and therefore should be used more often. – EDWIN HAISLET, *Boxing*, pages 35, 32

The Step In-Step Out: Is the start of an offensive maneuver, often used as a feint in order to build up an opening. The foot movement is always combined with the arm movement. The initial movement is directly in, as if to hit, then moving out quickly before the opponent can adjust his defense. – EDWIN HAISLET, *Boxing: The V5 Naval Aviation Training Manual*, page 47

The Quick Retreat: Here, again, is a technique which makes possible sudden retreat. It is a sudden forceful move backward, allowing further retreat if necessary, or a stepping forward to attack if desired. – EDWIN HAISLET, *Boxing: The V5 Naval Aviation Training Manual*, page 47

If it is necessary to combine a step back with a parry it is because one is pressed for time. The parry must, therefore, be made at the *beginning* of the retreating movement, that is to say, *when the rear foot moves.* – ROGER CROSNIER, *Fencing with the Foil*, page 198

When the opponent's offensive action is a compound one, the correct coordination will be to perform the first parry simultaneously with the movement of the rear foot, and the remaining parry, or parries, simultaneously with that of the retreating leading foot. – ROGER CROSNIER, *Fencing with the Foil*, page 199

The step back could be taken first, but this should only be the case when the attack has been *prepared* with a step forward and not when the attack has been made with a step forward. – ROGER CROSNIER, *Fencing with the Foil*, page 199

TAO FAST FACTS

Bruce Lee ending work on the *Tao of Jeet Kune Do* disappointed many in the martial arts, as indicated by comments in the February 1971 issue of *Black Belt* magazine: "There is a big movement underway to try and convince Bruce Lee to change his mind about not publishing his book on Jeet Kune Do. After we announced in this column he was going to shelve the book, a grassroots letter campaign was started, and now Bruce has so much mail pleading with him to go ahead with the book that he doesn't know where to put it all. In spite of these efforts, Bruce still remains firm about his non-publishing decision."

To a man with quick footwork and a good left hand the art comes easily enough. It is a continuous process of hit-and-away. As your opponent bores in, you meet him with a defensive-hit with the left and immediately step back; then as he follows up you repeat the process, continually retreating round the ring, and as you do so frequently checking yourself in your stride and temporarily stopping to meet him with a straight left or right or occasionally both. – NORMAN CLARK, *How to Box,* page 86

Success in "milling on the retreat" depends mainly on good judgment of distance and ability to stop in your retreat quickly and unexpectedly. The common fault is to deliver your blow whilst actually on the move, instead of properly stopping to do it; but this is quite useless, and often fatal, for your hit is too weak to stop your opponent, and slowing your retreat without stopping his advance, you play into his hands. The secret lies in great rapidity in passing from defence to attack, and then back to defence again. – NORMAN CLARK, *How to Box,* page 86

When retreating, do not make the common mistake of attempting to hit while you are actually moving back. Step back, halt, then hit. That is the only way of ensuring that punches delivered when back-pedalling carry any real authority. – PETER MCINNES, *Tackle Boxing This Way,* page 75

Sidestepping

Sidestepping is shifting the weight and changing the feet without disturbing balance. It is used to avoid straight rushes forward, and to move quickly out of range of attack. – EDWIN HAISLET, *Boxing,* page 50

It is a safe, sure, and valuable defensive tactic. It can be used to frustrate an attack simply by moving every time an opponent gets "set" to hit. It may be used as a method of avoiding blows or creating openings for a counter-attack. – EDWIN HAISLET, *Boxing,* page 50

Sidestepping may be performed by shifting the body forward which is called a forward drop. This is the safest position in boxing, that is, carrying the body and head to a place directly beneath the opponent's chest. Here, with the head in close, the bands carried high and ready to perform a double stop, is an area that is absolutely safe. ... *The Drop Shift* is a further

TAO FAST FACTS

Although uncredited in its pages, boxing expert Edwin Haislet is the author of the book *Boxing: Naval Aviation Physical Training Manual*, first published in 1943. A revised version was released in 1950. The book was written as the official training manual for the United States Navy's Iowa Preflight Training School during World War II. Haislet was the school's chief boxing instructor. Much of the content was borrowed from Haislet's previous boxing books. Haislet also appears as the principal boxer in the photographs illustrating the book, representing the only published images of Haislet engaged in boxing.

Boxing: Naval Aviation Physical Training Manual was among the numerous boxing books in Bruce Lee's personal collection.

refinement of the sidestep. It is used to gain the inside or outside guard position and is also useful in infighting. Mainly a vehicle for countering, it requires timing, speed, and judgment to properly execute. It may be combined with the left jab, the straight right, the right hook, and the left hook. – EDWIN HAISLET, *Boxing*, pages 50, 67

The same step may also be performed *directly* to the right or directly back, depending on the degree of safety needed or the plan of action. The sidestep should be perfected by every boxer. – EDWIN HAISLET, *Boxing*, page 50

Footwork does not mean leg, work nor does it mean jumping around. It means moving just enough to accomplish a purpose, in order to make an opponent miss or to deliver a counter blow effectively. – EDWIN HAISLET, *Boxing*, page 30

Properly used, sidestepping is not only one of the prettiest things in boxing, but a method of escaping all kind of attacks and countering an opponent whence he least expects it. ... The art of sidestepping, as of ducking and slipping, is to move late and quick. You wait until your opponent's blow is almost on you, and then take a quick step either to the right or left, according to which suits the situation best. – NORMAN CLARK, *How to Box*, pages 99, 100

In nearly all cases, you move first the foot nearest the direction you intend to go, and in order to do the step in the quickest possible manner the body should sway over in .the direction you are going slightly before the step is made. The rear foot then follows quickly and naturally, and in sidestepping a rush, the boxer turns immediately and counters his man as he flies past him. – NORMAN CLARK, *How to Box*, page 100

When sidestepping a lead the counter is naturally quite easy, but not so after sidestepping a rush, for to counter effectively here a boxer has to keep very close to his opponent, only moving just enough to make him miss and turning extraordinarily quickly to be on him before he has flashed past. – NORMAN CLARK, *How to Box*, page 100-101

By which I mean that when an opponent rushes you, it is not so much the rush you sidestep as some particular blow he leads during the rush; indeed, if you step to the side of your opponent without catching sight of some blow to get outside, you will be very liable to run into a hook or a swing. – NORMAN CLARK, *How to Box*, page 103

Sidestepping Left: Carry the left foot sharply to the left and forward, a distance of about 18 inches, Bring up the right foot an equal distance. The step serves to swing the body to the right, bringing the left side of the body farther forward and closer to the opponent's right. For that reason, the left sidestep is not used as frequently as the one to the right. Most of the weaving and sidestepping is to the right, keeping you closer to his left and farther away from his right hand. – PHILADELPHIA JACK O'BRIEN, *Boxing*, pages 64-65

Occasionally a left sidestep is taken just to vary the direction of the weaving and even less frequently in slipping a left lead, getting inside of it in order to counter with a right. It is also used in starting a right to the body. – PHILADELPHIA JACK O'BRIEN, Boxing, page 65

Sidestepping Right: From the fundamental position bring the right foot sharply to the right and forward a distance of about 18 inches. This should carry you to the outside or the opponent's left. You will find that as you take the step to the right, the right side of your body swings forward and the left side back, so that you rotate toward the opponents left flank, and as you complete this half-circle movement you will find that your left foot is again in its normal position, namely, ahead of the right. – PHILADELPHIA JACK O'BRIEN, Boxing, page 64

If you have taken the sidestep to the right in order to avoid the opponent's left lead, you should sway your body and duck your head in the direction of the step; that is, to the right. His left will swish by over your head and in the direction of your left shoulder. Now as you wheel left toward the opponent you have his whole left flank exposed and can quickly land a right to the heart or jaw with telling effect. – PHILADELPHIA JACK O'BRIEN, Boxing, page 64

– GEORGE F. JOWETT, *How to Knock 'Em Cold*, page 25

Remember always to retain the fundamental stance. No matter what you do with that moving pedestal, your turret carrying the artillery must remain well poised, a constant threat to your foe. ... Aim always to retain the relative position of the two feet. – PHILADELPHIA JACK O'BRIEN, Boxing, pages 65-66

Rocky Marciano

Rocky Marciano was born on September 1, 1923 as Rocco Francis Marchegiano. The son of Italian immigrants, Marciano was raised in Brockton, Massachusetts. He quit school after the 10th grade.

Marciano was drafted into the Army in 1943, where he was stationed in Wales. While serving his country, he fought in and won the 1946 Amateur Armed Forces boxing tournament. he was released from the Army in March of 1946.

Marciano continued his amateur boxing career after being released from military service, compiling a record of 8-4. Rocky Marciano had one professional fight in 1947, but his professional career really didn't begin until his July 12, 1948 bout with Harry Bilazarian, which he won by knockout. He would go on to win his first 16 professional fights by knockout.

Marciano became heavyweight champion on September 23, 1952 when he knocked out Jersey Joe Walcott in the 13th round. A rematch a year later resulted in Walcott being knocked out in the first round.

Rocky Marciano would defend his heavyweight title a total of six times, winning them all, the only heavyweight defender to ever do so. He retired on April 27, 1956, at the age of 32, with a professional record of 49-0.

Shortly after retiring from boxing, Rocky Marciano collaborated with Charley Goldman on a book, Rocky Marciano's *Book of Boxing and Bodybuilding*. The book, released in 1957, is the source of four passages and illustrations in Bruce Lee's *Tao of Jeet Kune Do*.

After retiring from boxing, Rocky Marciano hosted a weekly boxing show on television. He also worked as a boxing and wrestling referee and invested in a restaurant franchise.

Rocky Marciano died on August 31, 1969, a day before his 46th birthday, in a small plane crash in Newton, Iowa.

Mobility, rapidity of footwork and speed of execution are primary qualities which, together, make for a successful epeeist. – ROGER CROSNIER, *Fencing with the Epee*, page 31

No matter how simple the strokes may be which are being practised in the lesson, or whether they are of an offensive or defensive nature, the pupil must be made to combine footwork with them. He must be made to advance or retire, before, while, or after the stroke at which he is working has been executed. In. this way he will acquire a natural sense of distance and develop great mobility. – ROGER CROSNIER, *Fencing with the Epee*, pages 30-31

Slipping

Slipping is avoiding a blow without actually moving the body out of range. It is used primarily against straight leads and counters. It calls for exact timing and judgment and to be effective must be executed so that the blow is escaped only by the smallest fraction. – EDWIN HAISLET, *Boxing*, page 49

It is possible to slip either a left or a right lead, although more often used and safer against a left lead. The outside slip, that is, to the right of an opponent's left lead, or to the left of an opponent's right lead, is the safest position, leaving the opponent unable to defend against a counter-attack. – EDWIN HAISLET, *Boxing*, page 49

– EDWIN HAISLET, *Boxing*, page 80

– GEORGE F. JOWETT, *How to Knock 'Em Cold*, page 18

Slipping is an invaluable technique, the real basis of counter-fighting upon which depends the science of attack. – EDWIN HAISLET, *Boxing*, page 49

TAO FAST FACTS

Although this book represents the first time a comprehensive listing of the work of other authors appearing in the *Tao of Jeet Kune Do* has been published, that passages in the *Tao of Jeet Kune Do* were taken from other sources was first discovered by Joe Snyder shortly after the book's release in 1975. His discoveries briefly halted the continued publication of the book; when publication resumed, an acknowledgment was added to the front page of the book crediting the original authors (those who were identified at the time). In 2011, Ohara Publications and Bruce Lee Enterprises released the *Tao of Jeet Kune Do: Expanded Edition*. Curiously, the acknowledgment for the original authors was relocated to the back of the book. Although other authors were identified since the original acknowledgement, such as Jack Dempsey and Eric Hoffer, no additions were made to the acknowledgment.

You can learn more about Joe Snyder and his discoveries related to the *Tao of Jeet Kune Do* by turning to page 174 of this book.

As the opponent leads a straight right, drop the weight back to the right leg by quickly turning the left shoulder and body to the right. – EDWIN HAISLET, *Boxing*, page 54

The right foot remains stationary but the left toe pivots inward. This movement allows the right lead to slip over the left shoulder and obtains the inside vantage position. – EDWIN HAISLET, *Boxing*, page 54

As opponent leads a straight right, step forward and sideways with the left foot, shifting the body weight over the left leg. At the same time, turn the right shoulder smartly forward. The right hip swings forward and the right leg bends slightly. The left hand is carried to the right of the chin, and the right hand is dropped to waist position ready to counter with a right uppercut to the body. – EDWIN HAISLET, *Boxing*, page 55

The inside slip on the left jab - Assume the fundamental position. As the opponent leads a left jab, shift the weight over the left leg, thus moving the body slightly to the left and forward, and bring the right shoulder quickly forward. In so doing the left jab slips over the right shoulder, the right hip rotates inward and the right knee bends slightly. The movement gains the inside position which is the best position for attack. The left hand is placed over the opponent's right. The head is moved only if the slip is too close. – EDWIN HAISLET, *Boxing*, page 54

The outside slip on a straight left lead – Assume the fundamental position. As the opponent leads a left jab, drop the weight back to a straight right leg by quickly turning the left shoulder and body to the right. The right foot remains stationary but the left toe pivots inward. The left jab will slip harmlessly over the left shoulder. Drop the left hand slightly but hold it ready to hook to opponent's body. The right hand should be held high off the left shoulder ready to counter to the chin. – EDWIN HAISLET, *Boxing*, page 55

ABOVE: Examples of various translations of the *Tao of Jeet Kune Do* that have been published over the years.

TAO FAST FACTS

> The title of the *Tao of Jeet Kune Do* was likely inspired by the 1957 book, *The Tao of Science: An Essay on Western Knowledge and Eastern Wisdom*, which Bruce Lee owned. The prefix "Tao of" was only used a handful of times for book titles before the *Tao of Jeet Kune Do* hit the market. Since the release of Bruce Lee's book, the use of the prefix has exploded, including titles such as *The Tao of Pooh, The Tao of Long Life, The Tao of Acupuncture, The Tao of the Species, The Tao of Nursing Research, the Tao of Sex*, and *the Tao of Trading*, to name just a few. The author of the latter, investor Simon Ree, fully acknowledged he drew inspiration from the *Tao of Jeet Kune Do*.

Accordingly, the head must have assistance in slipping a punch. That assistance is provided by rolling the shoulders. In fact, the shoulder roll will do all the work in shifting your head. You need not try to tilt your head even slightly. – JACK DEMPSEY, *Championship Fighting: Explosive Punching and Aggressive Defense*, page 176

ALWAYS HIT ON THE SLIP! ... You can hit harder when stepping inside a punch than when you block and counter or parry and counter. – JACK DEMPSEY, *Championship Fighting: Explosive Punching and Aggressive Defense*, pages 184, 209

Few people realize that the real key to the successful slipping of blows lies in a little movement of the heel. If it is desired to slip a lead to the left so that it passes over the right shoulder the right heel should be lifted and twisted outwards. This transfers the weight on to the left foot and twists the shoulders, setting the defender nicely to counter. – PETER MCINNES, *Tackle Boxing This Way*, page 77

To slip a lead over your left shoulder with a defensive movement to the right your left heel should be twisted in similar fashion. The weight is thus shifted on to the right foot, the right shoulder is to the rear and the defender is favourably placed to counter with a left hook. – PETER MCINNES, *Tackle Boxing This Way*, page 77

Remember that the shoulder over which it is desired to slip a blow and the heel which should be twisted are one and the same and you will not go far wrong. The defensive movement will then follow naturally, and practice will enable you to make all these moves without the necessity of thinking first. – PETER MCINNES, *Tackle Boxing This Way*, pages 77-78

Ducking

Ducking is dropping the body forward under hooks and swings to the head. It is used as a means of escaping blows allowing the boxer to remain in range for a counter-attack. Neither ducking, slipping, nor weaving should be practiced without hitting or countering. It is just as necessary to learn to duck swings as it is to slip straight punches. Both are used for the same purpose, and both are important in counter-attack. – EDWIN HAISLET, *Boxing*, pages 49-50

The Snap Back

The *Rockaway* means rocking the body away from a straight blow enough to make the opponent miss and as the opponent's arm relaxes to the body it is possible to move in with stiff counters. This is a very effective technique against a left jab and may also be used as the basis of the one-two combination blow. – EDWIN HAISLET, *Boxing*, page 51

– THOMAS INCH, *Boxing*, page 49

Rolling

Rolling means nullifying the force of a blow by moving the body with the blow. Against a straight blow, the movement is backward; against hooks, to either side; and against uppercuts, it is backward and away. – EDWIN HAISLET, *Boxing*, page 50

The Sliding Roll

The fundamental asset of the clever boxer is the sliding roll. He spots the punch coming, perhaps instinctively, and takes one step back, sweeping his head back and underneath the contemplated punch. Even if it strikes him, it will be just a grazing blow. He is now in a position to come up with several handy blows into nice openings. – BARNEY ROSS, *Fundamentals of Boxing*, page 66

TAO FAST FACTS

Bruce Lee's *Tao of Jeet Kune Do* was originally intended by Lee to be published in 1967. In a response to a reader in the August 1968 issue, *Black Belt* magazine editors attributed the delay to Bruce Lee's "meticulous workmanship".

– EDWIN HAISLET, *Boxing*, page 87

The purposes of the bob are:

1. to sink under the swing or hook with a single, perfectly-controlled movement;
2. to bring your fists in toward your opponent;
3. to maintain nearly normal punching position with legs and feet, even at the bottom of the bob; and
4. to maintain at all times your normal slipping position with head and shoulders, for defense against straight punches.

It's extremely important that you be in position to slip at any stage of the bob. Your freedom to slip will enable you to employ the "bob and weave" in attacking. ... Generally, you will not be able to counter on the actual bob, if it's a straight-down bob that's not part of a weave. But you'll be in position to make delayed counters at the bottom of the bob with whirling straight punches to the body or with outside hooks. – JACK DEMPSEY, *Championship Fighting: Explosive Punching and Aggressive Defense*, pages 185-187

The objects of the weave are:

1. to make a moving target of your head (from side to side)
2. to make your opponent uncertain about which fist you will throw when you punch
3. to make your opponent uncertain about which way you will slip if he punches at you.

– JACK DEMPSEY,
Championship Fighting: Explosive Punching and Aggressive Defense, page 187

Weaving is an advanced defensive tactic which means moving the body in, out, and around a straight lead to the bead, making the opponent miss and using the opening thus created as the start of a two-fisted counter-attack. Weaving is based on slipping and thus mastery of slipping helps to obtain skill in weaving. It is more difficult than slipping but a very effective defense maneuver once perfected. It is a circular movement of the upper trunk and head, right or left as desired. – EDWIN HAISLET, *Boxing*, page 50

– EDWIN HAISLET, *Boxing*, page 87

Weaving to the inside position – Assume the fundamental position. On a left lead slip to the outside position (Figure 64, page 56). Drop the head and upper body and move in under the extended left lead and then up to the fundamental position. The left lead now approximates the right shoulder. Carry the hands high and close to the body. As the body moves to the inside position, place the open left glove on the opponent's right. Later, counter with a left blow, then a right and a left as the weave is performed. – EDWIN HAISLET, *Boxing*, page 57

Weaving to the outside position – Assume the fundamental position. As the opponent leads a left jab slip to the inside position. Move the head and body to the right and upward in a circular movement so that the opponent's left lead approximates the left shoulder. The body is now on the outside of the opponent's lead and in fundamental position. Both hands are carried high and close. – EDWIN HAISLET, *Boxing*, page 57

Weaving is based on slipping and thus mastery of slipping helps to obtain skill in weaving. It is more difficult than slipping but a very effective defense maneuver once perfected. – EDWIN HAISLET, *Boxing*, page 50

However, the weave is rarely used by itself. Almost invariably the weave is used with the bob. ... Nearly all fighters use the bob-weave to some degree as they shuffle toward their opponents. Most of them use it mildly. However, the genuine bobber-weaver uses it fully. He uses a deep bob and a wide sway. He uses it to slide *under* his opponent's attack. He uses it to get to close quarters; the real bobber-weaver always is a hooking specialist ... It was only natural that I should, for it is the perfect attack for one to use against taller opponents. .. When you use the bob-weave, watch your rhythm. As you near an opponent, break your rhythm. ... When you step inside a punch, you counter terrifically *as you step*. – JACK DEMPSEY, *Championship Fighting: Explosive Punching and Aggressive Defense*, pages 192, 203, 208, 209

While the punches are coming, keep your eyes open every minute. The punches will not wait for you. They will strike unexpectedly, and unless you are trained well enough to be able to spot punches, they will be hard to stop. – BARNEY ROSS, *Fundamentals of Boxing*, page 66

The elbows and forearms are used for protection against body punches. Blows aimed at the head are swept aside by the hand when you are not sliding and countering. – BARNEY ROSS, *Fundamentals of Boxing*, page 66

Almost every fighter at one time or another reaches a dangerous spot where he loses some of his command and must protect himself. When this time comes, it is wise to have learned good defense. – BARNEY ROSS, *Fundamentals of Boxing*, page 66

ATTACK

Don't worry. Take things as they are. Walk when you want to walk. Sit when you want to sit.

– PAUL WIENPAHL,
The Matter of Zen: A Brief Account of Zazen,
page 75

Strangely, there is little DIRECT attack in boxing. Practically all offensive action is INDIRECT, coming after a feint or taking the form of counter-blows after an opponent's attack is foiled or spent. ... The first method requires manœuvre, feinting and drawing an opponent together with a scientific plan. – PETER MCINNES *Tackle Boxing This Way*, pages 38-39, 38

Limitations of space prevent us from giving a detailed analysis of tempo, but we may establish without dissecting examples that there are two basic moments for attack:

1. When our own will decides the time of attack.
2. When the moment of attack depends upon the opponent's movement or the failure of his attention.

– JOHN KARDOSS, *Sabre Fencing: History, Theory, Practice*, page 59

If the fencer *concentrates* sufficiently, senses the moment to attack and *acts upon it swiftly and decisively*, the prospects of success are greatly enhanced. – JOHN KARDOSS, *Sabre Fencing: History, Theory, Practice*, page 75

Direct attacks with point or edge should naturally be launched when the opponent's sabre and swordhand are farthest from the part of the target which it is intended to hit. Ideally, they should be made when the opponent's hand is moving away from the line into which one intends to attack, to gain maximum time and distance for the attack over the defence. – CHARLES LOUIS DE BEAUMONT, *Fencing: Ancient Art and Modern Sport*, page 155

The Psychophysical Process of the Attack

The psychophysical process on analysis is found to consist of three phases:

1. *Survey.* It is entirely mental and could be sub-divided into two parts:
   a. *Definable.* For instance, the estimation of the distance between the opponents. What guard invitation or line position the adversary has taken.
   b. *Instinctive.* Whether the opponent will attack or retire, etc.
2. *Decision.* This is also a mental function, but the nerves and muscles are alerted in preparation for execution. During this phase the fencer decides how to attack. For example, should it be from a short distance with a direct attack or, should he, from a long distance, use a compound attack? Alternatively, he could attack with a second intention or in any other way he considers will be successful.
3. *Action.* The brain has given the muscles the order which they now execute, but even in the execution the fencer has to be prepared for the possibility of an intra - attack, a stop thrust, or a time cut. Thus, it is both essential and obvious that the mental and physical alertness, be maintained throughout the bout. – JOHN KARDOSS, *Sabre Fencing: History, Theory, Practice*, page 74-75

Primary and Secondary Attack

Various kinds of attack are here divided into, and briefly treated under, the following headings:

Primary, initiated by oneself with the intention of scoring by *pace, fraud, or force,* and which are therefore subdivided into:

1. Simple, made on the lunge, the object of which is by superior neatness and quickness to hit the opponent before he can parry, without any attempt to disguise the direction of the attack.
2. Feints, the purpose of which is to induce your opponent, by some preliminary movement of the hand, to think that you are going to hit him in one particular line, so that, on his offering a parry to protect that tine, you may deceive it and be free to complete the attack by lunging in another line; and-
3. Force, by which, finding your opponent covered, you attack his blade with sufficient vigour to turn it aside and make an opening for your point on the lunge; or by which, on some movement of his blade in the direction of one line, you encircle it with yours, and, carrying it off in an opposite line, urge your point home with strong opposition.

– H. A. COLMORE DUNN, *Fencing,* pages 61-62

Secondary, intended to out-manoeuvre or retaliate upon attacks initiated by the opponent in one or other of their different stages, and therefore subdivided into:

1. Attacks on the preparation, to arrest his movements before he matures his plans.
2. Attacks on the development, principally "time" attacks, whereby, having anticipated in what line your opponent's attack will be delivered, you intercept his blade as he gives in his attack, and go to meet it by straightening your arm and delivering in the point with a strong opposition on the lunge or half lunge, according to the distance between you; and
3. Attacks on the completion, when the opponent has brought himself within thrusting range on his lunge. These are called "ripostes," and are made from the position of the parry, whatever it may be, which has been used to stop the opponent's primary attack. As the point is delivered in while the opponent is extended on the lunge or in act to recover, they are, almost without exception, unaccompanied by any movement of the foot.

– H. A. COLMORE DUNN, *Fencing,* page 62

Decoy, or false attacks, not made with the intention of hitting the opponent, but only to lure him on, say, to attack you in some line, in order that, when he does so, you may, for instance, disconcert him by an emphatic parry, and lead up to an effective return. These attacks are, therefore, not made on the lunge, as a slight movement of the foot (if any) is all that is needed.
– H. A. COLMORE DUNN, *Fencing,* page 62

At sabre, as for any other weapon, a hit is brought about by using the stroke which corresponds to that of the opponent, taking advantage of the opportunity to deliver it and timing its execution correctly. – ROGER CROSNIER, *Fencing with the Sabre*, page 182

Against an opponent who opens up his target or makes wild actions, counter-timing into his actions or stop thrusting into his exposed arm or body as he moves forward are particularly effective. – EDITORS OF SPORTS ILLUSTRATED, *Sports Illustrated Book of Fencing*, page 45

But a sabreur who is observant will realize when he is found out. He will not carry on, stubbornly, with strokes which are no longer the right ones. So many fencers put down the failure of an offensive stroke to lack of speed, rather than to the incorrect choice of the stroke. – ROGER CROSNIER, *Fencing with the Sabre*, page 183

Each fencer, therefore, has to be studied from the several angles of style, tactics, and cadence, before a definite plan of action, involving a choice of strokes, is finally decided upon. – ROGER CROSNIER, *Fencing with the Sabre*, page 183

Fencers can be placed into two main categories, i.e. the 'mechanical' fencers and the 'intellectual' fencers. Advice can be more easily given against the former, whose fencing technique and fighting tactics are the result of the mechanical repetition of strokes bred of a lesson which was purely automatic, and lacking an intelligent explanation of the WHY, the HOW and the WHEN. Their fencing follows a similar pattern in each successive encounter. – ROGER CROSNIER, *Fencing with the Sabre*, page 185

The *intellectual* fencer, who has technique as well as the ability to analyse the game, is a different proposition. Probably, aware that he may be under observation, he will change his tactics as often as possible. His desire to deal with his opponents by using the correct strokes, will mean variations in his method of approach. … It must be apparent to the student, now, that the sabreur's decision to use any particular stroke must be influenced by his opponent's technique and method of fighting. – ROGER CROSNIER, *Fencing with the Sabre*, page 185

The on-guard position, the parries, the simple attacks, the advance and retreat, the lunge and the recovery must all be learned beyond the need of giving them more than passing attention so that concentration on the adversary, his play, and your solution of his attack and defense need not be diverted. Freedom of movement, balance, and confidence accompany a practised certainty of the fundamental movements. – JULIO MARTINEZ CASTELLÓ, *Theory and Practice of Fencing*, page 54

TAO FAST FACTS

When editor Gilbert Johnson began the assignment of editing the *Tao of Jeet Kune Do*, he was faced with a challenging task. Johnson was given seven volumes of Bruce Lee's written notes. His mission was to distill the essence of those seven volumes into one, cohesive book. "Between major blocks of copy were unnumbered pages of unused paper, each headed by simple titles," Johnson told *Black Belt* magazine in 1975. "Sometimes he wrote introspectively, asking questions of himself."

The important thing is to study the adversary's weakness and strength, and to take advantage of the former while avoiding the latter. If this is done, there is a great possibility of success. – JULIO MARTINEZ CASTELLÓ, *Theory and Practice of Fencing*, page 60-61

If the opponent has a good hand for parrying, the attacks should be preceded by a beat, press or some attack on the blade that might disorganize the functioning of the parry. – JULIO MARTINEZ CASTELLÓ, *Theory and Practice of Fencing*, page 60

All attacking movements must therefore be made as small as possible, that is with the least deviation of the blade necessary to induce the opponent to react. Caution demands that attacks should, whenever possible, be completed covered. – CHARLES LOUIS DE BEAUMONT, *Fencing: Ancient Art and Modern Sport*, page 119

> It will be recalled that, when studying the various weapons, we found that at fencing the form of an attack is generally dictated by the form of defence used by the opponent against it. In other words, between opponents of approximately the same standard, an attack can rarely be successful unless it deceives, or outwits, the defence. For example, an attack made with a circular movement, such as a double, cannot succeed if the defender meets it with a simple or lateral movement in his parry. It is therefore essential correctly to anticipate an opponent's reaction if an attack is to succeed. – CHARLES LOUIS DE BEAUMONT, *Fencing: Ancient Art and Modern Sport*, page 198
>
> His *final* choice of stroke should be based on the observation of his opponent's reactions, habits, and preferences. – ROGER CROSNIER, *Fencing with the Epee*, page 48

It is dangerous for the epeeist to launch himself into complicated compound attacks where there are several periods of fencing-time in which an opponent can land a stop-hit. – ROGER CROSNIER, *Fencing with the Epee*, page 49

The more the attack is complicated, the more chance there is of an unpremeditated counter-offensive movement being executed out of hand. This being the case, the attack proper must remain simple, whatever form the preparation may have taken. – ROGER CROSNIER, *Fencing with the Epee*, page 49

Preparation of Attack

This is due, mainly, to the need to gain time and distance on an adversary whose measure keeps him out of range of attacks delivered with a lunge. The gaining of distance has to be covered up by some blade action which will, momentarily, distract the opponent's attention. Thus, in most cases, two types of preparations are used simultaneously. They are either an attack on the blade or a taking of the blade *(prise de fer)*, executed at the same time as a step forward. By deflecting, or taking the blade while stepping forward, the possibility of a successful stop-hit from the opponent has been limited. – ROGER CROSNIER, *Fencing with the Sabre*, page 139

A preparation of attack is the action taken by a fencer to make an opening for his attack. It usually consists in making some movement which will either *deflect the opponent's blade, or obtain a desired reaction from it, but it may consist merely of a change of distance.* – CHARLES LOUIS DE BEAUMONT, *Fencing: Ancient Art and Modern Sport*, page 92

An aggressive opponent can often be drawn within distance by a series of steps back which are progressively shortened; a wary opponent can sometimes be manoeuvred into the same position by a series of steps forward and backward of varying length. – CHARLES LOUIS DE BEAUMONT, *Fencing: Ancient Art and Modern Sport*, page 132

At any weapon, fencers resort to preparations of attacks in an attempt to obtain some form of reaction from their opponent, when feints have failed to fulfil that purpose. – ROGER CROSNIER, *Fencing with the Sabre*, page 139

Feints preceded by beats or takings of the blade can upset the defender's confidence and force him to move to a defensive action against his will and be deceived. – ROGER CROSNIER, *Fencing with the Sabre*, page 140

Beats, change-beats, froissements, engagements and changes of engagement will be used. These will have as object either to fix the opponent's hand and blade in a particular line, which will cause him to contract and slow down his reactions or, on the contrary to make him react by the execution of a parry sooner, or with less control, than he intended. Whatever may be the reaction of the opponent a result will have been obtained which may pave the way for a successful simple attack. – ROGER CROSNIER, *Fencing with the Electric Foil*, page 50

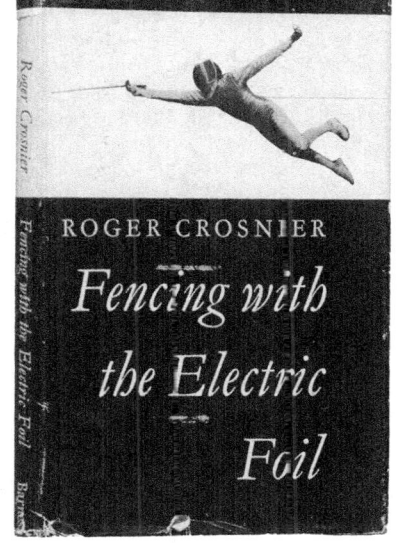

By deflecting, or taking the blade while stepping forward, the possibility of a successful stop-hit from the opponent has been limited. – ROGER CROSNIER, *Fencing with the Sabre*, page 139

Beats on the blade, pressures, expulsions, binds, envelopments, and glides -- all these make up the attacks on the blade. Their purpose is to make an opening for the attack by forcing the opponent's point out of line. In addition, these attacks also make it difficult for the adversary to parry by confusing his expectancy of where to parry. – JULIO MARTINEZ CASTELLÓ, *Theory and Practice of Fencing*, page 35

When a step forward and an action on the blade are made simultaneously, they are known as a compound preparation. ... Its success depends on perfect coordination of hand and feet. Much time must be given to the practice of this type of action, as well as to the different variations of blade movements which can be fitted into the footwork. – ROGER CROSNIER, *Fencing with the Sabre*, page 147

It must not be forgotten that, whether the lunge or the fleche is used after the step forward, the possibility that the opponent may stop-hit is always present. It is essential, therefore, that the sabreur should pay particular attention to his balance and foot control, so that he can halt his movement forward with the least possible effort. Short, rapid steps will ensure this, as his centre of gravity is less likely to be shifted than if he were to make long and rushed steps. He must not hurl himself at his opponent but gain and maintain distance in a calm and precise manner. – ROGER CROSNIER, *Fencing with the Sabre*, page 147

There is no doubt that, too often repeated, the attack on the blade will draw a stop-hit rather than a parry. – ROGER CROSNIER, *Fencing with the Epee*, page 57

In order to shorten the period of vulnerability as much as possible, the blade movements which constitute the attack should be made as the step forward is completed, that is to say as the rear foot reaches the ground, which is the first moment when the attacker is ready to make his lunge. – CHARLES LOUIS DE BEAUMONT, *Fencing: Ancient Art and Modern Sport*, page 101

By keeping in mind that preparation and attack are two separate movements, the fencer will be able to provide for, and take precautions against, the possible counter-attack. – ROGER CROSNIER, *Fencing with the Foil*, page 169

Simple Attacks

Simple Ripostes consist of single blade movements which are either direct or indirect. A *Direct Riposte* is one made from the position in which the parry was made to the opponent's target by the most direct route. – CHARLES LOUIS DE BEAUMONT, *Teach Yourself Fencing*, page 48

A *direct thrust* is more likely to be successful if it is made *as the line is opening* rather than when it is being closed. – CHARLES LOUIS DE BEAUMONT, *Fencing: Ancient Art and Modern Sport*, page 52

TAO FAST FACTS

Bruce Lee's widow, Linda Lee, had this to say about the release of the *Tao of Jeet Kune Do* when interviewed by Marlin Johnson in the November 1975 issue of *Black Belt* magazine: "The main thing is that Bruce didn't want it to be a 'how to' book, one that pretended to teach the martial arts in 10 easy lessons. The purpose of the book is to open a lot of questions and to let the person answer the questions for himself, to let him get to know himself."

When deceiving your opponent's blade, offensive blade actions are usually made up of semicircular or circular movements. – Maxwell R. Garret, *Fencing Instructor's Guide (Athletic Institute Series)*, page 59

The disengagement is an indirect simple attack. It consists of passing the point of the sword from the line of engagement into the opposite line. ... Fundamentally, the disengagement is attacking from a closed line into an open one, but, as we have explained above, the success of such a move is problematic. Why? ... To seize the opportunity, in other words to time this movement of sword and arm crossing from left to right, or right to left, for the execution of the attack, means that for a moment the defence is moving in an opposite direction to that of the attack. The defence has to recover and return to the line that is being threatened. The attacker is moving slightly ahead of the defence and has, therefore, a chance of getting there first. The attacker must initiate his disengagement whenever he feels the pressure on his sword. It is while the opponent's arm is travelling across that he must start his offensive action. If the covering up is terminated, then he is again attacking from a closed line into an open line and under adverse conditions. ... A similar sense of timing can be obtained on a fencer who is continually making an absence of blade and returning to the engagement. As he is returning to this latter position (moving across) the disengagement can be attempted. – ROGER CROSNIER, *Fencing with the Foil*, pages 76, 79, 80

For instance, it is noticeable that when going from a high to a low line, or a low to a high line, the disengagement with the edge is favoured, while going from right to left, or left to right, of the body, the attacks are done by cutting-over. – ROGER CROSNIER, *Fencing with the Sabre*, page 62

Here are a few examples of simple attacks, and the movements on the opponent's part which they must time.

1. Straight-thrust on:
   (a) the absence of blade;
   (b) the engagement;
   (c) the change of engagement;
   (d) the step forward with and without the above.
2. Straight-thrust on all the above, with opposition.
3. The disengagement and cut-over in the high, and also low line on:
   (a) the engagement;
   (b) the beat;
   (c) the change of engagement;
   (d) the step forward with an engagement;
   (e) the first three executed with a step forward.

– ROGER CROSNIER, *Fencing with the Electric Foil*, page 49

To counter-disengage is to deceive the opponent's change of engagement, or to deceive his attempt to parry with a counter-parry (Circular parry, Elementary Defence). ... The first thing to be noticed is that, contrary to the simple disengagement and the cut-over, it does not end in the line opposite to that of the engagement, but in the same line. Next, that it does not deceive a lateral opposition, but a circular movement of the opponent's blade. – ROGER CROSNIER, *Fencing with the Foil*, page 85

The other was that, prior to the electric foil, fencers were notoriously weak in low-line defence. Low parries were not taught, or practised, nearly enough. It was not surprising that, attacks being directed in that area more frequently, there should result a greater number of low-line hits. – ROGER CROSNIER, *Fencing with the Electric Foil*, page 44

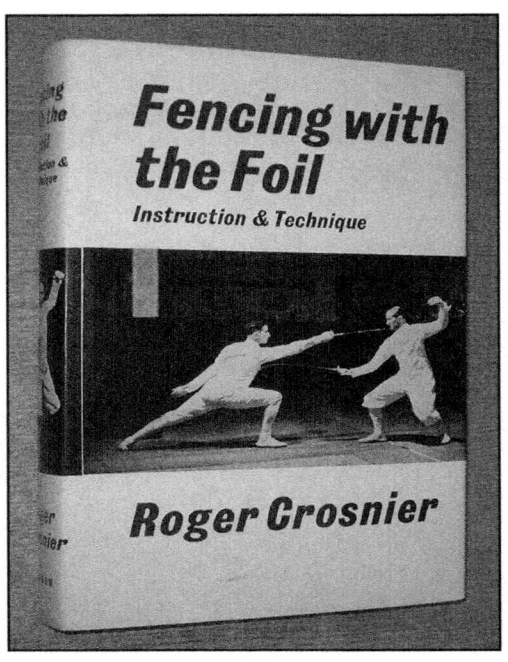

If we wish to make use of any form of attack, the opponent's habits and preferences must be observed and found out. This is a principle which will often be repeated. In the case of each of the simple attacks, direct or indirect, success lies in their correct selection. The attack must correspond to whatever movement is being, or may be, made by the adversary. It is always dangerous to attack with the first thing that comes to one's mind as it may not correspond to the defence and has, then, little chance of being successful. – ROGER CROSNIER, *Fencing with the Foil*, page 86

The success of a simple attack depends on the correct timing of the movement, which must naturally be related to the cadence of the opponent's movements if it is not to be caught up in them. – CHARLES LOUIS DE BEAUMONT, *Fencing: Ancient Art and Modern Sport*, page 56

Simple attacks started within reaching distance of the adversary should land, if properly made, provided that the adversary does not supplement the parry by retreating. The reason for this is that the one who attacks takes the initiative, and although the distance followed by the parry is a little shorter than the distance which the point of the attacking blade must travel, still the man on the defense is at a slight disadvantage. – JULIO MARTINEZ CASTELLÓ, *Theory and Practice of Fencing*, page 34

To ensure the success of the straight-thrust, the straightening of the arm and the lunge must be so well coordinated that they appear to be one movement, but the fencer who has practised the development assiduously can arrive at a state of near perfection if he has paid particular attention to the development of a continual condition of relaxation. The attack will then flow forward, all the speed being derived from the extension of the rear leg and the dropping of the rear arm. Any tension when awaiting the opportunity to launch the attack will only give a short and jerky movement. It is also more than likely that this tenseness, the result of over-eagerness to get off one's mark quickly, will cause one to move too soon, or to give some indication of one's intentions. – ROGER CROSNIER, *Fencing with the Foil*, page 75

Their acceleration can be increased by sheer practice and will power. Mechanical repetition is at the basis of this method. One can copy fencers from certain countries and lunge two or three hundred times per day, faster and faster each time. – ROGER CROSNIER, *Fencing with the Electric Foil*, page 48

For if you don't strike when you should, your opponent will. Nothing being more dangerous than a half-hearted attack, let your legs fly, concerning yourself only with the correct and most determined execution of your offensive. – ALDO NADI, *On Fencing*, page 243

As soon as you begin reducing your disadvantage you should look as boldly aggressive as a beast of prey-without becoming reckless-in order to bring pressure at once upon the adversary's morale. ... The great fencer follows Napoleon's advice. To exploit this doctrine to the utmost he should possess the eye of an eagle, the cunning of a fox, the agility and alertness of a cat, the courage, aggressiveness and fierceness of a black panther, the striking power of a cobra, and the resistance of a mongoose. Sissy game! – ALDO NADI, *On Fencing*, pages 261, 265

While much speed will be gained through this method of training, the success of simple attacks will not be assured against every opponent. It is more than certain that adversaries of equal, or superior, speed in defence will be met. Other means will have to be devised to gain time, if not speed. – ROGER CROSNIER, *Fencing with the Electric Foil*, page 50

TAO FAST FACTS

A timeline of the *Tao of Jeet Kune Do*, as seen through mentions in *Black Belt* magazine:

- January 1968 issue - *Black Belt* editors tell reader Paul Francis that the *Tao of Jeet Kune Do* is due to be published shortly; appears to be the first mention of the name of the book in the pages of *Black Belt*
- May 1968 issue - Reader Andy Pena inquires requests notification for when the *Tao of Jeet Kune Do* will be published; says he and 15 friends are anxiously waiting
- June 1968 issue - in response to reader Paul Hunter, *Black Belt* editors report that the *Tao of Jeet Kune Do* will be completed by June or July of 1968
- August 1968 issue - *Black Belt* editors tell reader Phil Davis that the *Tao of Jeet Kune Do* has been delayed but will be completed soon
- November 1970 issue - Bruce Lee suspends work on the *Tao of Jeet Kune Do*
- December 1970 issue - *Black Belt* editors write: "Unfortunately, Bruce got sidetracked from writing it, and even though it was almost completed, he has decided not to have it published."
- February 1971 issue - Martial artists launch a letter-writing campaign to convince Lee to reconsider publishing the book
- July 20, 1973 - Bruce Lee dies in Hong Kong
- October 1975 issue - The staff of Black Belt, under the leadership of Gilbert Johnson, complete work on *Tao of Jeet Kune Do*; the first ad for the book is run

Compound Attacks

Between fencers of equal speed and technique, and whose judgment of distance is maintained correctly, the simple attack is extremely difficult to bring off. ... He has to solve the problem of making up his disadvantage in distance, and simultaneously gain time. – ROGER CROSNIER, *Fencing with the Foil*, page 129

These are attacks of more than one action, and may be a feint of a simple attack, an attack on the blade, etc., followed immediately by the real attack. – JULIO MARTINEZ CASTELLÓ, *Theory and Practice of Fencing*, pages 34-35

Basically, compound attacks are a combination of the four forms of simple attack – the straight thrust, the simple disengagement, the cut-over, and the counter-disengagement. – CHARLES LOUIS DE BEAUMONT, *Fencing: Ancient Art and Modern Sport*, page 60

The complexity of the compound attack used is therefore directly related to the opponent's ability to parry the offensive movements made. ... When choosing the strokes to be used in a compound attack, success will depend on a correct anticipation of the form of parry-lateral or circular-which the opponent will make in answer to the feint. ... It is thus essential to gain some idea of the opponent's likely reaction before an attack is chosen. – CHARLES LOUIS DE BEAUMONT, *Fencing: Ancient Art and Modern Sport*, pages 58-60, 60

> Firstly, feints must be made sufficiently deep, that is with the attacker's point sufficiently close to the defender's target, to impress the latter and draw a reaction from him. Secondly, the least number of feints necessary to achieve success should be employed. – CHARLES LOUIS DE BEAUMONT, *Fencing: Ancient Art and Modern Sport*, page 62
>
> It must be evident that the more complicated the form of the compound attack, the less chance it has of being successful, and that it is dangerous to attempt attacks composed of more than two feints. – ROGER CROSNIER, *Fencing with the Foil*, page 131

Many students will be surprised at our use of the term "simple" in relationship to compound attacks. We have not forgotten our theory but wish to make a difference between complicated compound attacks and those comprising just one feint. ... They will have all the more chance of success if they are delivered on the opponent's preparation, in particular on the step forward. – ROGER CROSNIER, *Fencing with the Electric Foil*, page 51

Naturally, compound attacks are used against fencers whose defence is strong enough to deal with simple attacks. But even the former may be of no avail if they are badly timed, or if a favourable opportunity is not seized. – ROGER CROSNIER, *Fencing with the Sabre*, page 109

Many compound attacks fail because the attacker forgets that he must *regulate the speed of his feints* in such a way that they are just moving ahead of the defensive movement. ... If finding an opponent's cadence is essential, it is also very necessary to find his preferences for certain parries. – ROGER CROSNIER, *Fencing with the Foil*, pages 131-132

Roger Crosnier: Maître d'Armes

Roger Leon Lucien Crosnier was born in London, England on January 20, 1908. Crosnier was the son of Eugénie Désirée Marguerite Guedet and Professor Georges François Léon Crosnier, an accomplished fencer and instructor at the Scottish Fencing Club in Edinburgh and a finalist in the 1927 French Sabre Championship.

Roger Crosnier was raised in Scotland, where he learned to fence under his father's tutelage. Upon leaving school, he followed in his father's footsteps and became a fencing Instructor. Crosnier also distinguished himself as a competitor, defeating the Olympic and World Champion of 1924 and the German and French champions of 1928. Crosnier was three-time British Open fencing champion and five-time runner-up in the French Professional Championships. For his performance, he was awarded a special medal by the French Fencing Federation. He was also a graduate of both the British and French Academy of Arms.

Crosnier moved to France at some point in the 1920s and served with the French Army during the occupation of the Rhineland. While in France, he met his future wife, Marie Madeleine Yvonne Voisin. They were married on August 29, 1932 in Indre-et-Loire, Centre-Val de Loire, France.

Roger Crosnier again served in the French Army during World War II and was part of the French Resistance in Centre-Val de Loire. After the war, he founded the Salle Crosnier in Paris. During the 1940s, he relocated to England to teach fencing, but was recalled to France to coach the French Olympic fencing team in 1948.

After the 1948 Olympics, Roger Crosnier returned to London with his wife and son. A grant from the Ministry of Education to the British Amateur Fencing Association enabled the association to appoint Professor Crosnier to the position of national coach in January 1949. In addition to authoring the *National Training Method* to qualify amateur coaches, Professor Crosnier set about traveling through Great Britain to generate interest in the sport and scout for talent. The result of his "pioneering" efforts was a renewed interest in the sport of fencing. Due in great measure to his efforts, the number of fencing clubs and associations went from 100 in 1936 to 256 in 1950.

In 1949, fencing master Charles Louis de Beaumont was inspired to resurrect a defunct medieval fencing guild called the London Masters of Defence, founded in 1540 by King Henry VIII. Beaumont charged Professor Roger Crosnier with the task. Assisted by Professor Leon Paul and Mr. J. D. Aylward, the guild was re-established as the British Academy of Fencing.

In 1950, Professor Crosnier was appointed National Fencing Coach for Great Britain and vowed to raise British national fencing to continental standards in five years. He served in that capacity until 1956. He also coached the British Olympic fencing team in 1952.

By this point in his career, Roger Crosnier had cemented his reputation as a premier fencer. The *South Wales Echo and Express* called him one of the top three living swordsmen in the world. He was highly in demand as a fencing instructor, and many countries requested his services. In 1965, he traveled to Canada to train fencing coaches for the National Fitness Council.

Professor Crosnier also authored a number of important books on fencing, including *Fencing with the Foil*, *Fencing with the Epée*, *Fencing with the Electric Foil*, and *Fencing with the Sabre*. The books were hugely influential to Bruce Lee. Collectively, these books are the true source of 124 passages and illustrations in the *Tao of Jeet Kune Do*.

Crosnier mentored a number of fencers who went on to become champions and successful fencers themselves, such as Australian champion John Fethers, who served as Scottish National Coach and later Australian National Coach, and British champion Bob Anderson, who would later become the top sword choreographer in Hollywood, his choreography seen in such classics as *Star Wars*, *The Highlander*, and *Princess Bride*.

Former student Gerald O. Pring, the coach of the Trinity College fencing team in Dublin, Ireland, attributed his own success to Professor Crosnier, saying: "A fencer is only as good as his instructor."

Roger Crosnier spent his final years in his French home in the Chinon community in Indre-et-Loire, Centre-Val de Loire, France, where he died on December 24, 1981 at the age of 73. After his death, the Roger Crosnier Memorial Trophy was established by the

Scottish Amateur Fencing Union to recognize fencing coaches who make a substantial contribution to fencing in Scotland.
"He fenced a way that made you think twice," said fencing expert Rudi van Oeveren, "but it was impregnated with elegance and lightness."

"There is no conclusion to a fencing method, as even the best of masters continue to learn, during the course of his everyday work, some little point which adds to his experience."

Counterattack

– EDWIN HAISLET, *Boxing*, page 80

– EDWIN HAISLET, *Boxing*, pages 90-91

– EDWIN HAISLET, *Boxing*, page 80

– THOMAS INCH, *Boxing*, pages 142, 141

Counter fighting is desirable because it is safer to you and more damaging to your opponent. ... Often when you do succeed in landing excellent punches, they do little damage because your opponent is moving in the same direction and his going with the punches removes their sting even as in base, ball a fielder handles a liner with ease by giving with the catch when the hard hit ball strikes his glove. In boxing it is called "rolling the punch" when a boxer, not having time to avoid being hit, deliberately moves with the punch when it hits him. – FRANK GILMER, *Push Yourself: A Book for Amateur Boxers and Boxing Fans*, page 27

WHO WROTE THE TAO?

– JOHNSON SMITH & COMPANY, *The Art of Sparring and Boxing*, pages 23, 25, 10, 11, 15

Tao of Jeet Kune Do - A Tale of Multiple Covers

Fishkill, New York Jeet Kune Do instructor Richard Torres is mentioned multiple times throughout this book, and with good reason – he possesses an unparalleled library and archive of historical artifacts relating to Bruce Lee and Jeet Kune Do. Torres dived into his archives to provide this review of the various editions of the *Tao of Jeet Kune Do*.

October 1975 – The first edition of the *Tao of Jeet Kune Do* book. The picture seems inspired by a Beatle album. The cover was enhanced for the future versions. The first cover is more bland. There is no acknowledgement of other author contributions on the first page.

December 1975 – The hardbound version was released. It was beautifully done with a brown leatherette and gold letter. A dustcover was included which resembled the soft cover.

January 2007 – a limited hardbound edition was released. It came with a black slipcase and the book itself had a black hard-cloth cover. Unlike the original hardcover, there was no Jeet Kune Do symbol or Bruce Lee autograph on the cover or slipcase. This limited-edition copy came with a certificate of authenticity and was autographed by Linda Lee and Shannon Lee.

November 2011 – *Tao of Jeet Kune Do: The Expanded Edition* was released. The book was completely revamped for easier reading and comprehension of the material. A few copies of the expanded edition came with a Shannon Lee autograph, a numbered certificate of authenticity, and a glossy photograph of Bruce Lee as on the cover.

November 2019 – Hardcover edition of the deluxe version of the *Tao of Jeet Kune Do*. Encased in a hard-shell sleeve with red and gold embossed foil of the Jeet Kune Do symbol. The cover has gold lettering as well as an inlayed picture of Bruce Lee. Pages are all heavy paper with gold trimmed edges and a red silk ribbon bookmark.

Invitations - These are actions *provoking* the adversary to make an attack. Instead of making a false attack, the absence of the blade, change of engagement, beat on the blade, or any attack on the blade is used. The purpose is the same as that of the false attack-i.e., to parry the attack of the adversary followed by an immediate return or to make a counter-attack. Double thrust or double touch is the result of two correct simultaneous attacks. In foil fencing the double touch does not count and must be avoided. – JULIO MARTINEZ CASTELLÓ, *Theory and Practice of Fencing*, page 43

You must accomplish both; avoid being hit; succeed in hitting your opponent while he is still *out of position* as a result of missing you. … Learning the counterpunches, therefore, is obviously the most important part of learning how to box. To be able to do them in a fight you must be able to act *automatically* and *instantaneously*. You must have practiced each counterpunch so faithfully that when the appropriate situation presents itself you will counter properly without thinking and without previous planning. There is no substitute for the hard work and training involved. It must be done correctly, enthusiastically, and endlessly while you are a boxer. Once you do your countering automatically during your match your mind can devote itself to your broad plan of battle. – FRANK GILMER, *Push Yourself: A Book for Amateur Boxers and Boxing Fans*, pages 27-28, 28

In connection with the avoidance of your opponent's lead which is the first part of counter-fighting, there are three ways to avoid his punch. First, you can make his punch miss you altogether by slipping it, pulling away from it or ducking it. If it is a swing, you can also pull inside it. Second, if it is a straight punch you can guard or deflect it by turning its direction away from you causing it to miss and spend itself. Third, you can block the punch with a part of your body that can stand this punishment. You will notice in the pages to come that few blocks are recommended. It is much harder on your opponent and easier on you to make him miss altogether. – FRANK GILMER, *Push Yourself: A Book for Amateur Boxers and Boxing Fans*, page 28

First, then, let us talk about counters which are preceded by a right-hand guard, always bearing in mind that anticipation is the secret of success at the art, and that therefore it is preferable to feint your man into making a lead rather than to wait for him to do so. – PETER MCINNES, *Tackle Boxing This Way*, page 55

A counter-offensive movement is an offensive action delivered on the opponent's attack in such a way that it gains a period of fencing time on it. – ROGER CROSNIER, *Fencing with the Foil*, page 157

Counters are a simple combination of the most elementary defensive and offensive moves. To each there are two separate and distinct movements; first, avoidance of the opponent's lead by defensive means, and secondly deliverance of the counter-hit. The beauty of the science lies in the fact that its principle is so essentially simple. Yet for all its simplicity this is the most effective craft in all boxing. – PETER MCINNES, *Tackle Boxing This Way*, page 55

Samples

NUMBER	LEAD	COUNTER
1	Left Jab	Draw back, then left jab
2	Left Jab	Slip outside, left jab
3	Left swing	Guard with right forearm, left jab
4	Left Jab	Push aside lead with right, then left uppercut to body
5	Right swing or hook	Beat opponent to the punch with left jab
6	Left Jab	Right hand body blow
7	Left Jab	Right cross counter
8	Left Swing	Beat opponent to the punch with right cross
9	Right Cross	Duck under lead, right hand body blow
10	Right Cross or Swing	Guard with left forearm, right cross

– FRANK GILMER, *Push Yourself: A Book for Amateur Boxers and Boxing Fans*, page 82

When you first practice these counterpunches be concerned only with doing them in good form. Later you will work for speed and to a limited extent, punch, although you must always remember that your sparring partner is leading to you in an effort to help you and is necessarily open to the jolt you are countering with and must take the punishment involved. – FRANK GILMER, *Push Yourself: A Book for Amateur Boxers and Boxing Fans*, page 29

Having succeeded in making him miss and in jarring him with a well-placed counterpunch, what then? The answer is that you should follow up by pouring in well directed punches to your opponent's head and body until he goes down, clinches or succeeds in fighting back on even terms. – FRANK GILMER, *Push Yourself: A Book for Amateur Boxers and Boxing Fans*, page 50

Counter-Attack means fore-knowledge of specific openings which will result from attack by the opponent. The counter-attack is not a defensive action but a method of using an opponent's offense as a means to the successful completion of one's own attack. – EDWIN HAISLET, *Boxing*, page 72

Tao of Jeet Kune Do - Personal Impacts

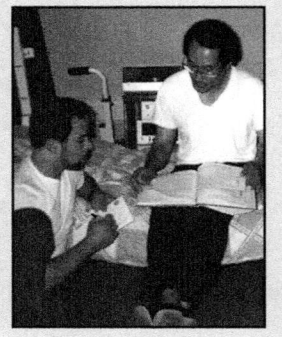

I received my *Tao of Jeet Kune Do* book back in 1975, when it was offered in *Black Belt Magazine*. Before the book even hit the stores, I was receiving my copy in the mail for $6.95. The book totally changed the way I looked at martial arts from punching, kicking, and the overall philosophy of not clinging to styles.

When training in Jeet Kune Do with my instructor, Sifu Ted Wong, the mental and the physical of the art all came together. Here is a picture of Sifu Ted Wong and I in Holland in 1995, going over the *Tao of Jeet Kune Do*. He pointed out to me what he thought was important in this book. I took notes.

To this day, I still read the *Tao* and something new always appears to me with better understanding.

Richard Torres
Jeet Kune Do Martial Arts Institute, Upstate New York

The counter-attack is an advanced phase of offense. It calls for the greatest skill, the most perfect planning, and the most delicate execution of all boxing techniques. It uses as tools all the main techniques of boxing, blocking, guarding, parrying, slipping, weaving, ducking, sidestepping, feinting, drawing, and shifting. It uses all phases of hitting, crisp, straight blows, clean hooks, and short uppercuts. Besides a mastery of technique, the counter-attack requires exact timing, unerring judgment, cool, calculating poise. It means careful thought, daring execution, and sure control. It is the greatest art in boxing, the art of the champion. – EDWIN HAISLET, *Boxing*, page 72

There are numerous counters which may be used for every lead, but for each particular occasion there is one counter which should be used. Such a counter is that one most effective for the particular situation at hand. Action must be instantaneous, and where there is a wide choice of action, instant action is difficult if not impossible unless the right action has been previously conditioned. Conditioning then becomes the keystone of the counter-attack. – EDWIN HAISLET, *Boxing*, page 72

Conditioning is a process whereby a specific stimulus will cause a specific reaction. A repeated stimulus eventually creates an action pattern in the nervous system. Once this pattern is established the mere presence of the stimulus will cause a specific action. Such action is instantaneous and almost unconscious which is necessary for effective countering. In boxing, conditioned action should be the result of intense and concentrated practice of planned action patterns in response to every lead. – EDWIN HAISLET, *Boxing*, page 72

Such action should be practiced slowly for hours, days, weeks, always in response to certain leads. Finally, the lead itself will automatically bring the right counter. – EDWIN HAISLET, *Boxing*, pages 72-73

Boxing should be done with the head, not with the hands. It is true that during the time of actual boxing one does not think of how to box but rather of the weakness or strength of the opponent, of possible openings and opportunities. Boxing will never reach the stage of a true art unless performance of skill is made automatic and the cortex freed to think and to associate, to make plans and to judge. The higher nerve centers always retain control and will act when necessary. It is like pressing a button to start or stop a machine. – EDWIN HAISLET, *Boxing*, page 73

In a consideration of counter blows there are three things that must be understood:

    a. the lead of the opponent.
    b. the method of avoiding the lead.
    c. the counter blow itself.

– EDWIN HAISLET, Boxing, page 73

The lead of the opponent is important in that it *determines the side of the body open to attack*. A left lead exposes the left side of the body, while a right lead exposes almost all of the upper trunk. ... *To avoid leads* it must be decided whether the counter-attack should be one- or two-handed. Blocking, guarding, stopping, parrying, all leave but one hand with which to counter. Such maneuvers as slipping, sidestepping, ducking, weaving, feinting, drawing, and shifting allow a two-handed attack. ... The counter blow depends upon the method used in avoiding the opponent's lead as well as the lead itself. In other words, if the opponent jabs and the blow is avoided by an inside slip, a right to the heart or a right cross is indicated. – EDWIN HAISLET, *Boxing*, page 73

WHO WROTE THE TAO?

Left Hand Counters for a Straight Left Lead

By Blocking or Stopping

1. On a straight left lead, catch the opponent's lead in the right glove, at the same time stepping left and drive a straight left to the chin. – EDWIN HAISLET, *Boxing*, page 75

By Parrying

1. On a straight left lead, parry to the outside guard position and hook the left to the solar plexus.
2. On a straight left lead, parry to the outside guard position and hook the left to the chin.
3. On a straight left lead, parry to the outside guard position and deliver a left uppercut to the chin.
4. On a straight left lead, parry to the inside position and drive a straight left to the chin.
5. On a straight left lead, parry to the inside guard position and hook the left to the solar plexus.
6. On a straight left lead, parry to the inside guard position and uppercut left to the solar plexus.

– EDWIN HAISLET, *Boxing*, page 75

By Slipping

1. Slip to the outside position and book the left to the chin.
2. Slip to the outside position and book the left to the solar plexus.
3. Slip to the outside position and drive a left uppercut to the solar plexus.
4. Slip to the outside position and drive a straight left to the chin.

– EDWIN HAISLET, *Boxing*, page 75

By Sidestepping

1. Sidestep to the outside position and drive a left hook to the chin.
2. Sidestep to t.he outside position and drive a left hook to the solar plexus.
3. Sidestep to the outside position and drive a left uppercut to the chin.
4. Sidestep to the outside position and drive a straight left-hand to the chin.

– EDWIN HAISLET, *Boxing*, page 76

Right-Hand Counters for a Straight Left Lead

By Parrying

1. On a straight left lead, parry to the inside guard position with the right hand, then drive the right hand to the opponent's chin.
2. Cross parry the opponent's left lead with the left hand and drive a straight right to the opponent's side.

– EDWIN HAISLET, *Boxing*, page 76

By Slipping

1. On a straight left lead, slip to the inside guard position and hook the right to the heart.
2. On a straight left lead, slip to the inside guard position and drive a straight right to the heart.
3. On a straight left lead, slip to the inside guard position and drive a straight right to the chin.
4. On a straight left lead, slip to the inside guard position and cross a right hook to the opponent's chin.
5. On a straight left lead slip to the inside guard position and drive a right to the solar plexus.

– EDWIN HAISLET, *Boxing*, page 76

By Sidestepping

1. Sidestep to the outside guard position and drive a right cross to opponent's chin.
2. On a straight left lead, sidestep to the outside guard position and drive a right to the heart.
3. On a straight left lead, sidestep to the inside guard position and drive a right uppercut to the chin.
4. On a straight left lead, sidestep to the outside guard position and drive a right uppercut to the chin.
5. On a straight left lead, sidestep to the inside guard position and drive a right uppercut to the solar plexus.

– EDWIN HAISLET, *Boxing*, page 76

Left-Hand Counters for a Straight Right Lead

By Parrying

1. On a straight right lead, cross parry with the right hand and hook left to the chin.
2. On a straight right lead, reach across with the right hand and parry the lead to the outside, hooking the left hand to the opponent's abdomen.

– EDWIN HAISLET, *Boxing*, page 77

By Slipping

1. On a straight right lead, slip to the inside guard position and hook the left to the solar plexus.
2. On a straight right lead, slip to the inside guard position and cross a left hook to the chin.
3. On a straight right lead, slip to the outside guard position and cross-left to chin or body.

– EDWIN HAISLET, *Boxing*, page 77

By Sidestepping

On a straight right lead, sidestep to the inside guard position and drive a straight left to the chin. – EDWIN HAISLET, *Boxing*, page 77

Right-Hand Counters on a Straight Right Lead

By Parrying

1. On a straight right lead, parry to the inside guard position with the left hand, then drive a straight right to the chin or body.
2. On a straight right lead, parry to the inside guard position with the left, then hook the right to the chin or body.
3. On a straight right lead, parry to the inside guard position with the left and drive a right uppercut to the chin or solar plexus.
4. On a straight right lead, parry to the outside guard position with the left and hook the right to the chin or solar plexus.
5. On a straight right lead, parry to the outside guard position with the left and drive a right uppercut to the chin or solar plexus.

– EDWIN HAISLET, *Boxing*, page 77

By Slipping

1. On a straight right lead, slip to the outside guard position and drive a right hook to the chin or body.
2. On a straight right lead, slip to the outside guard position and drive a right uppercut to the chin or body.
3. On a straight right lead, slip to the outside guard position and drive a straight right to face or body.
4. On a straight right lead, slip to the inside guard position and drive a left uppercut to the solar plexus.

– EDWIN HAISLET, *Boxing*, pages 77-78

By Sidestepping

1. On a straight right lead, sidestep to the outside guard position and hook the right to the chin or body.
2. On a straight right lead, sidestep to the outside guard position and drive a right uppercut to the solar plexus.

– EDWIN HAISLET, *Boxing*, page 78

The Inside Parry and Left Jab is a straight left so timed as to take advantage of the opening left by the opponent's jab. It is a fundamental counter used consciously or unconsciously by almost every boxer. It is used to avoid the opponent's jab and at the same time sting and jar him. It is also used to "set up" openings for other counters. It is best used against a slow left jab. – EDWIN HAISLET, *Boxing*, page 73

The Outside Parry and Jab is a jab delivered after slipping the opponent's lead over the left shoulder. It is a safe way to avoid a left lead while dealing out punishment at the same time. It is best used against the long-armed opponent as it adds length to the left arm. The left jab is parried and held momentarily to the left shoulder. The more the opponent steps in with his jab, the more severely he will be punished. It should be used in combination with jabbing from the inside position. – EDWIN HAISLET, *Boxing*, pages 73-74

The Inside Parry and Left Hook to the Liver is a jarring, sickening blow used to slow up an opponent. It is rather dangerous to execute as it brings the body into range of the opponent's right hand. As the left hand and shoulder is dropped, the left side of the body becomes a target for the opponent. Therefore, it must be used suddenly and depends entirely upon speed and deception for its success. – EDWIN HAISLET, *Boxing*, page 74

The Outside Parry and Left Hook to the Body - This is used to bring down the opponent's guard, to create openings for the right hand, and to slow up an opponent. It is easy, safe, and effective. It is really an uppercut rather than a hook. – EDWIN HAISLET, *Boxing*, page 74

The Inside Block and Right Hook is *first a block* and then a blow. It should be used against a slow jab or the boxer who carries his left hand well out from the shoulder. It is a powerful blow but requires more practice and more accurate timing than most counters. It requires blocking a left lead from the inside, then shifting the weight forward and hooking the right to the chin. It is not advisable to use unless the opening is very apparent. – EDWIN HAISLET, *Boxing*, page 74

The Right Cross is one of the most talked of blows in boxing and the counter most often used by all boxers. Delivered properly, it exerts terrific force. It is merely a right hook to the jaw crossed over an opponent's straight left lead. The opponent's jab is slipped over the right shoulder and the right hand then hooked from the outside across to the chin. It is easy to execute and is really a finishing blow. – EDWIN HAISLET, *Boxing*, page 74

The Straight-Inside Right is a straight right timed to cross under and inside an opponent's left lead. It is best used against an opponent who steps well in with his left lead. It then becomes a "set-up" or finishing blow. It is an easy blow to time, carries terrific power and is best used in conjunction with the outside parry and left jab or a right cross. The left hand must be carried high in position to stop or guard. – EDWIN HAISLET, *Boxing*, page 74

The Inside Right to the Heart is a "sucker" punch in that it takes advantage of a natural opening created by any left lead. It is difficult to guard against. It is a straight right timed so as to drive underneath an opponent's left arm as be jabs and is used to slow up an opponent or to "shorten his arms." – EDWIN HAISLET, *Boxing*, page 74

To Minimize the Danger of a Counter

While using one of these three methods which are at his disposal, he is vulnerable to a counter-attack. He must minimize this danger, either by causing his opponent to lose a period of fencing-time, or by protecting himself against a stop-hit while he is gaining distance – ROGER CROSNIER, *Fencing with the Epee*, page 57

Riposte

Basically, a riposte is an attack (or more accurately a counterattack) following a parry. – CHARLES LOUIS DE BEAUMONT, *Fencing: Ancient Art and Modern Sport*, page 78

The choice of the riposte, like the choice of the attack, is determined by the type of defensive movement one thinks that the opponent is likely to adopt against it. *The opponent's reactions can only be ascertained by observation of his usual blade movements when recovering from an unsuccessful attack.* – CHARLES LOUIS DE BEAUMONT, *Fencing: Ancient Art and Modern Sport*, page 78

When, after a parry, the riposte is executed without a change of line, in the same line as the parry, it is called a *direct riposte*. ... The riposte is called simple when it is delivered in the same line as that of the parry, or in the line opposite to it whether it be in the high or low line. It never comprises more than a single blade movement. ... The direct riposte is no different from any other stroke in fencing. Its choice depends on the reactions and habits of the opponent. ... Both cases are the result of training, for in applying the correct riposte, the fencer knows that he has been taught to observe, deduce, and apply the correct stroke. – ROGER CROSNIER, *Fencing with the Foil*, pages 112, 111-112, 113, 113

The *riposte by disengagement* is made in the line opposite to that of the parry, by passing the point under the opponent's blade. ... Now we are faced with a fencer who, expecting a direct riposte, covers in the line in which he has been parried. Sometimes he covers intentionally, often it is merely an instinctive movement. Whatever the reason may be, if this covering is successful, the riposter must anticipate and deceive it by a simple disengagement. – ROGER CROSNIER, *Fencing with the Foil*, pages 114, 116

Types of Riposte

The riposte can be made in simple or compound form, and it can also be immediate or delayed. We can tabulate them as follows:

1. Simple Ripostes.
   a. Direct.
   b. Indirect (disengagement, cut-over, counter-disengagement).
2. Compound Ripostes, i.e. those composed of one or more feints.
3. Simple or Compound Ripostes terminating in the low line.

– ROGER CROSNIER, *Fencing with the Foil*, page 111

Simple or Compound Ripostes terminating in the low line. As stated above, any of these ripostes can be executed *immediately* after a parry or can be *delayed*. The riposte can be given with, or without, the help of a lunge. That the latter should be used is determined solely by the speed of recovery of the opponent from his attack. – ROGER CROSNIER, *Fencing with the Foil*, page 111

Generally, the *immediate riposte* is the most effective as it forces the opponent on to the defensive. Its timing is, however, a delicate matter, for to ensure its effectiveness the parry and riposte must be made just as the attack is ending, and before the opponent has any opportunity of changing from offence to defence. This form of parrying and riposting is known as 'parrying and riposting on the final of the attack' and implies that the defender is morally certain of the line in which the attack will end. It is also known as parrying and riposting tack-to-tack, a sound picture of the two movements. – ROGER CROSNIER, *Fencing with the Foil*, pages 123-124

The *delayed riposte* usually occurs when the defender, having parried without preparing a riposte, hesitates in his choice of one, looking for his opponent's reaction; but it can be a very effective tactic as an occasional manner of riposting when, in general, the ripostes have been immediate. The attacker, expecting an immediate counter-offensive action, automatically goes for a parry, and finding no blade is apt to become flustered by this change of cadence and lose some control in his defence. The French term this type of riposte *Temps perdu* (lost, or broken time). The fencer will greatly add to his repertoire of strokes by the discriminating use of these two types of ripostes. – ROGER CROSNIER, *Fencing with the Foil*, page 124

En resume, now that we have studied the particular application of each of the simple ripostes, we can say with confidence that:

   a. The direct riposte is executed against a fencer who, when on the lunge, commits the error of bending his arm preparatory to recovery, thus leaving himself exposed in the line of the parry.
   b. The riposte in the low line is the choice made against an opponent who ends his attacks correctly covered, and who recovers with his arm extended, thus only leaving his lower target open.
   c. The disengagement and cut-over ripostes are used against an opponent who, when on the lunge, or while recovering, bends his arm and covers in the line of the parry, in anticipation of a direct riposte.
   d. The riposte by counter-disengagement is made against an opponent who, when on the lunge or recovering, does not remain in the line of the parry, but changes his engagement; in other words, takes a counter.

The counter-disengagement is the riposte which deceives the change of engagement taken by the attacker when recovering from his attack ... This form of riposte is particularly useful when dealing with left-handed fencers, who generally return to the line of quarte, where they have the top of the blade and more authority over it. ... Now we are faced with a fencer who, expecting a direct riposte, covers in the line in which he has been parried. Sometimes he covers intentionally, often it is merely an instinctive movement. Whatever the reason may be, if this covering is successful, the riposter must anticipate and deceive it by a simple disengagement. – ROGER CROSNIER, *Fencing with the Foil*, pages 124, 119, 121, 116

A *compound riposte* is the counter-offensive movement which follows a successful parry and is composed of one or more feints. ... Take as an example a compound riposte by one-two, following the parry of counter of sixte. The attacker, having been brought back to the line of sixte by the counter, and anticipating the direct riposte, covers in sixte, to which the riposter, maintaining his arm bent, feints of the disengagement, draws the attacker's parry of quarte, and, still with a bent arm, deceives it. Finally stretching his arm he ripostes. – ROGER CROSNIER, *Fencing with the Foil*, page 145

As with most fencing strokes, the *timing is all-important*. A parry and riposte is most effective if it is made *as the attack is completing its course*. At this point the time available to the opponent to change from attack to defence is cut to the minimum, and consequently the riposte has the best chance to succeed before the attacker can parry it. – CHARLES LOUIS DE BEAUMONT, *Fencing: Ancient Art and Modern Sport*, page 78

There is an opportunity here to exploit a counter-bluff. By reacting to an opponent's *exploratory moves* in one definite way, it is often possible to induce him to use a particular stroke. Knowing the nature of this stroke, it will not be difficult to turn it to one's advantage. – CHARLES LOUIS DE BEAUMONT, *Fencing: Ancient Art and Modern Sport*, page 199

A *counter-riposte* is the offensive movement which follows a successful parry of a riposte. It can be delivered by either the attacker or the defender and can be simple or compound. ... The attacker's counter-riposte can be done while on the lunge, while recovering, or after having recovered. They can, therefore, be executed by either fencer with or without a lunge according to their distance. – ROGER CROSNIER, *Fencing with the Foil*, page 151

A counter-riposte can also be the result of premeditation, in other words, it can be a *second intention*. When we say second intention, we mean that the original attack has been made not with the object of hitting, but on the contrary, to draw a parry and riposte from the defender, in order to riposte from it in turn. This succession of offensive and defensive actions executed by the attacker, is usually reverted to against an opponent whose original defence is very strong, and where it is hoped that a second offensive action will catch him unprepared. If we have advised the attacker to develop the habit of returning to guard automatically after an attack, this is a case where he will deliberately remain on the lunge to ensure that he is within reaching distance for his counter-riposte. But, if he is faced by a fencer with a rapid and precise riposte, he can make either a half recovery, or shift the weight of his body back on to his rear leg when parrying, then counter-riposte with a half lunge, or with a leaning forward of the body. Thus, he places himself out of range of the dangerous riposte. – ROGER CROSNIER, *Fencing with the Foil*, page 152

– THOMAS INCH, *Boxing*, page 30

Renewed Attack

The remise is a renewed cut or a replacement of the point on the target in the same line as that of the original offensive or counter-offensive action. ... The remise is a commonly used stroke at sabre. Usually aimed at the sword-arm, it is designed to penalize an opponent who, riposting indirectly, or compound, uncovers because his movements are controlled by the arm and therefore wide. – ROGER CROSNIER, *Fencing with the Sabre*, pages 153, 154

The redoublement is very effective against fencers who, although having a strong defence, hesitate to riposte or are slow in doing so. Often, this is because they are off balance when parrying. – ROGER CROSNIER, *Fencing with the Sabre*, page 157

Many sabreurs commit the fault of leaning back on their rear leg when defending themselves, instead of taking a short step back. – ROGER CROSNIER, *Fencing with the Sabre*, page 157

In either category each of the examples given is effective, but their success depends, to a very great extent, on the rapidity of the recovery forward. The opponent must be surprised by the speed by which the offensive is continued. He must be given no respite, nor must he be allowed to regain any loss of balance or control which the initial attack may have cost him. – ROGER CROSNIER, *Fencing with the Electric Foil*, page 77

Generally, the recovery forward is accompanied by an attack on the blade, or a *prise de fer*. These actions have the advantage, first of all, of filling in the time lag caused by the recovery forward. Secondly, they occupy the opponent's mind during that period, and minimize the risk that he might riposte belatedly, or stop-hit. Thirdly, especially in the case of the prise de fer, the fencer reprising finds some degree of support by holding his opponent's blade during his recovery. – ROGER CROSNIER, *Fencing with the Electric Foil*, page 77

The *remise* is a commonly used stroke at sabre. Usually aimed at the sword-arm, it is designed to penalize an opponent who, riposting indirectly, or compound, uncovers because his movements are controlled by the arm and therefore wide. In most cases, its choice as a stroke is premeditated, as a result of the observation of the opponent's habits and tactics. Although it is possible to execute, successfully, a remise on the spur of the moment, to do so does not make certain that a period of "fencing-time" will be gained. – ROGER CROSNIER, *Fencing with the Sabre*, page 154

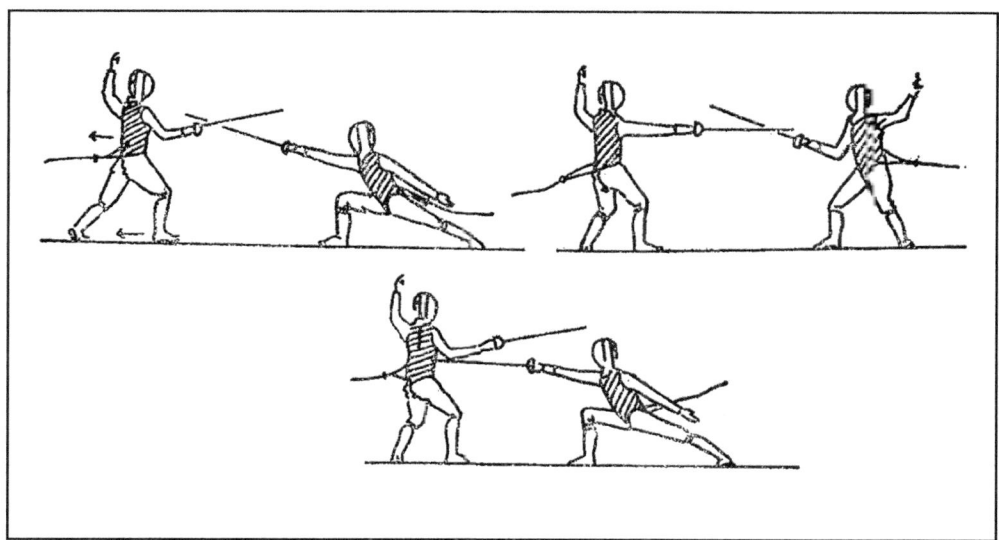

– ROGER CROSNIER, *Fencing with the Electric Foil*, page 76

They are to be attempted after the recovery forward.

- Straight-thrust;
- Feint of the straight-thrust followed by one of the indirect simple attacks, or a compound attack;
- A simple or a compound attack preceded by an attack on the blade; or a *prise de fer*.

– ROGER CROSNIER, *Fencing with the Electric Foil*, pages 76-77

Tactics

Tactics are the brainwork of fencing; they are based upon observation and analysis of the opponent and upon intelligent choices of actions against him. The tactical approach consists of three parts: *prelude or preliminary analysis, preparation, and execution*. ... The purpose of the prelude is to lay the foundation by scrutinizing the opponent's habits, virtues, and faults. The fencer should know whether his opponent is aggressive or defensive, whether he likes to make actions on time, and what his favorite attacks and parries are. Much of this can be learned by observing the other fencers who are likely to qualify for the next round. But even after a fencer knows his opponent's game thoroughly (e.g. when the two have fought with each other) it is often necessary to devote some time at the beginning of the bout for an analysis. The reason is that a fencer's physical and mental condition varies from day to day and from bout to bout. He may be fresher on one day than on another; his reactions may be quicker

– THOMAS INCH, *Boxing: Secret of the Knock-Out,* pages 139, 121, and 109

or slower, and even in the same competition he may move differently if he is not sufficiently warmed up, is tired, or is in the process of getting his "second wind." The process of testing out the opponent's current reactions, his physical and mental condition, his disposition and spirit must be carried out with caution. The fencer should shorten and lengthen the distance and make use of false attacks that are persuasive enough to force the opponent to reveal the quality and speed of his parries. – JULIUS PALFFY-ALPAR, *Sword and Masque*, pages 47-48

It is during the preparation of the action that each fencer looks for cues and tries to outwit his opponent. The variations are endless, but a few may be pointed out. For example, the fencer who plans to score on the attack has to take the initiative and keep control of the play. He attempts to mislead his opponent by sometimes making a false attack followed by a real attack to a different area or to the same target area. The lines and positions should be varied in order not to give the opponent a free moment in which to seize the initiative. – JULIUS PALFFY-ALPAR, *Sword and Masque*, page 48

The preparation of the attack should be cautious, and the fencer must always be ready to parry if the opponent tries to make a sudden stop-hit or counter-attack. The *execution* of the real attack must be done with proper timing, quickly without break or hesitation. It must be a conscious, accelerated, determined, and decisive movement. Surprise is vital, and the fencer must believe in its successful outcome. Preparation of actions used to score on the parry riposte or stop-hit follow the same principles. The opponent must be lured into the attack at the exact moment desired by the defender, so that the latter may score on a short, determined parry riposte or an action in time. ... If the opponent takes the initiative, the fencer must discourage him by constant threat of counter-attack, by short thrusts or cuts, by beating his blade, or by other legal means which will disturb his concentration. – JULIUS PALFFY-ALPAR, *Sword and Masque*, pages 48-49

If physical qualities between fencers are equal, intellectual superiority helps to achieve victory. Between equally intelligent fencers, mechanical and technical knowledge can be decisive. – JULIUS PALFFY-ALPAR, *Sword and Masque*, page 50

A *fencer* must reach a fair standard of technical ability before he can apply tactics successfully. The basic technique of the weapon used must be mastered by lessons, exercises, and loose play so that the various fencing strokes are made automatically as required. Only then can the mind be concentrated on discovering the opponent's reactions, anticipating his intentions and devising the strategy and tactics required to beat him. – CHARLES LOUIS DE BEAUMONT, *Fencing: Ancient Art and Modern Sport*, page 197

It is the tactical application of fencing movements which provides much of the absorbing interest of a fencing bout. This requires cool judgment, anticipation, opportunism, bluff, and counter-bluff and *the ability to think at least one move ahead,* combined with courage and controlled reaction of muscles and limbs which enables the fencer to carry out simple or complex movements with his weapon as required by the situation at any given moment. – CHARLES LOUIS DE BEAUMONT, *Fencing: Ancient Art and Modern Sport*, page 197

It has been said that, for the fencer, to think and to act must be like one flash of lightning. Coordination of mind and body is certainly the secret of success in competitive fencing. Mechanical perfection is useless in fencing without the ability to think – the most intelligent analysis of an opponent's game will not ensure success unless the requisite fencing stroke can be devised and applied in the proper manner. – CHARLES LOUIS DE BEAUMONT, *Fencing: Ancient Art and Modern Sport*, page 197

WHO WROTE THE TAO?

The key to fencing tactics is to take advantage of the weakness of the opponent. – EDITORS OF SPORTS ILLUSTRATED, *Sports Illustrated Book of Fencing*, page 12

The boxing adage "box a fighter-fight a boxer" has much force in fencing. In other words, use the tactics opposite those favoured by the opponent's game. ... It is obviously unwise continually to attack a fencer who relies on his defence, while one should attack without respite the opponent who himself favours strong and speedy attacks. Counter-time is the answer to the stop-hit addict, and the stop hit the counter to the fencer who uses many feints. – CHARLES LOUIS DE BEAUMONT, *Teach Yourself Fencing*, pages 113, 200

A fencer with a long reach, or who continually makes renewed attacks, or attacks with a balestra or step forward, generally requires a wide measure. It is a mistake to step back on the attack or preparation, since this will help the opponent to obtain the space which he requires to manoeuvre. Such an opponent will probably be disconcerted, and lose his precision, if the measure is shortened by a step forward into his attack – CHARLES LOUIS DE BEAUMONT, *Fencing: Ancient Art and Modern Sport*, page 200

A short fencer tries to make up for his shorter reach by using attacks on the blade and by taking his opponent's blade in binding actions. – EDITORS OF SPORTS ILLUSTRATED, *Sports Illustrated Book of Fencing*, page 61

There are variations of rhythm, such as slowing down the cadence of movements and then suddenly putting on a burst of speed, or even the reverse of this. – EDITORS OF SPORTS ILLUSTRATED, *Sports Illustrated Book of Fencing*, page 60

The master should point out that the fencer cannot use the same actions against every opponent. – JULIUS PALFFY-ALPAR, *Sword and Masque*, page 50

Against a calm, quiet fencer the feints must be longer; against a nervous fencer the feints shorter. With the calm fencer, one should remain calm; the nervous type should be agitated (while the fencer himself tries to remain calm). Tall fencers usually are slower, but their long lunges are dangerous, so it is essential to keep a safe distance. – JULIUS PALFFY-ALPAR, *Sword and Masque*, page 50

ABOVE: Purchase receipt for first edition of the *Tao of Jeet Kune Do*. (Courtesy of Richard Torres)

Unconventional fencers use wide, sometimes unexpected, motions. Against such opponents the fencer must keep his distance and the parries should be taken at the very last moment. Unorthodox fencers usually use simple actions and almost always execute these in the same tempo. The attacks are made with wide movements, giving a chance for timed or stop-hits. The loss of a bout against such an opponent frequently points to the fencer's inflexibility and his inability to adapt his style to the requirements of the moment. – JULIUS PALFFY-ALPAR, *Sword and Masque*, page 50-51

One often meets fencers, especially at epee, who habitually attack with a preparation on the blade which they time to perfection. At epee it is often difficult to time the ceding parry or counter-riposte against a forceful opponent who is an expert in such attacks. Fencing with absence of blade and varying the measure, in preference to giving the blade, will often disconcert the opponent and severely limit his game. – CHARLES LOUIS DE BEAUMONT, *Fencing: Ancient Art and Modern Sport*, page 200

It is sometimes difficult to deal with the patient epee fencer who remains on guard well covered, keeps out of distance and evades attempts to make preparations on the blade. Such fencers generally make very accurate stop hits at wrist; it is unsafe, therefore, to attack directly at the hand, because their well covered position requires the attacker to angulate his blade and thus expose his own wrist. The obvious answer is to draw the stop hit and complete a second-intention attack, taking the blade. – CHARLES LOUIS DE BEAUMONT, *Fencing: Ancient Art and Modern Sport*, page 200-201

Before attacking an opponent who fences with absence of blade, false attacks or well-marked feints can be used to draw his reaction. If this is a stop hit, one can proceed in counter-time, preferably taking the blade. If he reacts with a parry one can complete a compound attack or score by counter-riposte. On the other hand, the effect may be for him to return to engagement, when an appropriate attack can be used. – CHARLES LOUIS DE BEAUMONT, *Fencing: Ancient Art and Modern Sport*, page 201

His rhythm, probably irregular, is hard to gauge, rendering long phrases dangerous, as he is unlikely to follow the lead being given him. He will, most certainly, panic easily and parry at the slightest provocation. These parries, started too soon and lacking control, often take the form of whips directed in no particular direction. They are apt to catch the attacker's arm. As often as not, such hits are flat, but few judges appear to realize this, and, guided by the sound of the hit, rather than because they have seen it, will signal it. There is, therefore, every reason to be careful *not to attack with compound movements against a novice, but to wait for the opportunity to launch simple, rapid, economical technique.* – ROGER CROSNIER, *Fencing with the Sabre*, page 191

Quite unintentionally, the novice will deliver broken-rhythm attacks, which will fool the more experienced fighter who will not be expecting such a rhythm. Thus, it is essential to maintain a very carefully judged measure, which will force the novice, finally, to reach out in order to hit. – ROGER CROSNIER, *Fencing with the Sabre*, page 192

WHO WROTE THE TAO?

A golden rule is never to use more complex movements than are necessary to achieve the desired result. Start with simple movements and only introduce composed ones when you cannot otherwise succeed. To hit a worthy opponent with a complex movement is satisfying, and shows one's mastery of technique; to hit the same opponent by a simple movement is a sign of greatness. – CHARLES LOUIS DE BEAUMONT, *Fencing: Ancient Art and Modern Sport*, page 203

Half the battle is won when one knows what the adversary is doing. If, in spite of having correctly chosen the corresponding movement, the action fails, the reason must be due to faulty technique. – ROGER CROSNIER, *Fencing with the Epee*, page 76

If, on the other hand, the fencer is at a loss to know how to deal with his opponent then, either he has not seen what his opponent is doing, or he has an insufficient number of strokes at his command. – ROGER CROSNIER, *Fencing with the Epee*, page 76

Knowing that opponents are constantly trying to note one's habits and weaknesses, it is obvious that a conscious effort must be made to give variety to one's game. – CHARLES LOUIS DE BEAUMONT, *Fencing: Ancient Art and Modern Sport*, page 198

Right-Hander Versus Left-Hander

The right hook is very effective as an offensive punch; also, as a counter punch thrown immediately after a short hop-back. A southpaw who uses his right hand efficiently along with his normally effective left hand is hard to beat. – JOHN J. WALSH, *Boxing Simplified*, page 51

The right-hander must very definitely circle to his left, away from the southpaw's potent left hand. He must keep his left hand high, and either beat the southpaw to the punch with a sharp right, or feint with his right-hand punch, hop back, and then counter with a sharp right. After each right-hand, follow immediately with a left hook. – JOHN J. WALSH, *Boxing Simplified*, pages 51-52

Glides and beats in the engagement of the outside lines are advisable before any attack. – JULIO MARTINEZ CASTELLÓ, *Theory and Practice of Fencing*, page 63

TAO FAST FACTS

Ohara Publications is a book publisher based in Valencia, California. Established in 1966, the publisher's primary genre is martial arts books. One of its earliest books was *Wing Chun Kung Fu* by James Yimm Lee (Bruce Lee served as technical editor). The *Tao of Jeet Kune Do* is the publisher's best-selling book and the first book that it published in a large format. Previous books in the publishing company's catalog were published in smaller, more traditional sizes.

Since publishing the *Tao of Jeet Kune Do*, Ohara Publications continues to publish books on Jeet Kune Do and Bruce Lee, including *The Bruce Lee's Fighting Method* series of books by Mito Uyehara, *Bruce Lee: The Incomparable Fighter* also by Uyehara, *The Legendary Bruce Lee* by the editors of *Black Belt* magazine, and *The Bruce Lee Story* by Linda Lee and Tom Bleecker.

Glides and beats in the engagement of the outside lines are advisable before any attack. However, the best solution to the difficulty encountered in fencing left-handers is to fence with them as much as possible, and thus become acquainted with their weakness and strength. – JULIO MARTINEZ CASTELLÓ, *Theory and Practice of Fencing*, page 63

– ROCKY MARCIANO and CHARLEY GOLDMAN, *Rocky Marciano's Book of Boxing and Bodybuilding*, pages 98, 100

The best way in which a right-handed fencer can in part overcome these disadvantages is: first, to meet the opponent's blade with the engagement of FOURTH; second, to use the parries of FOURTH and COUNTER FOURTH, which are his strongest; and third, to return and attack to the opponent's outside high and low lines so as to compel him to use his weak parries. If the attack is made to the outside high line, he will use then weak parry of SIXTH or the slower counter parry of FOURTH. If the attack is to the outside low line, he will use the parry of SECOND, which will result in his leaving himself open in the high lines. This can become very effective if the right-handed fencer feints to the outside low line, forcing the left-handed fencer to parry SECOND, and leave an opening for the attack or counter return to the high lines. – JULIO MARTINEZ CASTELLÓ, *Theory and Practice of Fencing*, pages 62-63

TAO FAST FACTS

The news that editor Gilbert Johnson would be compiling a version of Bruce Lee's unfinished book, the *Tao of Jeet Kune Do*, was initially met with some skepticism from Lee's students. "When Linda Lee introduced Gil Johnson and said he was going to put Bruce's book together for publication, we were all a little skeptical," Dan Inosanto told *Black Belt* magazine in 1975. "We figured, since he studied different styles, that he would interpret everything in terms of what he already knew and make Jeet Kune Do another style. But he didn't. The way he put the book together was fantastic. ... He clarified things only where they needed it and left the rest to interpretation."

Epée fencing is par excellence a game of timing, tactics and bluff. Two of the most effective means to this end are:

- *The Simple Attack from Immobility.* This will often surprise the opponent, especially after a series of false attacks and feints have been executed, so that the defender is subconsciously expecting a preparation or more complex movement and fails to react in time to the swift and unannounced simple movement.
- *The Variation of Rhythm or Cadence.* Made prior to, or during an attack, this may achieve the same element of surprise. For example, a series of judiciously slowed-down feints to the arm and slow gaining and breaking ground may be used, as the French say, to 'put the opponent to sleep'. A final simple movement which suddenly erupts at highest speed will often take him unawares. Again, some rapid feints followed by a deliberately slowed-down or broken-time final movement will often disconcert a vigilant opponent.

– CHARLES LOUIS DE BEAUMONT,
Fencing: Ancient Art and Modern Sport, pages 119-120

Some fencers, especially foilists, form the habit of withdrawing the sword-hand when a hit is directed towards it. Such fencers are particularly vulnerable to an immediate renewal of the attack by fleche. – CHARLES LOUIS DE BEAUMONT, *Fencing: Ancient Art and Modern Sport*, page 120

Similarly, a number of feints in the high lines can pave the way for a sudden disengagement to the knee. – CHARLES LOUIS DE BEAUMONT, *Fencing: Ancient Art and Modern Sport*, page 120

Preparations on the blade and prises de fer are much used to reduce the fencing-time factor, which favours the stop hit when getting within distance for an attack. Conversely, attacks on preparation are particularly effective at epee. – CHARLES LOUIS DE BEAUMONT, *Fencing: Ancient Art and Modern Sport*, page 120-121

Again, a broken-time attack, for example making a pause before delivering the final movement, can be very effective in deceiving the opponent as to the attacker's intention. – CHARLES LOUIS DE BEAUMONT, *Fencing: Ancient Art and Modern Sport*, page 163

An opponent's reactions can be found by different means, but the obvious method is to execute simple attacks, which he will have to parry. Wait for his riposte, which will be deflected, and carefully select the target-area for the counterattack! – MAXWELL R. GARRET, *How to Improve Your Fencing*, page 48

Watch your opponent. Never look away from him during the actual fighting. To box successfully you must see everything that goes on in the course of your fight. The place to watch in long range fighting is your opponent's eyes. Notice where animals look when they fight. They were never taught from a book. They are acting instinctively and correctly. You will be able to see everything necessary if you watch your opponent's eyes in long arm fighting. His leads will be as obvious as if you were looking at his gloves. When infighting look either at your opponent's waist or at his feet. – FRANK GILMER, *Push Yourself: A Book for Amateur Boxers and Boxing Fans*, page 66

Take the play away from your opponent. Come out fast at the beginning of each round and push the fighting. This is aggressiveness and counts in your favor. Look fresh, unmarked and smart. Use your natural advantages of height and reach, if you have them. Take a few chances and once in a great while even. dare to sneak a right lead. Try to get him on the defensive wondering what you are going to do next. Never give him any rest if you can help it. Hit from all angles and when jabbing with your left fist always shoot more than one. The second will hurt where the first was avoided. ... Discover your opponent's weaknesses as a boxer. Try your various attacks and counterpunches and find out what bothers him most. It may be left hooks, right hand body blows, or just fast left jabs that he has never learned to avoid. Concentrate your attack on that flaw in his defense and never ease up. If he wants to infight, sharp, shoot at long range. If he prefers to box prettily, crowd him into the ropes and rough him around with sustained and vicious exchanges in close. – FRANK GILMER, *Push Yourself: A Book for Amateur Boxers and Boxing Fans*, pages 66-67

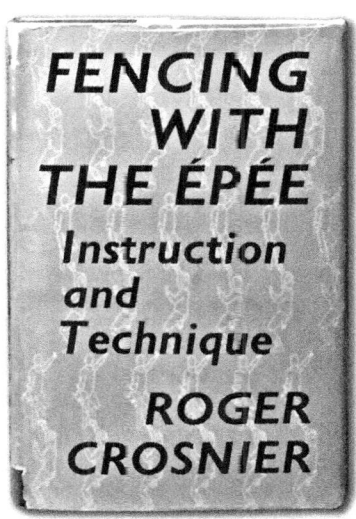

Keep moving there, by preventing him from getting set to punch and making him miss. Circle to your left. Sidestep his rushes and when he is off balance, go after him like a cat. Hit and run and occasionally, if he becomes careless, stop suddenly and catch him coming in with your hardest counterpunch. ... Follow up advantages. If you hurt your opponent, never let him get away or recover. – FRANK GILMER, *Push Yourself: A Book for Amateur Boxers and Boxing Fans*, pages 67, 68

Don't waste motion. Have a purpose in every action, of deception, defense or attack. Between rounds get all the rest and air you can. During the rounds learn to save your energy when you are not actually fighting. This ability to save yourself develops with experience. – FRANK GILMER, *Push Yourself: A Book for Amateur Boxers and Boxing Fans*, page 68

Whether or not these simple attacks are preceded by a preparation, they are dependent on great point accuracy and the fact that they are driven home confidently and with speed. – ROGER CROSNIER, *Fencing with the Epee*, page 51

In retrospect, therefore, all aggressive arm actions, no matter how simple or complex they become, stem from three fundamentals. ... the beat or an action on the blade ... the disengagement ... and the thrust. – MAXWELL R. GARRET, *How to Improve Your Fencing*, page 52

The classification of boxing as elementary and advanced has intentionally been avoided on account of its confusion. Any elementary offense or defense through proper strategy and ring generalship may under certain conditions be used in the most advanced type of boxing. – CLARENCE E. KENNEDY, *Boxing Simplified*, page iii

Training Aids

When for each stroke a pupil knows:

> HOW-it is done;
> WHY-it is done;
> WHEN-it is done;

and finally, can apply the answer to each question successfully, then he knows the stroke perfectly and can proceed to another. This is possible if the lesson progresses in the proper way. – ROGER CROSNIER, *Fencing with the Foil*, page 244

If the lessons have included the variety of circumstances in which a stroke may have to be used, then, again, the pupil is less likely to be surprised by an unfamiliar action. – ROGER CROSNIER, *Fencing with the Sabre,* page 180

We cannot repeat too often that the successful fencer is he who has learnt to select, *correctly,* the strokes which he has been taught. – ROGER CROSNIER, *Fencing with the Sabre*, page 191

Tao of Jeet Kune Do - Personal Impacts

My name is Lamar Davis and I am a certified Senior Instructor of Bruce Lee's fighting methods (Jun Fan Gung Fu and Jeet Kune Do). At the time that the *Tao of Jeet Kune Do* was released, I was a junior in high school. I was already into martial arts and was especially interested in Bruce Lee. I was buying martial arts books and magazines every month and saw in *Black Belt* magazine where Ohara Publications was going to release the works of Bruce Lee in a book to be titled, *Tao of Jeet Kune Do*. Needless to say, I was more than excited about this upcoming book!

I had ordered many books from Ohara Publications, so I was on their pre-publication list, meaning that I received ordering information just before a book was released. When I received the pre-publication notice, I immediately ordered three copies of the book. Of course, back then ordering books involved going to the post office and purchasing a money order, then mailing it in with the order form. This was the actual beginning of what I call my "Rule of Three" when it comes to any books on Bruce Lee's martial arts. I order at least three copies of any book about Jeet Kune Do or Jun Fan Gung Fu. This gives me one to read, one for my collection and one to put away for safe-keeping. As an Instructor, this has proven to be a great strategy for me!

The game of eagerly awaiting the book's arrival began. Every day I couldn't wait for the mail to arrive in hopes that the book had come. When it did arrive, I eagerly (but carefully) opened the package. When I got my hands on the actual book, I was totally ecstatic! I felt as if I was holding the "Holy Grail" of Jeet Kune Do knowledge. I opened the book and was immediately pleased with the formatting of the material within. I will have to say that my main disappointment was that there were no photographs. I had seen many photos (those later used for the *Bruce Lee's Fighting Method* books) that appeared to be instructional, so I was thinking that they would be in the book. There were no photos at all, but only drawings by Bruce Lee. I remember eagerly pouring through the material the first day, reading the entire book in just a few hours. The layout made for extremely easy reading. I know that simplicity is one of the guidelines for Jeet Kune Do, but it still felt like there was much missing material. The best way that I

can describe how I felt about the book is somewhat conflicted, like a "Is the glass half empty or half full?" feeling! Many years later, I realized that there was so much more to Bruce Lee's actual notes than what the *Tao* included, as well as many things that were attributed to him that were not actually his work.

Sifu Lamar M. Davis II
Hardcore Jeet Kune Do Academy
Oneonta, Alabama

Immobilization Attack

Stopping is the pinning of an opponent's hand or arm so that he is unable to deliver a blow. It may be used as a preventive measure when slipping or countering, or when an opponent actually intends to deliver a blow. – EDWIN HAISLET, *Boxing*, page 49

It may be used as a preventive measure when slipping or countering, or when an opponent actually intends to deliver a blow. Used in this manner, it requires a knowledge of when an opponent is going to lead and depends on speed and skill for execution. – EDWIN HAISLET, *Boxing*, page 49

Progressive Indirect Attack

It is, therefore, conceivable and quite possible to execute a compound attack with one feint, i.e. a one-two or a double, in one period of fencing time, on the condition that the blade movements are executed simultaneously with the lunge. It would take a fencer of greatly superior speed to gain a period of fencing time on an opponent delivering an attack in a progressive manner. – ROGER CROSNIER, *Fencing with the Foil*, page 133

The principal uses of a compound attack are (a) to overcome a strong defense against simple attacks, and (b) to offer variation in one's pattern of attack. – HUGO CASTELLÓ and JAMES CASTELLÓ, *Fencing,* page 39

He will have shortened the distance his point had to travel by a good half with his feint and leave to his second movement only the second half of the distance. Thus, he is at the same time gaining distance by starting his lunge with his feint, and simultaneously gaining time by deceiving the parry while doing so. The attack from the beginning is progressing towards the opponent, and for that reason is known as a progressive attack. – ROGER CROSNIER, *Fencing with the Foil,* page 130

Do not wait for the parry before completing your attack; keep ahead of it. But, prolong your feint enough so that the opponent has time to react. – HUGO CASTELLÓ and JAMES CASTELLÓ, *Fencing,* page 37

In doing so they are exerting a pressure upon their opponent's blade, creating an ideal condition for the disengagement. To seize the opportunity, in other words to time this movement of sword and arm crossing from left to right, or right to left, for the execution of the attack, means that for a moment the defence is moving in an opposite direction to that of the attack. The defence has to recover and return to the line that is being threatened. The attacker is moving slightly ahead of the defence and has, therefore, a chance of getting there first. The attacker must initiate his disengagement whenever he feels the pressure on his sword. – ROGER CROSNIER, *Fencing with the Foil,* page 80

All attacking movements must therefore be made as small as possible, that is with the least deviation of the blade necessary to induce the opponent to react. Caution demands that attacks should, whenever possible, be completed covered. – CHARLES LOUIS DE BEAUMONT, *Fencing: Ancient Art and Modern Sport,* page 119

To reach the target the attacker must deceive the adversary's blade. – ROGER CROSNIER, *Fencing with the Foil,* page 93

Gilbert Johnson

Gilbert Lee Johnson was the man chosen by Linda Lee to compile and edit the *Tao of Jeet Kune Do*. While little has been written about Johnson, mostly due to his relatively brief life, it seems appropriate to write a few words about him in this book.

Not much has been made publicly available about his life and upbringing. Born on January 10, 1951 in California, Johnson majored in writing in college. He served in the military and earned his black belt in Karate while studying in Hawaii. During his stay in Hawaii, he began developing a program to teach martial arts to blind students, a program he continued when he relocated to

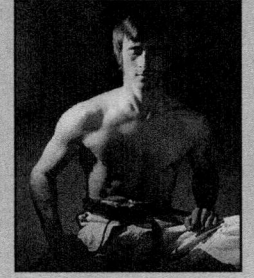

Albuquerque, New Mexico. In a fascinating article in the March 1974 issue of *Black Belt* magazine, Gilbert described his teaching of blind students, and how they were able to determine their surroundings through echolocation, not unlike Marvel Comics' crimefighting Daredevil.

By the mid-1970s, Johnson relocated to California and found work as an assistant editor for *Black Belt* magazine; he also edited a number of books, including *Advanced Nunchaku* by Fumio Demura. This brought him to the attention of Linda Lee, who decided he was the right man to put together Bruce Lee's notes.

While working on the editing of the *Tao of Jeet Kune Do*, Johnson was invited by Dan Inosanto to train in Inosanto's class at the Filipino Kali Academy along with classmates like Jerry Poteet, Chris Kent, and Cass Magda. He later co-wrote *The Filipino Martial Arts: As Taught by Dan Inosanto* along with Inosanto.

Gilbert Johnson was also a freelance journalist, and one of his notable assignments was covering the Iranian Revolution in 1979. While on an overseas trip in the early 1980s, Johnson was injured in a vehicular accident. In the hospital he was given a blood transfusion, one that turned out to be tainted with HIV-infected blood.

Rather than let his HIV status break his spirit, he became an AIDS activist. But it was difficult being publicly identified as HIV-positive in the 1980s. "(Johnson) came out (about being HIV-positive) to the notoriously conservative martial arts scene. It was unheard of," said Diana Lee Inosanto, who spoke of her fondness for him in a 2011 *Black Belt* article.

Gilbert Johnson lost his battle with AIDS on February 12, 1988. The following statement, written by Johnson in a 1974 *Black Belt* article, could just as well be applied to him:

"I used to watch my students as they left for home in the evening," recalled Gilbert Johnson. *"They would be exhausted, battered, and bruised from having been constantly forced to meet their own fears. I couldn't help but wonder if some time they might all just walk away and never come back. But they didn't. They have proven to me, to themselves, and so many others that they have something within them worth much more than the physical properties that they lack. They have the courage and determination to face their handicaps, to overcome them, and to become something extraordinary."*

– THOMAS INCH, *Boxing and Physical Cullture,* page 155

Attack By Combination

The term "set-ups" denotes a series of blows delivered in a natural sequence. The object is to maneuver the opponent into such a position, or create such an opening, that the final blow of the series will find a vulnerable spot thus rendering the opponent helpless and "setting him up" for the finishing or knockout blow. – EDWIN HAISLET, *Boxing,* page 85

The difference between an expert and a novice boxer is that the expert makes use of each opportunity and follows up each opening. He delivers bis blows in a well-planned series, each opening creating another, until finally a clean "shot" is obtained. – EDWIN HAISLET, *Boxing*, page 85

Some blows seem to be "follow" blows in that they come after certain leads. For instance, the straight right is a "follow" blow for the left jab, and a left hook is a "follow" blow for the straight right. – EDWIN HAISLET, *Boxing*, page 85

It seems natural to punch straight and then hook, and it seems natural to punch first to the head and then to the body. – EDWIN HAISLET, *Boxing*, page 85

"Follow" blows or "set-ups" have rhythm and "feel" as their basis. Punching in rhythm is an important factor in boxing. – EDWIN HAISLET, *Boxing*, page 85

The *Triple Blows* are combinations of three different punches which have slipping as their basic technique. Always the first two blows are to the body, followed by a blow to the chin. There are two triples, one which starts with a slip to the inside guard position, and one which starts with a slip to the outside guard position. Both are effective, but the inside triple is used more often. Jack Dempsey used this triple to "bit 'em in the stomach, then hit 'em on the jaw." The first two blows are designed to bring down the guard to create an opening for the final or finishing blow. – EDWIN HAISLET, *Boxing*, page 85-86

The *High-Lows* are a series of blows which have rhythm as their basis in punching first to the body and then to the head, or vice versa. The wide hook is used to open a path for the final straight blow. The main thing to remember is that the last blow will be to the spot of the first blow. If the first blow is to the jaw, the last blow will also be to the jaw. – EDWIN HAISLET, *Boxing*, page 86

Aikido and The Dynamic Sphere, by A. Westbrook & O. Ratti. "The gentleman's fighting art" is a sophisticated style, particularly in its essential motivations. This book goes into the complete range of aikido activities with emphasis on non-aggression. Over 1200 illustrations show you exact moves and counter moves. In its twelfth printing. $12.75.

ABOVE: Advertisement for *Aikido and the Dynamic Sphere*. The book is the source of the Aikido images seen in the *Tao of Jeet Kune Do*.

Attack By Drawing

It is usually best, whenever possible, to "draw" your opponent into a lead before hitting out on your own account. The advantages gained thereby are four in number. In the first place, you have forced your opponent to commit himself to a decided step and can therefore be moderately certain of what he is about to do. Secondly, you have to a very large extent deprived him of the ability to change his position and guard swiftly enough to deal successfully with any offensive you may yourself adopt. – JIM DRISCOLL, *The Straight Left and How to Cultivate It*, page 63

Thirdly, by his mere action of hitting out, you will or should secure an opening of sorts, can or should make him present you with a fair target at which to aim. – JIM DRISCOLL, *The Straight Left and How to Cultivate It*, page 63

His lunge forward accompanying his punch will have almost, if not quite, finished, and you will then have very little additional force to borrow from him. ... The whole secret of hard hitting lies in accurate timing and in mental application. – JIM DRISCOLL, *The Straight Left and How to Cultivate It*, page 66

Tao of Jeet Kune Do
by Bruce Lee

The martial arts book of the century!
Entirely written & illustrated by Bruce Lee!

This is the book that has been talked and whispered about for several years. It took time to gather Bruce's notes and drawings and arrange them with the seven volumes into a single, massive book. But here it is, the most comprehensive work ever written on the martial arts and written by the most famous martial artist that ever lived! Bruce Lee discusses the principles, observations and training that make Jeet Kune Do. His own sketches and finished drawings illustrate the work throughout. Now, with his wife Linda Lee's authorization, Ohara presents it to the public, impressively bound and artistically crafted.

ORDER YOUR COPY NOW!
No. 401-$6.95

ABOVE: Advertisement for the *Tao of Jeet Kune Do*.

TAO FAST FACTS

The movie *Dragon: The Bruce Lee Story* was released in May 1993. Made for $16 million, it would eventually gross $65.3 million at the box office. The movie featured the *Tao of Jeet Kune Do* book, and during one scene an opponent tells Bruce Lee, "I read your book. I learned all your secrets." The appearance of the book in the movie resulted in increased demand, and the book sold out everywhere. Ohara Publications could not keep up with the demand and the book could not be found for many weeks.

Circle with No Circumference

Swordsmanship is, after all, not a matter of petty technique but of highly developed personal spirituality. Hence Ichiun's declaration to the effect that there is no one who can be his equal. ... Resolute-mindedness applies to the work of restoration in which the "fully developed" are now engaged. It is not a question of developing what has already been developed but of recovering what has been left behind, though this has been with us, in us, all the time and has never been lost or distorted except for our misguided manipulation of it. But the swordsman, perhaps first instigated by the Zen masters and after a long trial experience of his own, has come to recognize the presence in himself and the importance of this "unknown quantity," which we now strive in every way to describe. ... It may sound strange that he wishes to be a philosopher, but in Japan and also in China the arts are not a matter of technology but of spiritual insight and training. Swordsmanship is no exception. – D. T. SUZUKI, *Zen and Japanese Culture*, pages 182, 184, 143

> Being a swordsman, he inevitably emphasizes the activity aspect of the sword instead of its substantiality. That is to say, he wants to see the sword moving functionally. When the sword is held in his hands, it is at an undifferentiated center of a circle that has no circumference. It is ready either to assert itself or to negate itself. – D. T. SUZUKI, *Zen and Japanese Culture*, page 158
>
> When the situation is analyzed intellectually, we can never escape a contradiction in one form or another: moving and yet not moving, in tension and yet relaxed, seeing everything that is going on and yet not at all anxious about the way it may turn, with nothing purposely designed, nothing consciously calculated, no anticipation, no expectation—in short, standing innocently like a baby and yet with all the cunning and subterfuge of the keenest intelligence of a fully matured mind: how can this be achieved? No amount of intellection can ever be of any help in this paradoxical situation. – D. T. SUZUKI, *Essentials of Zen Buddhism*, pages 453-454

This latter fact is therefore described as leaving sagehood behind and entering once more into ordinary humanity. ... P'u-yiian makes the statement: "After coming to understand the other side, you come back and live on this side." ... After the completion of cultivation, however, one's thoughts continue to be detached from phenomenal things, and one still remains "amid the phenomenal yet devoid of the phenomenal." – FUNG YU-LAN, *A History of Chinese Philosophy. Vol. II*, pages 403, 405

The first step of leaving mortal humanity behind and entering sagehood is that in which "both the man and his surroundings are eliminated," in other words, in which neither subject nor object longer exist for him. – FUNG YU-LAN, *A History of Chinese Philosophy. Vol. II*, page 405

However well a man may be trained in the art, the swordsman can never be the master of his technical knowledge unless all his psychic hindrances are removed and he can keep the mind in the state of emptiness, even purged of whatever technique he has obtained. The entire body together with the four limbs will then be capable of displaying for the first time and to its full extent all the art acquired by the training of several years. They will move as if automatically, with no conscious efforts on the part of the swordsman himself. – D. T. SUZUKI, *Zen and Japanese Culture*, page 152

The mind, it may be said, does not know where it is. When this is realized, with all the training thrown to the wind, with a mind perfectly unaware of its own workings with the self vanishing nowhere anybody knows, the art of swordsmanship attains its perfection, and one who has it is called a meijin ("genius"). – D. T. SUZUKI, *Zen and Japanese Culture*, page 153

You see, it is only when the mind is free from the burden of knowledge that it can find out what is true; and in the process of finding out, there is no accumulation, is there? The moment you begin to accumulate what you have experienced or learnt, it becomes an anchorage which holds your mind and prevents it from going further. In the process of inquiry, the mind sheds from day to day what it has learnt so that it is always fresh, uncontaminated by yesterday's experience. – JIDDU KRISHNAMURTI, *Think on These Things*, page 161

Learning of the technique corresponds to an intellectual apprehension in Zen of its philosophy, and in both Zen and swordplay a proficiency in this does not cover the whole ground of the discipline. Both require us to come to the attainment of ultimate reality, which is the Emptiness or the Absolute. The latter transcends all modes of relativity. – D. T. SUZUKI, *Zen and Japanese Culture*, page 153

In swordplay, all the technique is to be forgotten and the Unconscious is to be left alone to handle the situation, when the technique will assert its wonders automatically or spontaneously. – D. T. SUZUKI, *Zen and Japanese Culture*, page 153

For learning and knowledge are after all meant to be "forgotten," and it is only when this is realized that you feel perfectly comfortable in your transaction of business of any kind. ... Learning is needed, but the point is not to become its slave. You must be its master so that you can use it when you want it. You have to apply this psychology to swordplay. The swordsman must not harbor anything external and superfluous in his mind, his mind must be perfectly purged of all egocentric emotions. ... An idea, however worthy and desirable in itself, becomes a disease when the mind is obsessed with it. – D. T. SUZUKI, *Zen and Japanese Culture*, pages 152, 153

An idea, however worthy and desirable in itself, becomes a disease when the mind is obsessed with it. The diseases or obsessions that the swordsman has to get rid of are: (1) the desire for victory, (2) the desire to resort to technical cunning, (3) the desire to display all that he has learned, (4) the desire to overawe the enemy, (5) the desire to play a passive role, and lastly, (6) the desire to get rid of whatever disease he is likely to be infected with. When any one of these obsesses him, he becomes its slave, as it makes him lose all the freedom he is entitled to as a swordsman. – D. T. SUZUKI, *Zen and Japanese Culture*, pages 153-154

For instance, we can say, "I desire this" or "I do not desire this." "To desire" is an attachment, "to desire not to desire" is also an attachment. To be unattached then means to be free at once from both statements, positive and negative. In other words, this is to be simultaneously both "yes" and "no," which is intellectually absurd. – D. T. SUZUKI, *Zen and Japanese Culture*, page 154

So let us desire nirvana as though we desired not. When this paradox is understood we are in possession of nirvana, which is to be as if not possessing it. To be consciously unconscious, or to be unconsciously conscious, is the secret of nirvana, out of which issues the *myoyu* of creativity. *Myo* or *myoyu* is a Japanese word signifying "something defying the challenge of man's thinking powers." In other words, it is a mode of activity which comes directly out of one's inmost self without being intercepted by the dichotomous intellect. The act is so direct and immediate that intellection finds no room here to insert itself and cut it to pieces. – D. T. SUZUKI, *Zen and Japanese Culture*, page 140

The spirit is no doubt the controlling agent of our existence, though altogether beyond the realm of corporeality. The Sword of Mystery must be mode to occupy tills invisible "seat" of spirit and control every movement in whatever external situation it may happen to find itself. – D. T. SUZUKI, *Zen and Japanese Culture*, page 159

It is the ego that stands rigidly against things coming from the outside, and it is this ego rigidity that makes it impossible for us to accept everything that confronts us. – D. T. SUZUKI, *Zen and Japanese Culture*, page 144

Art lives where absolute freedom is, because where it is not, there can be no creativity. Freedom and creativity and myoyu are synonymous. – D. T. SUZUKI, *Zen and Japanese Culture*, page 144

Very few of us ever stop to look in silence at a tree, or at the evening sky. Our minds are chattering, deteriorating all the time. Why? Why is there no innocence—not the cultivated innocence of a clever mind that wants to be innocent, but that state of innocence in which there is no denial or acceptance, and in which the mind just sees what is? In this state of innocence there is moving, unbounded energy. But we grow old in the pattern of society, with its ambitions, frustrations, joys, sorrows; our minds become more and more dull, and when old age comes upon us, we are destroyed. – JIDDU KRISHNAMURTI, *Talks by Krishnamurti January - June 1960: (Verbatim Report) Bombay - Banaras - New Delhi - Ojai*, page 89

All goals apart from means are therefore an illusion and becoming is a denial of being. – CARLO SUARÈS, *Krishnamurti and the Unity of the Man*, page 2

By an error repeated throughout the ages, truth, becoming a law or a faith, places obstacles, in the way of knowledge. Method, which is in its very substance ignorance, encloses it within a vicious circle which, Krishnamurti says, we should break not by seeking knowledge, but by discovering the cause of ignorance. – CARLO SUARÈS, *Krishnamurti and the Unity of the Man*, page 3

Recollection and anticipation are fine qualities of consciousness which distinguish the human mind from that of the lower animals. They are useful and serve certain purposes, but when actions are directly related to the problem of life and death they must be given up so that they will not interfere with the fluidity of mentation and the lightening rapidity of action. – D. T. SUZUKI, *Essentials of Zen Buddhism*, page 460

Action is not departmental, or partial; it is a total thing. Action is our relationship to everything: to people, to nature, to ideas, to things. ... And action, surely, is not a matter of right and wrong. It is only when action is partial, not total, that there is right and wrong. – JIDDU KRISHNAMURTI, *Talks by Krishnamurti January - June 1960: (Verbatim Report) Bombay - Banaras - New Delhi - Ojai*, pages 88-89, 89

It is important not to get your attention arrested by the sword or by the measure of its movement. ... In spite of all the concern he has or ought to have, he is above himself, he transcends the dualistic comprehension of the situation, yet he is not a contemplative mystic, he is in the thickest of the deadly combat. – D. T. SUZUKI, *Zen and Japanese Culture*, pages 96, 96-97

Give up thinking as though not giving it up. Observe the techniques as though not observing. ... But when a man is born into the samurai family, he is not to shun learning the art of swordplay, for it is his profession to be trained in it. The point is, however, to utilize the art as a means to advance in the study of the Way (tao). When it is properly handled, it helps us in an efficient way to contribute to the cultivation of the mind and spirit. – D. T. SUZUKI, *Zen and Japanese Culture*, pages 165, 132

Prajna is possessed by all Buddhas and also by all sentient beings. It is transcendental wisdom flowing through the relativity of things and it remains immovable, though this *does not mean the immovability or insensibility* of such objects as a piece of wood or rock. *It is the mind itself endowed with infinite motilities*: it moves forward and backward, to the left and to the right, to every one of the ten quarters, and *knows no hindrances* in any direction. *Prajna Immovable* is this mind capable of *infinite movements*. – D. T. SUZUKI, *Zen and Japanese Culture*, page 97

In the case of the perfect swordsman, this becomes possible because he has realized that all movements come out of emptiness and that the mind is the name given to this dynamic aspect of emptiness, and further that here is no crookedness, no ego-centered motivation, as the emptiness is sincerity, genuineness, and straightforwardness allowing nothing between itself and its movements. It is *veni, vidi, vici*. – D. T. SUZUKI, *Zen and Japanese Culture*, page 164

The right mind is equally distributed over the body and not at all partitive. The partial mind on the other hand is divided and one-sided. Zen dislikes partialization or localization. When the mind is kept hardened at one place it fails to pervade or flow over every part of the body. When it is not partialized after any schematized plan, it naturally diffuses itself all over the body. It thus can meet the opponent as he moves about trying to strike you down. – D. T. SUZUKI, *Zen and Japanese Culture*, page 107

The swordsman is thus advised to retain this state of mentality even when he is engaged in a deadly combat. He forgets the seriousness of his situation. He has no thought of life and death. His is an "immovable mind" (fudo-shin). The fudo-shin is like the moon reflected in the stream. The waters are in motion all the time, but the moon retains its serenity. The mind moves in response to the ten thousand situations but remains ever the same. The art culminates here. All the scheming of the intellect has been quieted, and no artifice finds room for its demonstration. – D. T. SUZUKI, *Zen and Japanese Culture*, page 148

The stillness in stillness is not the real stillness; only when there is stillness in movement does the universal rhythm manifest. – Trevor Leggett, *A First Zen Reader*, page 229

Nothingness cannot be confined; the softest thing cannot be snapped. – Lieh-Tzu, *The Book of Lieh-Tzu* (translated by A. C. Graham), page 33

But the fact is far from this, for what he really intends here is to free the mind from every possible psychic obstruction or inhibition and to restore it to its pristine purity in order to display its native activities to the utmost limit. – D. T. SUZUKI, *Zen and Japanese Culture*, page 148

WHO WROTE THE TAO?

Would that we could at once paint with the eyes! In the long way from the eye through the arm to the pencil, how much is lost! – GOTTHOLD LESSING, *A Dictionary of Thoughts: Being a Cyclopedia of Laconic Quotations from the Best Authors of the World, Both Ancient and Modern* (edited by Tryon Edwards), page 31

But the fact is far from this, for what he really intends here is to free the mind from every possible psychic obstruction or inhibition and to restore it to its pristine purity in order to display its native activities to the utmost limit. In the case of swordsmanship, this is to sharpen the psychic power of seeing in order to act immediately in accordance with what it sees. – D. T. SUZUKI, *Zen and Japanese Culture*, page 148

But as soon as his mind is fixed on anything, for instance if he desires to do well, or to display his skill, or to excel others, or if he is too anxiously bent on mastering his art, he is sure to commit more mistakes than are actually necessary. Why? Because his self-consciousness or ego-consciousness is too conspicuously present over the entire range of his attention—which fact interferes with a free display of whatever proficiency he has so far acquired or is going to acquire. He must get rid of this obtruding self- or ego-consciousness and apply himself to the work to be done as if nothing particular were taking place at the moment. When things are performed in a state of "no-mind" *(mushin)* or "no-thought" *(munen)*, which means the absence of all modes of self- or ego-consciousness, the actor is perfectly free from inhibitions and feels nothing thwarting his line of behavior. – D. T. SUZUKI, *Zen and Japanese Culture*, page 147

The swordsman calls this unconscious "the mind that is no-mind" *(mushin no shin)*, or "the mind that knows no stopping" *(tomaranu kokoro)*, or "the mind abandoned and yet not abandoned" *(sutete sutenu kokoro)*, or "the everyday mind" *(heijo-shin)*. The secret of swordsmanship consists in attaining to this state of mentality—or, we may call it, spirituality, because it is beyond the realm of psychological phenomenalism. – D. T. SUZUKI, *Zen and Japanese Culture*, pages 146-147

Thinking is possible, surely, only when there is room in the mind for observation. We must have space to think. The mind must be wide open in order to function freely in thought. For a limited mind cannot think freely. A mind that is free can think freely, but not the other way around. – JIDDU KRISHNAMURTI, *Talks by Krishnamurti January - June 1960: (Verbatim Report) Bombay - Banaras - New Delhi - Ojai*, page 99

A concentrated mind is not an attentive mind, but a mind that is in the state of attention can concentrate. Attention is never exclusive, it includes everything. – JIDDU KRISHNAMURTI, *Talks by Krishnamurti January - June 1960: (Verbatim Report) Bombay - Banaras - New Delhi - Ojai*, page 100

"Meditation" is not quite the right word for this in English, because no thinking is involved, as the term might suggest, but a state the swordsman, the judo fighter, or sumo wrestler must have —*that of not being tense but ready, not thinking but not dreaming, not being set but flexible*. André Gide calls this being *disponible*, available. Zen appealed to the samurai because it taught him, when his life depended on it, not to watch the enemy's sword too closely, not to become fascinated and fastened, hence unable to shift, avoid, and strike back. The same thing holds for boxing, basketball, baseball, and other sports. ... It is also what William James would call immersion in "pure experience." It is not problem-solving or having anything "on the mind." It certainly is not slackness. *It is being wholly and quietly alive, aware and alert, ready for whatever may come.* – VAN METER AMES, *Zen and American Thought*, pages 9, 7

By this, says Yagyi, Lao-tzi wants to make us see into the interfusion of being and nonbeing. Being does not remain as such, nor does nonbeing. They are always ready to change from one state to the other. This is the "fluidity" of things, and *the swordsman must always be on the alert to meet this interchangeability of the opposites. But as soon as his mind "stops" with either of them, it loses its own fluidity.* The swordsman, therefore, is warned to keep his mind always in the state of emptiness so that his freedom in action will never be obstructed. Fluidity and emptiness are convertible terms. – D. T. SUZUKI, *Zen and Japanese Culture*, page 158

The "abiding stage" means "the point where the mind stops to abide." In Buddhist training we speak of fifty-two stages, of which one is a stage where the mind attaches itself to any object it encounters. This attaching is known as tomaru, "stopping" or "abiding." *The mind stops with one object instead of flowing from one object to another* (as the mind acts when it follows its own nature). – D. T. SUZUKI, *Zen and Japanese Culture*, page 95

The delusive mind may be defined as the mind intellectually and affectively burdened. It thus cannot move on from one topic to another without stopping and reflecting on itself, and this obstructs its native fluidity. – D. T. SUZUKI, *Essentials of Zen Buddhism*, page 454

The wheel revolves when it is not too tightly attached to the axle. When t is too tight, it will never move on. If the mind has something in it, it stops functioning, it cannot hear, it cannot see, even when a sound enters the ears or a light flashes before the eyes. To have something in mind means that it is preoccupied and has no time for anything else. But to attempt to remove the thought already in it is to refill it with another something. The task is endless. ... When we tie a cat, being afraid of its catching a bird, it keeps on struggling for freedom. But train the cat so that it would not mind the presence of a bird. The animal is now free and can go anywhere it likes. *In a similar way, when the mind is tied up, it feels inhibited in every move it makes, and nothing will be accomplished with any sense of spontaneity. Not only that, the work itself will be of a poor quality, or it may not be finished at all.* – D. T. SUZUKI, *Zen and Japanese Culture*, pages 111, 114

As we have seen, all life is action; living is action, thinking is action, and not-thinking is also action. And we also see that any action from a centre creates conflict. When the mind is tethered to a centre, naturally it is not free, it can move only within the limits of that centre. ... There is no human being who is isolated. If he is isolated, he is dead; he is paralyzed within the fortress of his own ideas. – JIDDU KRISHNAMURTI *Talks by Krishnamurti January - June 1960: (Verbatim Report) Bombay - Banaras - New Delhi - Ojai*, page 90

When you are looking at something with complete attention *there is no space for a conception, a formula, or a memory.* This is important to understand because we are going into something which requires very careful investigation. It is only a mind that looks at a tree or the stars or the sparkling waters of a river with *complete self-abandonment* that knows what beauty is, and when we are actually seeing we are in a state of love. – JIDDU KRISHNAMURTI, *Freedom from the Known*, page 90

When there is no obstruction of whatever kind, the swordsman's movements are like flashes of lightning or like the mirror reflecting images. There is not a hairbreadth interval between one movement and another. When in his mind there is any shadow of doubt, any sense of fear or insecurity, this indecisiveness at once reveals itself in his sword's movements, which means a defeat on his part. When the Sword of Mystery is off its original "seat," no myo (miao) can ever be expected to manifest itself. – D. T. SUZUKI, *Zen and Japanese Culture*, page 159

So long as there is a centre creating space around itself there is neither love nor beauty. When there is no centre and no circumference then there is love. And when you love you are beauty.
– JIDDU KRISHNAMURTI, *Freedom from the Known*, page 94

It's Just a Name

There is a powerful craving in most of us to see ourselves as instruments in the hands of others and thus free ourselves from the responsibility for acts which are prompted by our own questionable inclinations and impulses. Both the strong and the weak grasp at this alibi. The latter hide their malevolence under the virtue of obedience: they acted dishonorably because they had to obey orders. The strong, too, claim absolution by proclaiming themselves the chosen instrument of a higher power—God, history, fate, nation or humanity. – ERIC HOFFER, *The Passionate State of Mind*, page 54

We have more faith in what we imitate than in what we originate. We cannot derive a sense of absolute certitude from anything which has its roots in us. The most poignant sense of insecurity comes from standing alone; we are not alone when we imitate. – ERIC HOFFER, *The Passionate State of Mind*, page 84

To become different from what we are, we must have some awareness of what we are. Whether this being different results in dissimulation or a real change of heart—it cannot be realized without self-awareness. ... Yet it is remarkable that the very people who are most self-dissatisfied and crave most for a new identity have the least self-awareness. They have turned away from an unwanted self and hence never had a good look at it. The result is that the most dissatisfied can neither dissimulate nor attain a real change of heart. They are transparent, and their unwanted qualities persist through all attempts at self-dramatization and self- transformation. ... Lack of self-awareness renders us transparent. A soul that knows itself is opaque; like Adam after he ate from the tree of knowledge it uses words as fig leaves to cover its nakedness and shame. – ERIC HOFFER, *The Passionate State of Mind*, pages 93, 96

Fear comes from uncertainty. When we are absolutely certain, whether of our worth or worthlessness, we are almost impervious to fear. Thus, a feeling of utter unworthiness can be a source of courage. ... Everything seems possible when we are absolutely helpless or absolutely powerful—and both states stimulate our credulity. – ERIC HOFFER, *The Passionate State of Mind*, pages 56, 52

Pride is a sense of worth derived from something that is not organically part of us, while self-esteem derives from the potentialities and achievements of the self. We are proud when we identify ourselves with an imaginary self, a leader, a holy cause, a collective body or possessions. There is fear and intolerance in pride; it is sensitive and uncompromising. The less promise and potency in the self, the more imperative is the need for pride. The core of pride is self-rejection. It is true, however, that when pride releases energies and serves as a spur to achievement, it can lead to a reconciliation with the self and the attainment of genuine self-esteem. – ERIC HOFFER, *The Passionate State of Mind*, page 23

Secretiveness can be a source of pride. It is a paradox that secretiveness plays the same role as boasting: both are engaged in the creation of a disguise. Boasting tries to create an imaginary self, while secretiveness gives us the exhilarating feeling of being princes disguised in meekness. Of the two, secretiveness is the more difficult and effective. For in the self-observant boasting breeds self-contempt. Yet it is as Spinoza said: "Men govern nothing with more difficulty than their tongues and can moderate their desires more than their words." ... Humility is not renunciation of pride but the substitution of one pride for another. – ERIC HOFFER, *The Passionate State of Mind*, pages 117, 128

A fateful process is set in motion when the individual is released "to the freedom of his own impotence" and left to justify his existence by his own efforts. The autonomous individual, striving to realize himself and prove his worth, has created all that is great in literature, art, music, science and technology. The autonomous individual, also, when he can neither realize himself nor justify his existence by his own efforts, is a breeding call of frustration, and the seed of the convulsions which shake our world to its foundations. The individual on his own is stable only so long as he is possessed of self-esteem. The maintenance of self-esteem is a continuous task which taxes all of the individual's powers and inner resources. We have to prove our worth and justify our existence anew each day. When, for whatever reason, self-esteem is unattainable, the autonomous individual becomes a highly explosive entity. He turns away from an unpromising self and plunges into the pursuit of pride—the explosive substitute for self-esteem. All social disturbances and upheavals have their roots in crises of individual self-esteem, and the great endeavor in which the masses most readily unite is basically a search for pride. – ERIC HOFFER, *The Passionate State of Mind*, page 18

We acquire a sense of worth either by realizing our talents, or by keeping busy, or by identifying ourselves with something apart from us—be it a cause, a leader, a group, possessions and the like. Of the three, the path of self-realization is the most difficult. It is taken only when other avenues to a sense of worth are more or less blocked. Men of talent have to be encouraged and goaded to engage in creative work. Their groans and laments echo through the ages. – ERIC HOFFER, *The Passionate State of Mind*, page 19

Action is a highroad to self-confidence and esteem. Where it is open, all energies flow toward it. It comes readily to most people, and its rewards are tangible. The cultivation of the spirit is elusive and difficult, and the tendency toward it is rarely spontaneous. Where the opportunities for action are many, cultural creativeness is likely to be neglected. The cultural flowering of New England came to an almost abrupt end with the opening of the West. The relative cultural sterility of the Romans might perhaps be explained by their empire rather than by an innate lack of genius. The best talents were attracted by the rewards of administrative posts just as the best talents in America are attracted by the rewards of a business career. – ERIC HOFFER, *The Passionate State of Mind*, page 19

The propensity to action is symptomatic of an inner unbalance. To be balanced is to be more or less at rest. Action is at bottom a swinging and flailing of the arms to regain one's balance and keep afloat. And if it be true, as Napoleon wrote to Carnot, that "the art of government is not to let men grow stale," then it is an art of unbalancing. The crucial difference between a totalitarian regime and a free social order is perhaps in the methods of unbalancing by which their people are kept active and striving. – ERIC HOFFER, *The Passionate State of Mind*, page 14

We are told that talent creates its own opportunities. But it sometimes seems that intense desire creates not only its own opportunities, but its own talents. – ERIC HOFFER, *The Passionate State of Mind*, page 10

The times of drastic change are times of passion. We can never be fit and ready for that which is wholly new. We have to adjust ourselves, and every radical adjustment is a crisis in self-esteem: we undergo a test; we have to prove ourselves. A population subjected to drastic change is thus a population of misfits, and misfits live and breathe in an atmosphere of passion. – ERIC HOFFER, *The Passionate State of Mind*, page 7

That we pursue something passionately does not always mean that we really want it or have a special aptitude for it. Often, the thing we pursue most passionately is but a substitute for the one thing we really want and cannot have. It is usually safe to predict that the fulfillment of an excessively cherished desire is not likely to still our nagging anxiety. – ERIC HOFFER, *The Passionate State of Mind*, page 2

Our sense of power is more vivid when we break a man's spirit than when we win his heart. For we can win a man's heart one day and lose it the next. But when we break a proud spirit, we achieve something that is final and absolute. – ERIC HOFFER, *The Passionate State of Mind*, page 58

It is compassion rather than the principle of justice which can guard us against being unjust to our fellow men. – ERIC HOFFER, *The Passionate State of Mind*, page 86

It is doubtful whether there is such a thing as impulsive or natural tolerance. Tolerance requires an effort of thought and self-control. And acts of kindness, too, are rarely without deliberateness and "thoughtfulness." Thus, it seems that some artificiality, some posing and pretense, are inseparable from any act or attitude which involves a limitation of our appetites and selfishness. We ought to beware of people who do not think it necessary to pretend that they are good and decent. Lack of hypocrisy in such things hints at a capacity for a more depraved ruthlessness. ... If we want people to behave in a certain manner, we must set the stage and give them a cue. This is true also when it is ourselves we want to induce. There is no telling how deeply a mind may be affected by the deliberate staging of gestures, acts and symbols. Pretense is often an indispensable step in the attainment of genuineness. It is a form into which genuine inclinations flow and solidify. – ERIC HOFFER, *The Passionate State of Mind*, pages 122, 121

The control of our being is not unlike the combination of a safe. One turn of the knob rarely unlocks the safe. Each advance and retreat is a step toward one's goal. – ERIC HOFFER, *The Passionate State of Mind*, page 120

> Viewed in this manner, art becomes only a pretext through which life opens up its secrets to us. – Violetta Adorable, "The Zen Concept of Emptiness" from the journal *Asian Studies, v 9 issue 1 April 1971*, page 54
>
> We can see through others only when we see through ourselves. – ERIC HOFFER, *The Passionate State of Mind*, page 97

By an error repeated throughout the ages, truth, becoming a law or a faith, places obstacles, in the way of knowledge. Method, which is in its very substance ignorance, encloses it within a vicious circle which, Krishnamurti says, we should break not by seeking knowledge, but by discovering the cause of ignorance. – CARLO SUARÈS, *Krishnamurti and the Unity of the Man*, page 3

Joseph J. Snyder, Jr:
The First *Tao of Jeet Kune Do* Scholar

Although completely unheralded in the Jeet Kune Do community, Joseph Snyder deserves a great deal of credit. He is the original scholar on the text of the *Tao of Jeet Kune Do*. In 1975, he became the first person to recognize that the book released under Bruce Lee's name contained passages from the work of other authors. His research resulted in an acknowledgement added to the front page of the *Tao of Jeet Kune Do* by the Bruce Lee Estate and Ohara Publications that gave a handful of rightful authors their due credit.

Joe Snyder remains a bit of an enigma, as there is a paucity of information available on him. There is also no indication what martial art he practiced - or if he practiced martial arts at all. Information about Joe Snyder provided in this section was compiled from recollections of Jeet Kune Do instructors active in the 1970s, articles that Joe Snyder wrote for a handful of publications in the late 1970s and early 1980s, correspondence written by Snyder, genealogical resources, and government records.

Joseph John Snyder, Jr. was born on April 16, 1927 in Pittsburgh, Pennsylvania to Joseph John Snyder, Sr. and Ethel Baker Snyder. Snyder spent his early childhood in nearby Mt. Lebanon, but by the time he reached his teens, he was living in Pittsburgh.

In July of 1945, at the age of 18, Joseph Snyder (or "Joe" as he was often called) was drafted into the US Army. Due to the ending of World War II he served only briefly, from July 1945 to November 1946, and was discharged as a private first class. Snyder served at Keesler Field in Biloxi, Mississippi.

There is little public record of Joseph Snyder beyond this point. After his discharge from the military, Snyder returned to Pittsburgh for a time before relocating to Levittown, Pennsylvania. He married and became a father to a daughter, although there is no indication that he had other children. His occupation post-military service is unknown.

Joseph Snyder was 48 years old when the *Tao of Jeet Kune Do* was released in 1975. Snyder pre-ordered the book with the intention of using it to guide his daughter, who recently began martial arts classes. "I knew that she was too young to understand the material that probably would be presented," recalled Snyder, "but I thought that it might help as a reference."

Due to his pre-ordering, Snyder was one of the first fans to get a copy of the *Tao of Jeet Kune Do* in October of 1975. In one of his later articles for *Official Karate* magazine, Snyder spoke about his excitement to receive the book: "I eagerly tore open the cover of my newly-arrived treasure, retired to my bedroom, turned on the reading lamp, and thumbed through the pages. I was amazed at the mass of information presented, for it seemed to have it all."

Nonetheless, his excitement was soon replaced with a sense of disquiet. "After dozing off later that evening, I suddenly awoke with a feeling of strange restlessness and was bothered by something that made me go to my bookshelf and select a book at random. It turned out to be a book about boxing, written by Edwin L. Haislet, which I had purchased during the wars years at the Army PX."

He began thumbing through the book. "I noticed a section on training. It seemed so familiar – yes, I had read it earlier in Bruce Lee's masterpiece! I compared the passages, and sure enough, they matched word for word. I must admit I was a little shaken by the experience, for my arms were covered with goosebumps."

Having made this discovery, and knowing that it was possible the book contained other passages lifted from other authors, Snyder began looking at the *Tao of Jeet Kune Do* again with a different eye.

"Every field of endeavor has its own special vocabulary," explaned Snyder in one of his later articles. "If you were to close your eyes in front of any TV set and switch from talk show to talk show, I am certain that you would be able to envision whether the featured guest is a doctor, sports writer, or rock star. The same separation of mode of expression changes almost from paragraph to paragraph in Bruce Lee's masterwork, the *Tao of Jeet Kune Do*. It doesn't take long to come to the realization that you are reading something that has been assembled from different sources. Further investigation revealed to me that much of this was done word for word."

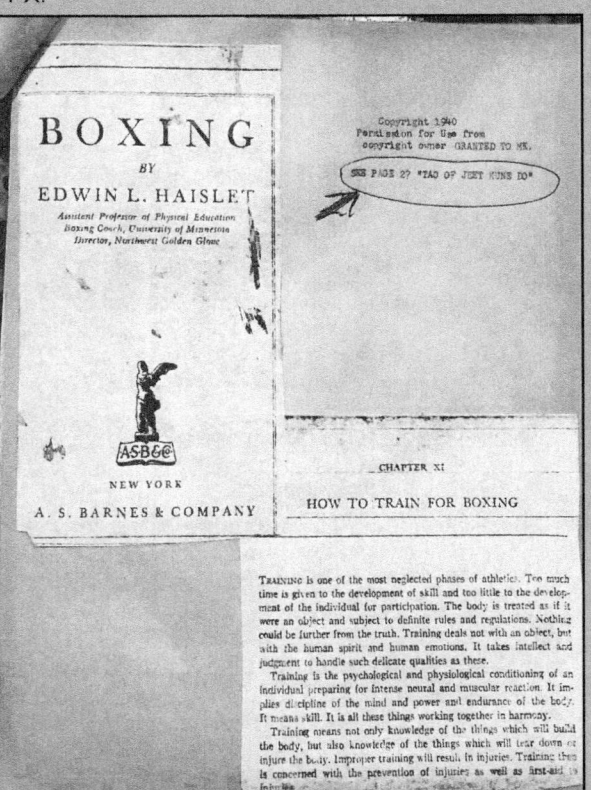

ABOVE: Photograph of a sample page from the research Joseph Snyder submitted to the Bruce Lee Estate. *(Courtesy of the Richard Torres Archives)*

Joseph Snyder's initial discoveries were passages and drawings lifted from the books *Boxing* by Edwin Haislet, *Fencing* by Hugo and James Castello, *Fencing with the Foil* by Roger Crosnier, and *The Theory and Practice of Fencing* by Julio Martinez Castelló.

Snyder compiled this information and attempted to reach the Lee family to make them aware of the verbatim borrowing. He sent his findings to Mito Uyehara, the founder of Black Belt magazine. Uyehara then passed the information along to Linda Lee, Bruce Lee's widow, and shortly thereafter Joseph Snyder was contacted by Adrian Marshall, the attorney for Linda Lee and the Bruce Lee Estate.

"Because of what I had uncovered," said Joseph Snyder, "the book was temporarily withdrawn from the market. I was in constant contact with Adrian Marshall, who called me frequently from Los Angeles, with prolonged conversations concerning my discoveries."

"Ohara Publications halted printing of the book until the real authors were contacted and permission given to use the material," said Jeet Kune Do instructor Richard Torres, who was in contact with Snyder during the late 1970s.

By March of 1976, Linda Lee offered Joseph Snyder compensation, personally paid by her, for his discoveries – first with a check for $500 and later another check for $300 – along with a legally-worded letter from Adrian Marshall declaring the matter resolved and no obligations outstanding on the parts of Linda Lee and Ohara Publications.

"Ask The Globe" will study every inquiry, but it isn't possible to answer or acknowledge every one. They will be chosen for general interest and shared with all readers of The Globe.

MONEY COMING BACK

A. G., Cambridge.—A new copy of "Tao of Jeet Kune Do," a refund check for $41.35 and a letter of apology from R. K. Hosokawa, operations manager. All three from Ohara Publications Inc. of Burbank, Calif.

ABOVE: When printing was halted on the Tao of Jeet Kune Do in late 1975/early 1976, the orders kept coming in, leading to a backlog of orders and a lot of frustrated customers, such as A. G. Cambridge, who sought out the assistance of the Boston Globe in early 1978.

Over the next seven years, Joe Snyder would continue to study the Tao of Jeet Kune Do and expanded his list of borrowed passages. He also began to reach out to the original authors, recording interviews with them and making them aware of their work appearing uncredited in the Tao of Jeet Kune Do. Later, he announced plans to sell a cassette tape, which he titled The Sources of Bruce Lee's Techniques and offered for the price of $10. Snyder promised the tape would weave a discussion of his findings with his recorded interviews of the original authors. "My tape gives the precise sources of those techniques Bruce Lee described in his seven handwritten volumes entitled The Tao of Jeet Kune Do, upon which he formulated the characteristic applications of his now famous style." It is unknown if Snyder's tape was ever sold and none seem to remain in existence.

At first, Joseph Snyder was quick to defend Bruce Lee, suggesting that Bruce Lee should not be judged for the Tao of Jeet Kune Do lifting from other authors. "Don't forget," said Snyder, "when we speak of Bruce Lee, we are speaking of a man to be respected, and his 'copying' habits do not detract from that." However, over a period of several years, as Snyder found more and more examples, his perspective on them began to change. And when he saw the erroneous quotes start to circulate in Black Belt and other publications, Snyder tried to sound the alarm. But when he attempted to inform the previously appreciative parties, he found himself rebuffed. "Although I have attempted to contact Linda Lee and Mito Uyehara concerning embarrassing inaccuracies appearing in subsequent publications based on the Tao of Jeet Kune Do, my pleas were not registering."

This only added to Joseph Snyder's growing disillusionment. "When I made my first discoveries, I must admit that I felt what I have since clearly recognized as a misguided obligation to protect the 'legend of Bruce Lee,'" wrote Snyder. "I sweated out a great deal of writing-time attempting to somehow justify the fact that Bruce used the ideas of those to whom he gave absolutely no credit. This may have furthered his career, but it did not give credit where it was due."

Joseph Snyder was planning and appears to have written a book, which was to be titled *The Sources and Application of Bruce Lee's Techniques*. In 1983, he described it as the product of seven years of research. He had a publishing contract with C.V. Mosby Company, a well-established publisher. "A prerequisite for the proper application of Bruce Lee's techniques is knowing and studying the theories of his sources - i.e. written by those whose expertise in their chosen fields is unquestioned," said Snyder.

Yet, despite mentioning it in multiple articles, the book was, mysteriously, never published. And Joe Snyder never wrote about Bruce Lee again.

"He wanted to write a book," said Richard Torres, "but that never came to fruition."

It is possible that Snyder reached an agreement with the Bruce Lee Estate that prevented the release of his findings. There is no way of determining if that is the case, so it remains conjecture.

Joseph Snyder seemed to have developed on open resentment toward the *Tao of Jeet Kune Do* as his scholarship reached completion, and he was unapologetic about his work to expose the misattributions. "The publication of the *Tao of Jeet Kune Do* was a mistake," said Snyder. "I'm certain Bruce Lee himself would have approved of my actions to avoid misunderstandings." Snyder must have surely bristled when, in 1993, Universal Pictures released the biographical movie *Dragon: The Bruce Lee Story* which prominently featured the *Tao of Jeet Kune Do* in a bit of obvious product placement – despite the fact that the book was never published in Bruce Lee's lifetime.

Joseph Snyder passed away in Levittown, Pennsylvania on January 9, 2004 at the age of 76. His scholarly work, including the cassette tape of interviews and the book he compiled, will almost certainly never be seen by the public.

Nonetheless, Joe Snyder revealed enough in his short period of activity to earn his recognition as a true scholar. I leave the final word to him:

> *"Having talked to some of the originators of these ideas, I have found that they would appreciate the recognition, and would be proud of having it known that they have had a hand in developing one of the greatest martial artists of all time."*

Afterword

When I began this research five months ago, my goal was to look at the philosophical writings attributed to Bruce Lee. As my findings grew, I realized that I needed to make a momentary detour and concentrate on the entire contents of the *Tao of Jeet Kune Do*. In the *Tao of Jeet Kune Do*, I found the sources for nearly 1,000 passages and illustrations, representing roughly 85% of the content of the book.

Yet, while that may sound like a lot, that only scratches the surface of what I have discovered. My goal, ultimately, is to put under the microscope every single statement that has ever been attributed to Bruce Lee. As I continue my research into the texts attributed to Lee, I will undoubtedly continue to make more discoveries of misattribution. This will likely include more discoveries about the *Tao of Jeet Kune Do*. I suspect, in the next few years, I may be publishing an updated edition of this book.

Not everyone will appreciate the release of this information. Some people may benefit personally or financially from the lack of awareness, others may know much of this information but zealously guard it for themselves, while some people – particular some members of Bruce Lee's fandom – may not want their vision of Bruce Lee to be disturbed. But I believe that the release of this information serves the greater good. And I also believe that the visionaries who originated these ideas deserve to be recognized for their genius.

Some people may argue that I am just a "Bruce Lee basher" who wants to redefine Bruce Lee as an unoriginal, uninspired posturer. Nothing could be further from the truth. Bruce Lee remains, to me, one of the most important intellectual influences on my life. These findings have not changed that. What these findings do, though, is give me a better understanding of Bruce Lee and expand my own intellectual journey.

These findings also correct the public record, insomuch as the public is willing to embrace them. I am wise enough at this point to recognize that the Bruce Lee quote machine is a leviathan that is very reluctant to change its course; indeed, it now possesses a life of its own, generating its own misattributions in the form of memes drawn from the great sea of the Internet, no longer dependent upon the publishing industry's misattributed scraps. It now makes up its own quotes, like some wild artifical intelligence that has grown beyond its need for a master.

So why then do I continue my course? To enlighten people, even though some people are not prepared to hear the message. I am reminded of a story of the Buddha: Mara, the evil one, tried to dissuade the Buddha from his mission of enlightening others, arguing that it is a wasted exercise and that the masses were not prepared for his message, to which the Buddha replied, "There will be some who will understand."

Sound familiar? It may for some of you. That last story is not Bruce Lee's, by the way. It is an old story of the Buddha and can be found in Christmas Humphreys' books *Buddhism*, *The Wisdom of Buddhism*, and *The Way of Action*, as well as in Huston Smith's *The Religions of Man*. Bruce Lee owned those books as well.

James Bishop, Ph.D.
September 4, 2022

List of Publications Found in the *Tao of Jeet Kune Do*

The following list includes the information of all texts that were found to have contributed to the *Tao of Jeet Kune Do*.

BOOKS

Allanson-Winn, R. G. (Lord Headley). *Boxing*. G. Bell and Sons, Ltd., 1920.
Ames, Van Meter. *Zen and Amerian Thought*. University of Hawaii Press, 1962.
Anonymous. *Chandogya Upanishad*.
Barbasetti, Luigi. *The Art of the Foil: With a Short History of Fencing*. E. P. Dutton & Company, 1932.
Barbasetti, Luigi. *The Art of the Sabre and the Épée*. E. P. Dutton & Company, 1936.
Barr, Robert. "Fighting with Four Fists." *McClure's Magazine Illustrated, Volume III*. S. S. McClure, Ltd., 1894, pp. 294-303.
Bartlett, E. G. *Judo and Self-Defense: One Hundred Lessons Arranged as a Two-Year Practical Course, for Private or Class Study*. ABC Books, Inc, 1963.
Joe Begala, Wesley Brown, Jr., and Harold Lowe. *Hand-To-Hand Combat*. United States Naval Institute 1962.
Blanchard, Robert G. *The Mechanics of Judo: Analytical Studies of Selected Standing Techniques*. Charles E. Tuttle Company, 1961.
Briggs, William. *Anthology of Zen*. Grove Press, Inc., 1961.
Brown, Robert L. and Thomas E. Robertson. *Illustrated Guide to Takedown in Wrestling*. Parker Publishing Company, Inc., 1968.
Buddhaghosa. *Visuddhimagga*.
Castelló, Hugo and James Castello. *Fencing*. The Ronald Press Company, 1962.
Castelló, Julio Martinez. *The Theory and Practice of Fencing*. Charles Scribner's & Sons, 1933.
Chang Chung-Yuan. *Creatiivity and Taoism*. Julian Press, 1970.
Clark, Norman. *How to Box*. Metheun & Co., Ltd., 1922.
Clark, Norman. *Boxing*. C. Arthur Pearson, 1921.
Colmore Dunn, H. A. *Fencing*. George Bell and Sons. Inc., 1906.
Conze, Edward. *Buddhist Texts Through the Ages*. Philosophical Library, Inc., 1953.
Crosnier, Roger. *Fencing with the Electric Foil*. Faber & Faber, 1961.
Crosnier, Roger. *Fencing with the Épée*. Faber & Faber, 1958.
Crosnier, Roger. *Fencing with the Foil*. A. S. Barnes and Company, 1955.
Crosnier, Roger. *Fencing with the Sabre*. Faber & Faber, 1954.
De Bary, William Theodore. *Sources of Chinese Tradition, Volume 1*. Columbia University Press, 1960.
De Beaumont, Charles Louis. *Fencing: Ancient Art and Modern Sport*. Nicholas Kaye, Ltd., 1960.
De Beaumont, Charles Louis. *Teach Yourself Fencing*. The English Universities Press, 1968.
Dempsey, Jack. *Championship Fighting: Explosive Punching and Aggressive Defense*. Prentice-Hall, 1950.
Driscoll, Jim. *The Straight Left and How to Cultivate It*. Athletic Publications Ltd., 1945.

Edwards, Tryon. *A Dictionary of Thoughts: Being a Cyclopedia of Laconic Quotations from the Best Authors of the World, Both Ancient and Modern.* F. B. Dickerson Company, 1908.
Enelow, Gertrude. *Body Dynamics: The Zen and Zest of Self-Development.* Information Incorporated, 1960.
Feldenkrais, Moshe. *Higher Judo: Groundwork.* Frederick Warne & Company, Ltd., 1962.
Fung Yu Lan. *A History of Chinese Philosophy. Vol. II.* Princeton University Press, 1952.
Fung Yu-Lan. *The Spirit of Chinese Philosophy.* Beacon Press, 1962.
Garret, Maxwell R. *Fencing Instructor's Guide (Athletic Institute Series).* Sterling Publishing Company, 1961.
Garret, Maxwell R. *How to Improve Your Fencing.* The Athletic Institute, 1934.
Gilbey, John F. (Robert W. Smith). *Secret Fighting Arts of the World.* Charles E. Tuttle Company, 1963.
Gilmer, Frank. *Push Yourself: A Book for Amateur Boxers and Boxing Fans.* Frank Gilmer, 1941.
Gotch, Frank. *Wrestling and How to Train.* Richard K. Fox, 1908.
Griffith, Coleman Roberts. *Psychology of Coaching: A Study of Coaching Methods from the Point of View of Psychology.* Charles Scribner's & Sons, 1926.
Gruzanski, Charles V. *Spike and Chain: Japanese Fighting Arts.* Charles E. Tuttle Company, 1968.
Haislet, Edwin. *Boxing.* The Ronald Press Company, 1940.
Haislet, Edwin. *Boxing: The U.S. Naval Aviation Training Manual.* The United States Naval Institute, 1950.
Hasumi, Toshimitsu. *Zen in Japanese Art: A Way of Spiritual Experience.* Philosophical Library, Inc., 1962.
Hoffer, Eric. *The Passionate State of Mind.* Harper & Row Publishers, 1954.
Hoffman, Bob. *Bob Hoffman's Daily Dozen.* The Bob Hoffman Foundation, 1958.
Hoffman, Bob. *Functional Isometric Contraction: Book One.* The Bob Hoffman Foundation, 1961.
Humphreys, Christmas. *Zen Comes West: The Present and Future of Zen Buddhism in Britain.* George Allen & Unwin, Ltd., 1960.
Inch, Thomas. *Boxing.* Sir Isaac Pitman & Sons, Ltd., 1948.
Inch, Thomas. *Boxing for Beginners: From Novice to Champion.* Kingswood: The World's Work, 1913.
Inch, Thomas. *Boxing: The Secret of the Knock-Out.* Sir Isaac Pitman & Sons, Ltd., 1953.
Johnson Smith & Company. *The Art of Sparring and Boxing: The Noble Art of Self Defense Without a Teacher.* Johnson Smith & Company, 1935.
Jowett, George F. *How to Knock 'Em Cold.* George F. Jowett, 1943.
Kardoss, John. *Sabre Fencing: History, Theory, Practice.* Hicks Smith and Sons Pty., Ltd., 1955.
Kennedy, Clarence E. *Boxing Simplified: Prepared Especially for Teachers.* The Antioch Press, 1929.
Krishnamurti, Jiddu. *Commentaries on Living, First Series.* Harper & Row Publishers, 1956.
Krishnamurti, Jiddu. *Commentaries on Living, Second Series.* Quest Books, 1967.

Krishnamurti, Jiddu. *The First and Last Freedom*. Harper & Brothers, 1954.
Krishnamurti, Jiddu. *Freedom from the Known*. Harper & Row Publishers, 1969.
Krishnamurti, Jiddu. *Krishnamurti's Talks in India 1948 (Verbatim Report) Series II - Bangalore*. Krishnamurti Writings, Inc., 1961.
Krishnamurti, Jiddu. *Talks by Krishnamurti January-June 1960: (Verbatim Report) Bombay - Banaras - New Delhi - Ojai*. Krishnamurti Writings, Ojai, 1961.
Krishnamurti, Jiddu. *Think On These Things*. Harper & Row Publishers, 1964.
Lawther, John Dobson. *The Psychology of Coaching*. Prentice-Hall, 1951.
LeBell, Gene and L. C. Coughran. *The Handbook of Judo*. Thomas Nelson & Sons, 1962.
LeBell, Gene and L. C. Coughran. *Your Personal Handbook of Self-Defense*. Whiting & Wheaton, 1966.
Leggett, Trevor. *A First Zen Reader*. Charles E. Tuttle Company, 1960.
Leonard, Hugh F. *A Handbook of Wrestling*. E. R. Pelton, 1897.
Liederman, Earle. *The Science of Wrestling and the Art of Jiu Jitsu*. Earle Liederman, 1923.
Lieh-Tzu. *The Book of Lieh-Tzu: A Classic of the Tao*, translated by A. C. Graham. John Murray, 1960.
Maraini, Fosco. *Meeting with Japan*. Penguin Publishing Group, 1960.
Marciano, Rocky and Charley Goldman. *Rocky Marciano's Book of Boxing and Bodybuilding*. Prentice-Hall, 1967.
McInnes, Peter. *Tackle Boxing This Way*. Stanley Paul, 1960.
Metheny, Eleanor. *Body Dynamics*. McGraw-Hill, 1952.
Mikinosuke Kawaish. *My Method of Self Defense*. W. Foulsham & Company, Ltd., 1957.
Morehouse, Laurence E. and Philip J. Rasch. *Scientific Basis of Athletic Training*. W. B. Saunders Company, 1958.
Morehouse, Laurence E. and Philip J. Rasch. *Sports Medicine for Trainers*. W. B. Saunders Company, 1963.
Morehouse, Laurence E. and Augustus T. Miller, Jr. *The Physiology of Exercise*. C. V. Mosby, 1953.
Nadi, Aldo. *On Fencing*. G. P. Putnam and Sons, Inc., 1948.
National Association for Girls and Women in Sport. *Bowling-Fencing-Golf Guide*. American Association for Health, Physical Education, and Recreation, 1962.
Neill, Bobby. *Instruction to Young Boxers*. Museum Press, 1961.
O'Brien, Philadelphia Jack and S. E. Bilik. *Boxing*. C.Scribner's & Sons, 1928.
O'Neill, Frank F. *Boxing: A Guide to the Manly Art of Self Defense*. American Sports Publishing Company. Inc., 1926.
Palffy-Alpar, Julius. *Sword and Masque*. F. A. Davis Company, 1967.
Peterson, Wilferd Arlan. *The New Book of the Art of Living*. Simon and Schuster, 1963.
Reps, Paul. *Zen Flesh, Zen Bones*. Charles E. Tuttle Company, 1957.
Ross, Barney. *Fundamentals of Boxing*. Ziff-Davis Publishing Company, 1942.
Ross, Nancy Wilson. *Three Ways of Asian Wisdom: Hinduism, Buddhism, Zen and Their Significance*. Simon and Schuster, 1966.
Schott, Carl P., editor. *The 1947 Official National Collegiate Athletic Association Boxing Guide*. A. S. Barnes and Company, 1946.
Selden, Elizabeth. *Elements of the Free Dance*. A.S. Barnes & Company, 1930.

Skinner, Harry H. *Jiu-Jitsu: A Comprehensive and Copiously Illustrated Treatise on the Wonderful Japanese Method*. The Baker and Taylor Company, 1904.
Smith, Robert W. and Donn Draeger. *Asian Fighting Arts*. Kodansha International, 1969.
Sports Illustrated, editors. *The Sports Illustrated Book of Fencing*. J. B. Lppincott Company, 1962.
Stryk, Lucien, editor. *World of the Buddha: An Introduction to Buddhist Literature*. Grove Press, Inc., 1968.
Suares, Carlo. *Krishnamurti and the Unity of the Man*. Chetana Ltd., 1969.
Suzuki, D. T. *The Essentials of Zen Buddhism*. E. P. Dutton & Company, 1962.
Suzuki, D. T. *Zen and Japanese Culture*. Pantheon Books, 1960.
Suzuki, D. T. *Zen Buddhism, Selected Writings*. Doubleday, 1956.
Swann, Jeffrey. *Toehold on Zen*. World Publishing Company, 1963.
Viscount Knebworth. *Boxing: A Guide to Modern Methods*. Seeley, Service & Co., Ltd., 1951.
Von Durckheim, Karlfried Graf. *Hara: The Vital Centre of Man*. George Allen & Unwin, Ltd., 1962.
Walsh, John J. *Boxing Simplified*. Prentice-Hall, 1951.
Watanabe, Jiichi and Lindy Avakian. *The Secrets of Judo: A Text for Instructors and Students*. Charles E. Tuttle Company, 1961.
Watts, Alan. *Beat Zen, Square Zen, and Zen*. Subterranean Company, 1959.
Watts, Alan. *This is It*. Vintage Books, 1960.
Watts, Alan. *Zen*. James Ladd Delkir, 1948.
Wells, Katharine F. Kinesiology. *The Scientific Basis of Human Motion*. W. B. Saunders Company, 1971.
Westbrook, A. and O. Ratti. *Aikido and the Dynamic Sphere*. Charles E. Tuttle Company, 1970.
Wienpahl, Paul. *The Matter of Zen: A Brief Account of Zazen*. New York University Press, 1964.
Williams, Jesse Feiring and Eugene White Nixon. *The Athlete In the Making*. W. B. Saunders Company, 1932.
Wong Hon Fan and Guangyu Luo. *Praying Mantis Book #01: Secrets of the Mantis Boxing Art* 螳螂拳術闡秘. Meiyi Publishing Company, 1946.

ARTICLES

Adorable, Violetta. "The Zen Concept of Emptines." *Asian Studies*, vol. 9, No. 1, 1971, pp. 37-54.
Ames, Van Meter. "Art for Zen and Dewey." *Proceedings of the IV International Congress of Aesthetics, Athens*, 1960, pp. 745-48.
Delcourt, J. "The French Manly Art of Self-Defense." *Black Belt*, Mar. 1967, pp. 16-23.
Kenneth, Gene. "Mat Work - Judo's Neglected Art." *Black Belt*, Sept. 1970, pp. 23-25.

Statistics on the *Tao of Jeet Kune Do*

An interesting result of the research I have conducted is that I am able to compile the data, code it, and then analyze it. Here are some simple analyses I have run on the information.

Table 1. An Analysis by Subject Matter

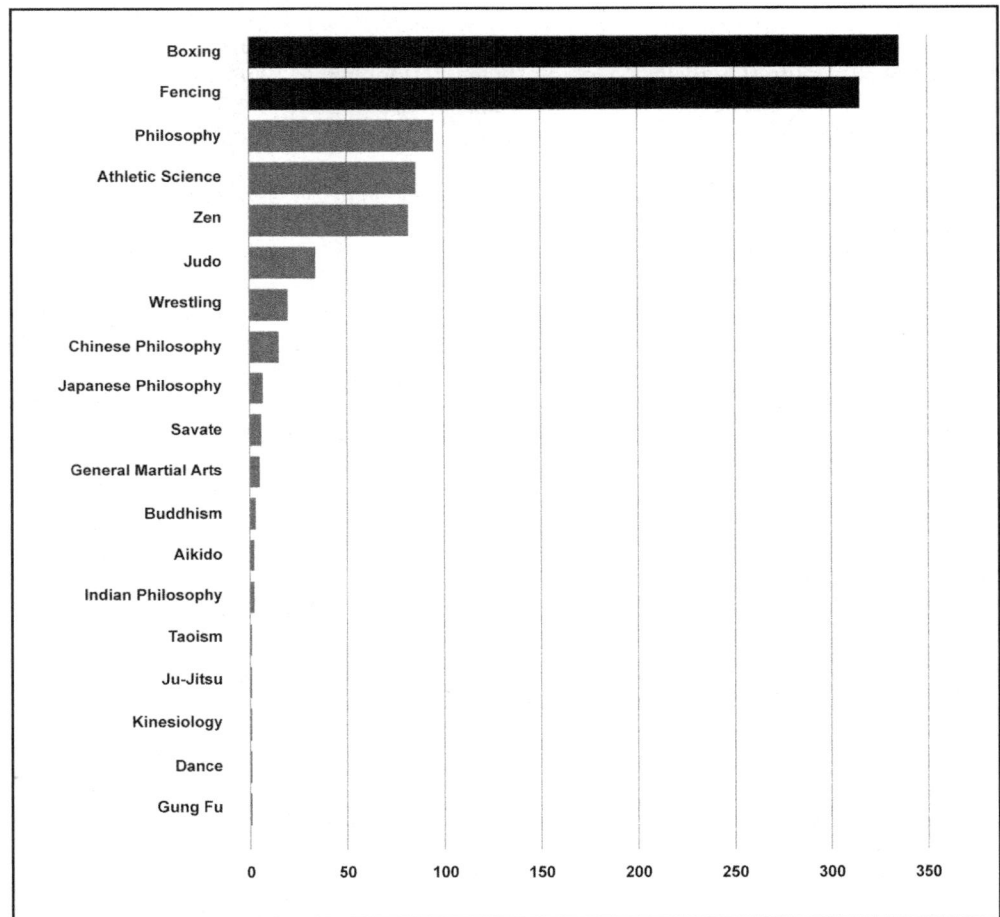

Table 1 above graphically illustrates how the content of my discoveries breaks down by subject matter. I say the "content of my discoveries" rather than the "content of the *Tao of Jeet Kune Do*" because the data only looks at items in the *Tao of Jeet Kune Do* for which I have identified the source. However, given that I have identified about 85% of the contents of the *Tao of Jeet Kune Do*, this graph is reasonably reflective of the entire book, with the most notable exception being the passages and illustrations regarding kicking, for which I have only identified the Savate elements.

Table 2. An Analysis by Author

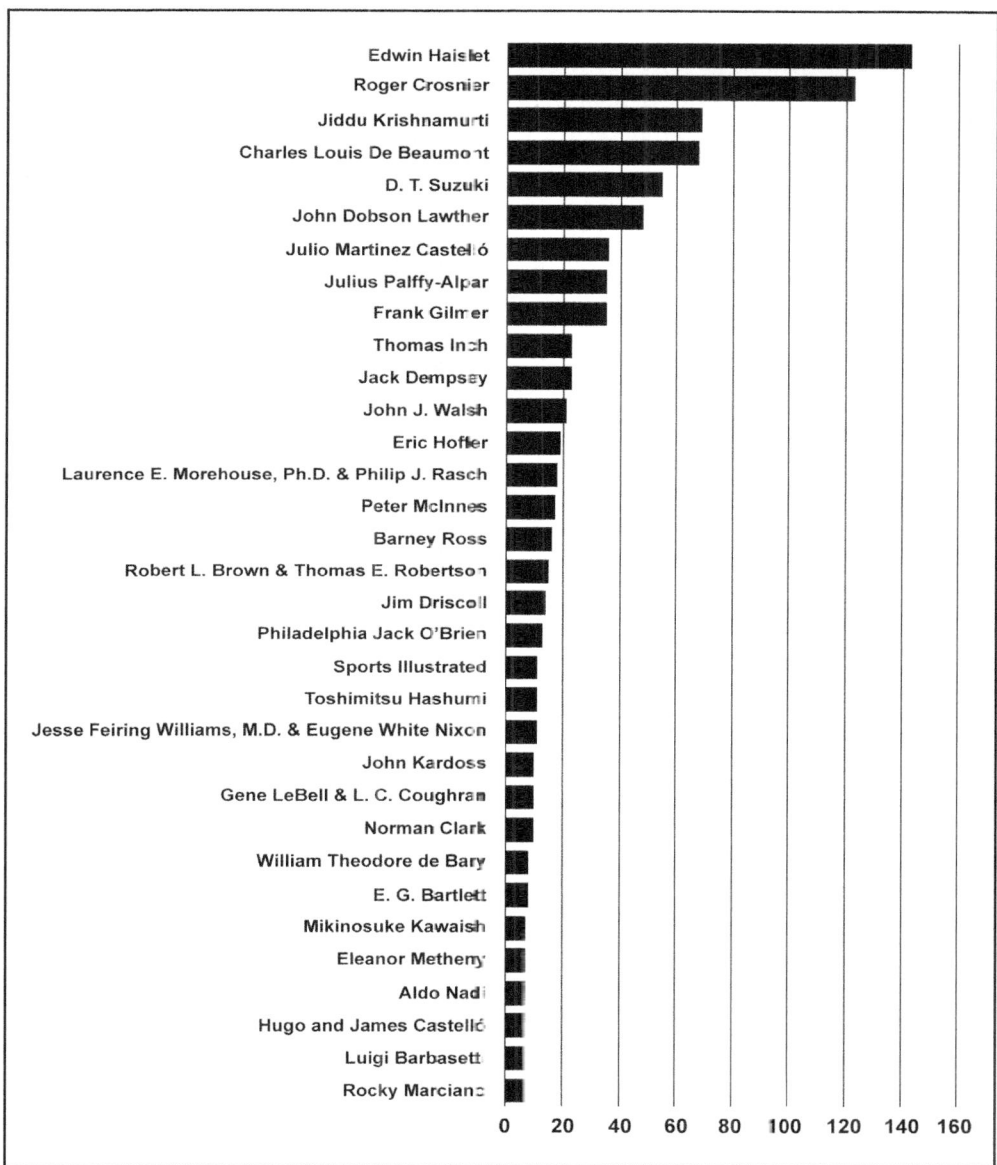

Table 2 shows the frequency of appearance in the analyzed data by author. Unsurprisingly, Edwin Haislet and Roger Crosnier appear most frequently, followed distantly by Krishnamurti. It is particularly interesting that Charles Louis de Beaumont is the second most referenced author on the subject of fencing. The same can be said for Frank Gilmer on the subject of boxing. John Dobson Lawther is the most referenced expert in the fields of athletics and sports science.

Table 3. Analysis by Source

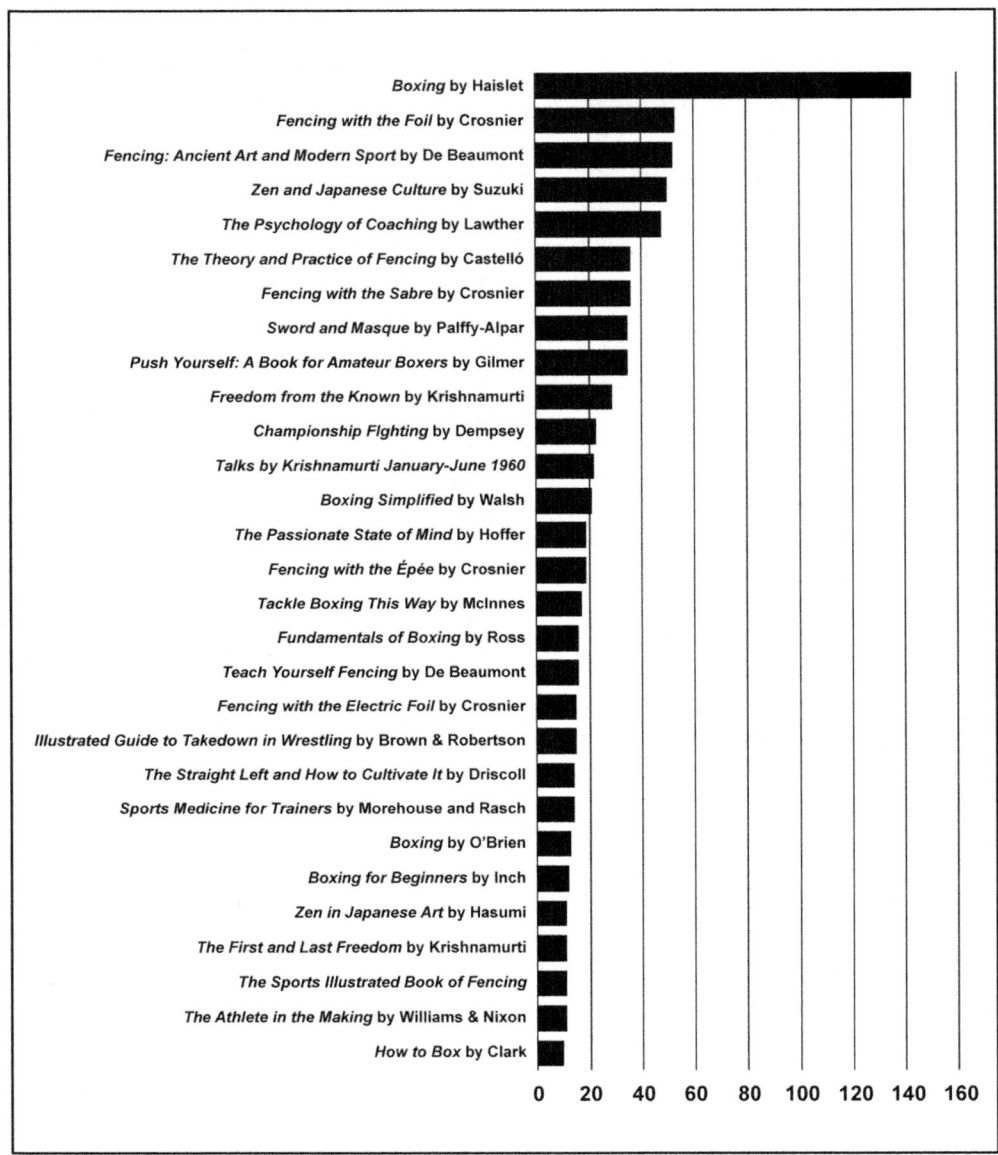

Table 3 represents the number of appearances each particular book or article made in the *Tao of Jeet Kune Do*. As expected, Edwin Haislet's book *Boxing* topped the list. Roger Crosnier's *Fencing with the Foil* was the most represented fencing book in the data. I limited the graph to only the top 30 titles in the data due to space, but you will note that Aldo Nadi's *On Fencing* is nowhere in the top 30. It came in at number 40, revealing that the common belief that Nadi was a significant influence on Jeet Kune Do is not backed up by the data.

Word Usage in the *Tao of Jeet Kune Do*

Below is a look at the frequency of 100 key words in the text that I gathered from the *Tao of Jeet Kune Do* for this project. The frequency gives an idea of the emphasis Bruce Lee placed on certain subjects or ideas. Note that I did not include every bit of text from the *Tao of Jeet Kune Do* in my data set; simple phrases or notes, such as Bruce Lee's fitness program list (i.e. "push-ups", "running in place") were not included because they are so basic in their language that they were unlikely to yield any identifications. Interestingly enough, the word "Tao" appears only once in the actual text of the *Tao of Jeet Kune Do* (not counting front matter or the title of the book) on page 11 under the header "The Path to Truth"; the word "Taoism" also appears once under the header "Mental Cultivation" on page 75 of the book.

Opponent: 514
Attack(s) or Attacking: 417
Movement: 263
Lead: 221
Position: 187
Parry or Parrying: 155
Punch, Punching, or Punches: 155
Feint or Feinting: 140
Fighter: 123
Speed: 123
Kick or Kicking: 122
Hook: 109
Hit or Hitting: 108
Action: 91
Balance: 83
Jab: 71
Fight or Fighting: 71
Target: 68
Power: 64
Counter: 62
Defense: 62
Art: 53
Timing: 51
Motion: 48
Footwork: 48
Preparation: 47
Technique: 46
Thrust: 46
Combination: 44
Force: 44
Guard: 44
Riposte: 44
Rhythm: 42

Strike or Striking: 42
Counter or Countering: 40
Blows: 38
On-Guard: 38
Sidestep: 38
Defensive: 36
Slipping: 35
Stop-Hit: 33
Adversary: 32
Relaxed or Relaxation: 29
Engagement: 28
Attention: 25
Awareness: 25
Training: 25
Counterattack: 24
Attacker: 23
Boxing: 23
Disengagement: 23
Freedom: 23
Economical: 22
Openings: 22
Retreat: 22
Method: 21
Tactics: 21
Cadence: 19
Powerful: 18
Flow: 16
Martial: 16
Mental: 16
System: 15
Deception: 14
Boxer: 12
Circling: 12
In-Fighting: 12

Weaving: 12
Advancing: 11
Explosive: 11
Guarding: 11
Defender: 10
Instinctive: 10
Trapping: 10
Covering: 9
Ducking: 9
Totality: 9
Artist: 8
Automatic: 8
Blocking: 8
Immobilization: 8
Neutrality: 8
Rapidity: 8
Weapons: 8
Efficiency: 7
Flexibility: 7
Grappling: 7
Penetration: 6
Speedy: 6
Artistic: 5
Long-Range: 5
Mastery: 5
Psychological: 5
Spiritual: 5
Teacher: 5
Telegraphing: 5
Cobra: 4
Explode: 4
Doctrine: 2
Taoism: 1
Tao: 1

OTHER BOOKS IN THE DRAGON LIBRARY SERIES

The Art of Boxing and Manual of Training: The Deluxe Edition
by William Edwards

Bruce Lee: Dynamic Becoming
by James Bishop

*The Bruce Lee Society:
A Retrospective Look at Bruce Lee Mania
and the Kung Fu Craze of the 1970s*
Edited by Carl Fox

Out-Fighting Or Long-Range Boxing: The Deluxe Edition
by Jim Driscoll

Ringcraft: The Deluxe Edition
by Jim Driscoll

Scientific Boxing: The Deluxe Edition
by James J. Corbett

The Straight Left and How to Cultivate It: The Deluxe Edition
by Jim Driscoll

The Text Book of Boxing: The Deluxe Edition
by Jim Driscoll

Printed in Great Britain
by Amazon

23921613R00130